*To Bill
In appreciat.
Friendship.*

18-03-2025

A journey of growing, re-inventing,
and recreating oneself.

CRESCENDO TO BECOMING

*A Memoir
of My Life*

Cav. Francesco Fiorentino

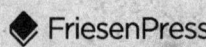
One Printers Way
Altona, MB R0G 0B0
Canada

www.friesenpress.com

Copyright © 2024 by Francesco Fiorentino
First Edition — 2024

All rights reserved.

No part of this publication may be reproduced in any form, or by any means, electronic or mechanical, including photocopying, recording, or any information browsing, storage, or retrieval system, without permission in writing from FriesenPress.

ISBN
978-1-03-832023-0 (Hardcover)
978-1-03-832022-3 (Paperback)
978-1-03-832024-7 (eBook)

1. BIOGRAPHY & AUTOBIOGRAPHY, PERSONAL MEMOIRS

Distributed to the trade by The Ingram Book Company

• • • • • • •

*"Man's main task in life is to give birth, to himself,
to become what he potentially is,."*
—Erich Fromm

• • • • • • •

*"We can have more than we got, because we can
become more than we are."*
—Jim Rohn

• • • • • • •

*"Have the courage to follow your heart and intuition.
They somehow already know what you truly want
to become. Everything else is secondary."*
—Steve Jobs

• • • • • • •

A person should visualize the future and see himself not as he is, but as he can become.
—**F. Fiorentino**

To Giacinto Graziano
In appreciation of your acceptance, caring, and support over the years.
Frank Fiorentino, 29/01/25

DEDICATION

TO JOSEPHINE, THE ONE AND only love and companion of my life, who has always been in my heart since I was sixteen and she was thirteen.

To my son Tony, my "rock" and pillar of joy, strength and support.

To my first princess Franca in heaven, who gave us real happiness and demonstrated real caring, love, and devotion during her forty-five years with us.

To my second princess Elisa, who personifies dedication and excellence, and the highest qualities of a caring human being, i.e. being loving and lovable.

To my twelve GRAND children, four of whom are also GREAT grandchildren, all very much valued members of my family, the reason for being, and my inspiration for writing this memoir in the first place.

To those that I have loved and loved me, particularly my dear mother and father, including my one brother and four sisters.

To the Graziano extended family, in Canada and in Italy, who welcomed and embraced me as one of their own.

To my four hero teachers: Mrs. Keith, Mr. Leavens, Mr. Potter and Mr. Pierce, who inspired, helped, and encouraged me to become who I am.

To my many students, colleagues, and friends, who taught me (the teacher), a great deal.

·······················

"It takes courage to grow up and turn out to be who you really are."
—E.E. Cummings

·······················

SPECIAL DEDICATION TO MY GRANDCHILDREN

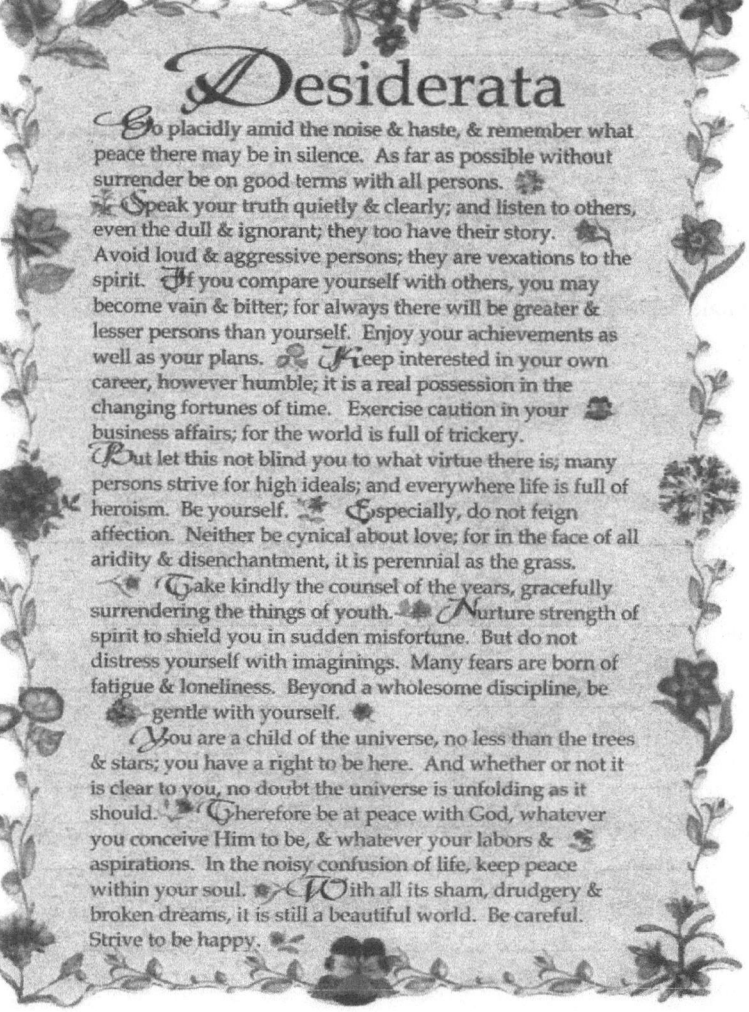

Desiderata

Go placidly amid the noise & haste, & remember what peace there may be in silence. As far as possible without surrender be on good terms with all persons. Speak your truth quietly & clearly; and listen to others, even the dull & ignorant; they too have their story. Avoid loud & aggressive persons; they are vexations to the spirit. If you compare yourself with others, you may become vain & bitter; for always there will be greater & lesser persons than yourself. Enjoy your achievements as well as your plans. Keep interested in your own career, however humble; it is a real possession in the changing fortunes of time. Exercise caution in your business affairs; for the world is full of trickery. But let this not blind you to what virtue there is; many persons strive for high ideals; and everywhere life is full of heroism. Be yourself. Especially, do not feign affection. Neither be cynical about love; for in the face of all aridity & disenchantment, it is perennial as the grass. Take kindly the counsel of the years, gracefully surrendering the things of youth. Nurture strength of spirit to shield you in sudden misfortune. But do not distress yourself with imaginings. Many fears are born of fatigue & loneliness. Beyond a wholesome discipline, be gentle with yourself. You are a child of the universe, no less than the trees & stars; you have a right to be here. And whether or not it is clear to you, no doubt the universe is unfolding as it should. Therefore be at peace with God, whatever you conceive Him to be, & whatever your labors & aspirations. In the noisy confusion of life, keep peace within your soul. With all its sham, drudgery & broken dreams, it is still a beautiful world. Be careful. Strive to be happy.

By Max Ehrmann

CREDITS: Image, Story, and Other

Vivian Albo	Charles Sherbo	Mary Mushinski
Father Sam Argenziano	Linda Smith	Don Pepe
Primo Augellone	Mary Sutherland	Franco Petrelli
Joe Bova	Anna Torchia	Cristina Povoledo
Franca Bova	Lorenzo Torchia	Sal Rapisarda
Giannino Calista	Dr. Luigi Villa	Dr. Edris Sabbadini
Ralph Cantafio	Valerie Andree	Mario Silvari
Stanislao Carbone	Amanda Asmundson	Valerie Sontag
Mark Charbonneau	Gail Bagnall	Tony Tascona
Francesca Colosimo	Robert Bend	Lorenzo Torchia
John Couture	Debbie Brown	Francesca Possia
Virginia D'Amico	Bruce Cairns	Zane Zalis
Tom DeNardi	Gregorio Cantafio	Phillip Andree
DiBiaggio Ermenegildo	Colleen Carswell	Mario Audino
Pasquale Falvo	Anna Cianflone	Todd Baraniuk
Frankie Fiorentino	Raimon Cosentino	Warren Bend
Onofrio Fiorentino	Phil Cramer	Frank Bueti
Adam Ferman	Anna Dell'Acqua	Teresa Campanelli
Joe Grande	Ugo/Maria DeNardi	Angela Caputo
Linda Hughes	Terry Duguid	Marianne Cerilli
Adriana Kiz	Angie Fiorentino	Lina Colosimo
Rob Kiz	Greg Fiorentino	Teresa Cotroneo
Lorne Kramble	Tonina Fiorentino	Francesca Creta
Carmine LaRosa	Rosemarie Gagliardi	Domenico Deluca
Josie Lucidi	Stefano Grande	Frank DeMarchi
Franco Masi	Delfina Jaffri	Nick Falvo
Peter Maruca	Austin Kiz	Dylan Fiorentino
Bobby Mottola	Ray Knowles	Luigino Fiorentino
George Pelletier	Felicia Kriegl	Tony Fiorentino
Dr. Glen Pierce	Debbie Loschiavo	Franco Grande
Dr. G. Potter	Franco Magnifico	Dan Heindl
Mario Raimondi	Giovanni B. Masi	Tina Jones
Don/Anna Romano	Stella Mazza	Evan Kiz

Barry Kramble	Art Miki	Angelamaria Silvestrin
Earnie Kyliuk	Tony Pesce	Wally Stoyko
Dr. Sam Loschiavo	Jackie Porco	Anna Maria Toppazzini
Peter Martin	Gianfranco Riva	Annette Trimbee
Raffaele Masi	Don Reece	Luigi Vendramelli
Ferruccio Moscarda	Tom/Mary Scerbo	Carmine Zirino

<u>Amato History of a Town And its Treasures</u>; Centro Caboto Centre; Italian Canadian League of Manitoba; <u>From Slate to Computer</u> by Nan Shipley; Daniel McIntyre Collegiate yearbooks, 1953–1956; H.M.S. Chippawa, Winnipeg, Manitoba; <u>Italians in Winnipeg</u> by Stanislao Carbone, 1998; Murdoch MacKay Collegiate yearbooks, 1968-1975; Transcona Collegiate Yearbooks, 1959–1968; Transcona News; Transcona-Springfield School Division; <u>Transcona 100th Anniversary publication</u>; Winnipeg Free Press.

*"Writing a life story is a sacred and spiritual experience,
It's more than just creative expression – it's a spiritual lifeline"*
**—Joanne Klassen, Founder and Director of Winnipeg's
Heart Space Writing School**

Table of Contents

DEDICATION	vii
SPECIAL DEDICATION TO MY GRANDCHILDREN	ix
1. INTRODUCTION	1
2. CRESCENDO, GROWING, AND BECOMING	4
3. ROOTS OF MY BECOMING	8
4. BECOMING ITALIAN: MY BIRTH AND EARLY YEARS IN ITALY	25
5. BECOMING A PROUD CANADIAN CITIZEN	37
6. BECOMING A STUDENT, A MUSICIAN, AND A YOUNG ATHLETE	56
7. BECOMING A TEACHER, A PRINCIPAL, AND A SUPERINTENDENT OF EDUCATION	83
8. BECOMING A HUSBAND, FATHER, GRANDFATHER, AND A GREAT-GRANDFATHER	174
9. BECOMING "FREE" AT "FREEDOM 55"	211
10. BECOMING A TRAVELLER	230
11. BECOMING A VOLUNTEER COMMUNITY BUILDER	248
12. BECOMING "ITALIANISSIMO" AS VICE-CONSUL FOR ITALY	275
13. BECOMING HONORED AND ESTEEMED	321
14. BECOMING A VICTIM OF HEART AND CANCER DISEASES!	349
15. BECOMING LOVING AND LOVABLE: THE ULTIMATE HUMAN	367
16. AT THE END: A NEW BECOMING?	371
POSTSCRIPT: SOME OF MY SPECIAL PEOPLE	373

"Whatever the mind of man can conceive and believe, it can achieve."
—Napoleon Hill

*The author **Cav. Frank Fiorentino**, Vice Consul of Italy for Manitoba, 1998–2006*

"Education, then, beyond all other devices of human origin, is a great equalizer of conditions of man-the balance wheel of the social machinery."
—Horace Mann

1.
INTRODUCTION

IT IS NOW EARLY 2024. Once again, I am finally attempting to finish writing this book, my labor of love, the same memoir that I began almost 15 years ago. It was originally entitled "***Becoming***", and I consequently abandoned this title and the writing of the book itself, some thirteen years ago, when my dear daughter Franca was diagnosed with terminal cancer, a tragedy that impacted and changed me and my family forever. With her passing, I lost every desire to continue with my beautiful life itself, as I had known it, to that dreadful point in time.

I have by now slowly re-kindled somewhat my desire to live, thanks mainly to my twelve grandchildren, but I am now eighty-eight years of age, with time fast being of the essence. It is for sure, now, a last opportune time to share with you, (my readers) some of my beliefs, some of my knowledge, and some of my feelings that provide the rationale for what I am about to share which is the central theme of this book, captured in the meaning of three words: *Crescendo (Growing) and Becoming*.

My motivation for writing the story of my life and times comes directly and primarily from my grandchildren, who have been and continue to be, the source of most of my inspiration, especially at this late point in my life. I am writing "my story", for I want to leave them something tangible about "my interesting life's journey", and in this way perhaps, they get to know something not only of their roots, but also something about who and what I was, and hopefully in so-doing, they can understand more fully, who they are, and perhaps more importantly still, who and what they can become.

In writing my memoirs, I have found that you cannot cut one's life into precise slices or sections, for one's life journey is usually complex and full of peaks and valleys, and my life journey is no exemption. It seems to me however, that I have lived two lives, as it were, in two distinct places, embracing two loves, Italy and Canada. For me, Italy is the epicenter of culture, art, and beauty. Yes, I am proud of my Italian heritage, but I also feel lucky that we found acceptance and received a warm embrace in Canada, one of the best and greatest countries in the world today. Because of this enriched background, I believe that I have become a multi-dimensional person, and one of the luckiest people on earth.

People that know me will attest that I have always gravitated toward what is different and good, and not toward what is common, convenient, and easy, for I have always been motivated by challenging and difficult work. There are always times in one's life when one must *"seize the opportunity"* and this is something that has given me immeasurable pleasure and strength, as my life's theme, both as an educator and as a person. Ever since I can remember, ***"Carpe Diem"*** has been my personal rallying cry and my own life's theme, both as an educator, and as a person. Today this slogan still forms part of the "coat of arms" of Murdoch MacKay Collegiate, when as the school's second principal in 1968, I urged its students to adopt the motto and live by it. As the reader will see, the story of my life is of my personal (but not private) interaction and involvement with many people, many places, and many things.

INTRODUCTION

POWERFUL ME

"If it is to be, it is up to me!"
Everything depends on me.
"I think, therefore I am."
Because I am, therefore, I can.
Because I can, I can be,
And because I can be, I can become.
It's my personal approach,
That determines the me to be.
I have power to burn,
With the power of choice.
The power to re-invent me,
To the me I really want to be.
It is my attitude that becomes
my altitude.
I am, I can, I will."
The commitment is within me
To let these beliefs empower me.
The power is within me,
To understand and be understood.
The power to re-create me,
To be loving and loveable
the ultimate me.

Frank Fiorentino

THE ROAD NOT TAKEN

Two roads diverged in a yellow wood,
And sorry I could not travel to both.
And be one traveler, long I stood.
And looked down at one as far as I could.
To where it bent in the undergrowth.

Then took the other, as just as fair,
And having perhaps the better claim,
Because it was grassy and wanted wear;
Though as for that the passing there
Had worn them really about the same,

And both that morning equally lay
In leaves no step had trodden black.
Oh, I kept the first for another day!
Yet knowing how way leads on to way,
I doubted if I should ever come back.

I shall be telling this with a sigh
Somewhere ages and ages hence;
Two roads diverged in a wood, and I –
I took the one less traveled by,
And that has made all the difference.

Robert Frost

2.
CRESCENDO, GROWING, AND BECOMING

TO BEGIN WITH, LET ME be clear about one thing: I believe in God as the creator of all things visible and invisible. I believe that God created us to be always in what I call a *crescendo(growing) mode*, that is, that we grow and become more than what we are able to think, more than what we can see, more than what we can hear, more than what we can sense, and more than what we can feel. Either we are growing, or we are dying. I believe that growing into being who we are, growing and being who we **can be**, and being able to determine who we become, is ultimately God's will, but probably not without a lot of input on our part. In any case, I have now concluded that while there is a lot that I *cannot* control in my life, I also know that there is also a great deal that I *can* control: what I think, what I do, what I say, and what I can become.

I also believe in some tenets of evolution. With my life-long dedication to learning and education, it is abundantly clear to me, that we can learn today something that we didn't know before and conclude that we are born with a propensity to become tomorrow that which today we still are not. Yes, everything we think, everything we are, and everything we can become is only possible because we have the ability to grow, learn, and change.

My life has always been characterized by learning and growing in all my life's many varied manifestations. But the one theme that has always been ever-present in my life has been the school. Since my sixth year of my life up to about seventy years of age, I have always "gone to school". Before and after my university graduation I was involved directly with education up to some twenty years ago. I have been involved in a truly life-long process of learning

CRESCENDO, GROWING, AND BECOMING

and growing which has allowed me to become many things and thus carry out many roles and functions, each of which has contributed immeasurably to the development and the defining of who and what I have become.

In summary, in my lifetime, I have performed roles or "become" the following:

- Alter Boy in the Roman Catholic Church, Amato Italy, at age 6.
- Member of the Eaton's Good Deed Club, 1952–1953.
- Grandson, son, brother, nephew, father, husband, uncle, grandfather (**nonno**), great grandfather. (**bisnonno**)
- School patrol boy at Montcalm Elementary School, Winnipeg;1953.
- Student (23 years), 1942–1965.
- **Classical and popular musician.**
- Singer (tenor).
- **Ballroom dance band leader.**
- Choirmaster.
- Athlete (soccer, football, track and field, softball, bowling.)
- University graduate with **B.A., B.Ed., M. Ed. degrees,** and a Professional Certificate in Education.
- Life-long learner and educator.
- **Teacher** (at the middle/senior years and adult levels).
- **School principal** (middle and senior years levels), 9 years.
- Administrative assistant to the superintendent of education.
- **Assistant superintendent of education,** 15 years.
- **Superintendent of education,** (2 years).
- Staff advisor, faculty of education, University of Manitoba.
- President of the Italian Canadian League of Manitoba, 1992–93.
- Continuing Education program coordinator, University of Manitoba.
- Native Youth pre-employment trainer (federal government).
- **Businessman** (Algonquin Travel, People Developers.)
- Consultant of Education and Training, 1992–2014.
- Board Member, Creative Retirement Manitoba.
- Board member of Villa Cabrini, a care home for seniors in Winnipeg.
- **Vice Consul of Italy** for Province of Manitoba, 1998–2006.
- Candidate for "Outstanding Young Man Award" sponsored by the Transcona Jaycees (1970).

- *Recipient of the "Queen Elizabeth II Golden Jubilee Medal", 2002.*
- *Recipient of the "Ordine Della Stella della Solidarietà Italiana"* **the Order of Italy)** *with the title of "Cavaliere", i.e. Knight, (2005).*
- *Recipient of two "Eccellenza Awards" of the Italian Community of Winnipeg (the first October 5, 2007) in recognition of my "remarkable career and volunteer effort.*
- **Workshop and seminar facilitator**; *motivational speaker.*
- **Volunteer/community builder/worker.**
- *Adult Ambassador (host) for the Italian Pavilion of Folklorama, the largest folk festival in the world held annually in Winnipeg.*
- **Member board of directors, Heart and Stroke Foundation of Manitoba** *(2010–2014).*
- *River East/Transcona Community Health Advisory Council (2013– 2016);*
- *Member of pensions, public relations and membership committees of the Retired Teachers Association of Manitoba, (2013–1915).*

The story of my life is also the story of my family and, interwoven with that, are the hardships and challenges that one usually attributes to immigrants as they struggle for survival in a new and challenging land. **But my life is not only a story of conflict, struggle, and survival; it is also a tale of personal growth, development, fulfillment and success... all represented by the word** *crescendo, i.e. growth.* . . My life is proof positive that given the willingness to learn, one can believe that a solid education is the greatest equalizer and foundation in one's life. I must say that I was lucky to have parents that had the audacity and the tenacity, to keep their children in school, together with the fact that I had the inborn drive to succeed, recognizing the fact that Canada is the great land of opportunity. It allows one to plan and design his own life, and become what he chooses and longs to be, for Canada provides the setting and support for the realization of one's own dreams and goals. This is especially true, if one is willing to take "the road less travelled". Yes indeed, **I thank God it was in Canada, that I was given the real opportunity to become who I am.**

CRESCENDO, GROWING, AND BECOMING

"I am a part of this, part of Canada.
Mine are the unlimited forests.
Mine the thousands of lakes,
Mine the riches of mountains and mines,
Mine the span of earth holding firm grasp two oceans.
This is Canada and it belongs to me –A Canadian"
From ***"Song of a Canadian"***

by Eva-Lis Wuorio

. . . .

God empowered us by giving us the power to live, to think, to choose, to touch, to feel, to laugh, to imagine, to create, to speak, to see, to taste, to smell, to will, to become, to pray, to love, to die, and to be born again.
—**Frank Fiorentino**

. . . .

3.
ROOTS OF MY BECOMING

Amato Mio!

Il mio paese e sopra una collina
Non tanto in alto sul livel del mare
Ci sono gli uliveti a la marina
Ci sono cose che ti fan sognar."
"Io ti amo o Amato e ti adoro
Con tutto l'affetto del cuore
E di te io ne faccio un tesoro,
Sempre più sei il verso valor".

My Amato ! (translation)

My little town is perched on a hilltop
Not too high above the level of the sea
There are olive groves right near the sea
There are things there that make one dream.
I love you and adore you, Amato
With all the affection in my heart
As for me you are my real treasure
You will always be worthy of my writings.

Antonio Fiorentino (my father)

It is said that where you come from has a great influence and significance as to determine what you will become, and where you are going to end up in life, for the environment you are in plays such a big part. I think without question, that this applied to my own situation. The setting for my life and times story began in the ancient town of Amato, Italy, and likely will end in the relatively new City of Winnipeg where I have lived since my arrival to Canada in 1949. Both locations in both countries have been quite a significant factor in my existence, my development, and my life. Italy gave me a sense of pride in my roots with its history-rich and with unbelievable culture and heritage, and Canada, a great natural beauty with a varied and shared mosaic of ethnic balance, justice, and freedom, long-recognized as a land of opportunity in the world. With such a supportive background, it is no wonder that I could become what, and who I wanted to be.

The word *"amato"*, which translates in English *"the loved place"*, *is* a small and an historic ancient town that dates back to somewhere between 300 to 800 B.C when it, and the whole region of Calabria, was occupied by Greece and constituted an integral part of what was then known as *Magna Grecia"*

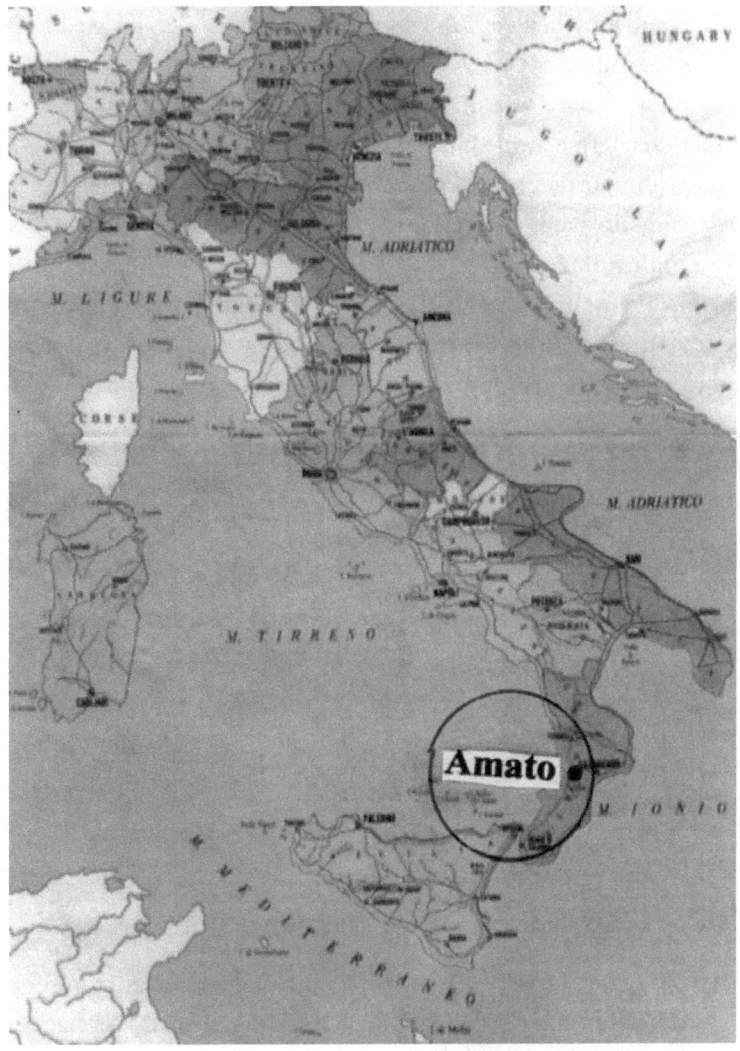

Location of the town of Amato in southern Italy where I was born.

Crescendo to Becoming

The town of Amato is in the Province of Catanzaro, in the region of Calabria in southern Italy. More specifically, in the *"boot"* that is Italy, Amato is in the "ankle" of Italy, precisely where the landform is the narrowest distance in all the peninsula of Italy, between the Mediterranean Sea to the West and the Adriatic Sea to the East. Today Amato rests up on higher ground than was the case during earlier civilizations, high enough on the hillside hugged by mountains and blessed with a most beautiful view of the valley beneath it, and enriched with the deep *"mare azzurro"* i.e. the Mediterranean blue of its Isthmus.

Apparently, Amato was once a thriving city located much closer to the sea at Lamezia Terme at the Gulf of Sant'Eufemia and the Gulf of Squillace. Its strategic importance had been noted by none other than the great Aristotle himself. Later of course, the region all became part of the great Roman Empire.

The inhabitants of Amato have relocated several times over the centuries as readjustment responses to the catastrophes and disasters such as floods, fires, and other calamities that have occurred there. In more recent times, specifically in 1783, Amato was again destroyed, this time by a horrific earthquake.

Looking back at the end of the Roman period, the region, like all other regions on the peninsula, was overrun by barbarian hordes including the Saracens in the year 827 A.D. It was during this period that apparently the area under the Normans' occupation underwent significant development and positive growth.

Part of the Panorama of Amato, taken from the by–pass road "Variante" now Via del Progresso, in the year 2011

From what we know now, it was from the year 1400 A.D. that the history of Amato becomes much more clearly defined. It is interesting to note also, that Amato was part of what was known as the *Kingdom of Naples* and was under the auspices of the King of Spain. At that time the territory that included Amato was known as the *"Marquis of*

ROOTS OF MY BECOMING

Amato" and belonged to Donato A. Mottola, given to him directly by the King of Spain himself. Still later on, after his death, the region was inherited by his son Orazio Mottola, whose time and influence are very well-known in the annals of the history of Amato.

In 1675 the territory of Amato became known as the *"University of Amato"* and later as the *Comune di Amato* and the lands thereto, were subdivided into smaller units of considerable size, (except for one third of the lands which were given to the Mottolas) and granted to the families who became the richest families in the area. These landowners that numbered about twenty-five families, included popular names that persist to this day in the Amato municipality whether they still live in Amato itself, in Winnipeg, Manitoba, or in other places on earth where *amatesi* now reside. Listed in alphabetical order, most of these family names are well recognized today, including: Anania, Caligiuri, Cantafio, Cianflone, Cosentino, D'Amico, Falvo, Fiorentino, Grande, Graziano, Jenzi, Loscerbo, Loschiavo, Masi, Mauro, Mazza, Mottola, Pallone, Papucci, Rossi, Todaro, and Torchia.

The *Comune di Amato* was finally granted a Charter, and the municipality consisted mainly of the *Montagna Soprana* (the Upper Mountain) and the *Montagna Sottana* (the lower mountain) within the boundary of the community of Amato.

With the passage of years and the continuous growth of the number of families and population, the lands in the Amato region underwent subdivision after subdivision, and eventually the reformatted land parcels became so small that they became insufficient in size to be able to sustain human family

"Don Orazio Mottola, Marquis of Amato, Baron of Ioppolo, of Coccorino and of Monterossa, poet and man of letters, was born in Tropea in July 9, 1640, son of Donna Felicia Braccio-Medici and Marquis Donato Antonio Mottola. He died in Amato, August 17, 1765"

By Joseph Mottola, Brooklyn New York, 1977 in his book entitled: <u>*"The Days and Life of Marchese Orazio Mottola of Amato, Italy*</u>

life for the ever-growing number of inhabitants. The result of the on-going reduction and fragmentation of the lands resulted in many people becoming *"coloni"* or *"sharecroppers"*, that is, people who looked after and worked other peoples' lands for a meager return that made it arduous if not impossible to provide for one's family.

Original Official Emblem of Amato    *Today's Official Emblem of Amato*

These were the conditions in the late 1880's and early 1900's when many people of Calabria and Amato immigrated to faraway places around the globe such as Australia, Argentina and Canada, in search of an opportunity to work, work that would ensure the survival of their loved ones and often the members of their extended families. Because of immigration during the twentieth century, Amato of today numbers fewer than 600 inhabitants, (from over 2300 when I was there) and it's ironic, I think, that the dead in its *campo santo* (cemetery) outnumber the living by a very large margin.

Arcangelo Sherbo 1877–1960 (originally spelled "Scerbo")

The background for the story of my life and times in many ways begins with my maternal grandfather Arcangelo Scerbo, who more than anyone else set and changed the course of my destiny, as well as the destiny of many other members of my family and many needy people of Amato. Interestingly, as well, Arcangelo Scerbo was born in Amato in 1877, the son of Pietro Scerbo the town miller, and Carmela Talarico, who is said (by my grandfather and other reliable sources), to have been the daughter of an actual brigand named Arcangelo Talarico. Carmela Talarico was born while her father Arcangelo Talarico was a fugitive from the law, the same Carmela who later married my great grandfather Pietro Scerbo, and together they had eight children: Arcangelo, Tommaso, Antonio, Serafina, Rosina, Concetta, Isabella, and Antonietta. Of these, Arcangelo Scerbo would later become my grandfather.

Arcangelo Scerbo, my grandfather, came to Canada as early as 1891 as a brave boy barely fourteen years of age, and was the youngest of the very first Amatese small group to come to Winnipeg. Just imagine such a brave young lad, venturing out with a few older men, across the vast expanse of the Mediterranean Sea and the Atlantic Ocean, as far as Ellis Island in New York, and proceeding then by train, to the distant land of Western Canada. Everyone in Southern Italy had heard that there was work to be had in Canada, as they knew that Canada was in the process of building the *Grand Trunk Railway*. So, desperate but motivated to find a job and earn some money, many men left Italy boarding a cheap ship in Naples, and courageously ventured out across the Atlantic Ocean to New York, and from there continued their long journey to Winnipeg.

With the money that my grandfather had accumulated by working hard in Canada, the newly-weds built a wonderful new house in Amato with the full intention of raising their family there. But it wasn't too long afterwards while in Italy, that my grandfather realized that conditions in Italy were again quickly deteriorating and that opportunities to raise a family seemed to him to be much more favorable in Winnipeg, a booming city that by now he knew only too well.

After no less than four miscarriages in Amato, Grandmother Maria was again pregnant with child and so in 1912, they embarked for Winnipeg where soon after, they celebrated the arrival of their first child, a girl named Carmela, who would become none other than my dear mother.

My mother, Nonno Arcangelo's first child, was named Carmela (but was affectionately known all her life as *Carmelina*,) for my grandfather wanted to renew his mother's name. Interestingly, my mother, who incidentally, was born in Winnipeg in 1912 in the St. Boniface General Hospital, died twenty-two years ago, on September 26, 2002, in the very same hospital

Crescendo to Becoming

Front Entrance of Arcangelo Scerbo's House in Amato, Built Circa 1910 (my grandfather)

where she had been born some 90 years earlier. She too loved both countries, but there is no doubt that having lived in both countries for a good period of her life, she preferred and loved living in Italy, if she had a choice to make.

Carmelina, my mother, was destined to be the first of seven children and was followed by a rather large number of six siblings (quite large comparatively to today). Subsequently after the birth of my mother came Anthony in 1913, Peter in 1915, Angelarosa in 1917, and Adelina in 1919. All five were born in Winnipeg and were therefore Canadian citizens by birth. With such a large family to raise, life was rough and challenging to say the least, and to make things even more difficult, my grandmother was not in good health, having undergone several miscarriages during her many pregnancies which were also prevalent in those days.

In the hope of finding better things in Italy, my grandparents, their five children including my mother (age nine), returned to Amato in 1921 with the intention of staying and really trying things there. They did have a relatively new house that they had built when my grandparents got married some ten years earlier, so their accommodation was quite good relatively speaking. But the region of Calabria in the early 1920's was economically quite depressed, Benito Mussolini was consistently gaining momentum and political support, and there was already talk of a dreaded world war all over again.

So, in 1923 my grandfather took off for Winnipeg for the ninth time no less, this time alone so as to make some headway economically speaking, leaving behind in Italy his whole family: my grandmother and her five children. To complicate things further, my grandmother was again pregnant to cap a family of already five children, but this time expecting twins no less, who were to become aunt Sera and Aunt Virginia. But after a remarkable nine trips back and forth to Italy, Nonno Arcangelo had had enough of Italy and was never to return to his beloved country ever again!

In Winnipeg, Nonno Arcangelo attacked life with all the determination and vigor that he could muster. His firm goal was to amass enough money, but not to go back and be able to live in Italy as had been the case before, but to be able to afford to rent a house in Winnipeg where he and his family would have permanent residence. He worked feverishly, but with a lot of enthusiasm and hope, he set up his own shoemaker shop *"Perfect Shoemaker"*, first on Notre Dame Avenue and later on Osborne Street, right in the middle of the block on the west side, on the landmark that is well-known today as the *Osborne Village* between River and Stradbroke Avenues, where he was located for many, many years. In the middle block location, he occupied a property that was then owned by the father of Duff Roblin, a well-respected former Premier of Manitoba. ... In the 1920's my grandfather felt rather strongly that all those that came to live in Canada should learn the English language and assimilate totally with other people the way it was usually expected in the United States. He took extraordinary measures to ensure that he and members of his family would not "stick out" in any way. Accordingly, he even went to the trouble of legally changing his name from "Scerbo" to what is still now "Sherbo", to anglicize it somewhat, and make it easier for Anglo-Saxons to pronounce it correctly. He decided that all the members of his family would become Canadian citizens and be deliberately committed to become the best Canadian citizens that they could be.

After seven years of separation from his family my grandfather was able to send for his family from Italy in 1930, and so all of them came to Winnipeg as a family unit, arriving in Winnipeg on November 6, 1930, all that is, except my own mother Carmelina, who at the young age of 18, had just married my father Antonio Fiorentino and was happy to remain and live in beautiful, sunny Amato, Italy.

As we can see from all accounts, my grandfather Arcangelo Sherbo had a choice, as to where to live and lucky for me and others, he deliberately chose Canada. He was a true pioneer in "his" adopted country of Canada. He foresaw Canada's greatness and understood its potential for those that were determined to make it work, and for those that appreciated freedom. Once so committed, he became a true and proud Canadian in every sense of the word. Because of his sacrifices, initiative and determination, I and members of my family, have had the opportunity and the privilege to have a wonderful, meaningful, and rewarding life in Canada, a country that is reputedly without question still today, one of the very best in the whole world.

Personally, I feel that I/we owe Arcangelo Sherbo a great deal. But how does one ever repay the great sacrifice he and his large family had to endure to establish the family on a solid footing in Canada? In a small way, here, through this book, I wish to recognize the great contribution he made for all our well-being. My grandfather Arcangelo Sherbo shall always be my first hero, for I shall never forget that during the Second World War, when the large Sherbo family was itself under great economic duress, my *nonno* and *nonna* saw to it that parcels of food and other basics would reach us in Italy when things there were scarce and miserable for all. I shall always remember his great generosity until we reached Canada, and the difference that he has made not only to me in my life, but also to the lives and survival of his extended family, and to many Amatesi and others well beyond his own family.

Arcangelo Sherbo's Immediate Family

Name	Relationship	D.O.B.	Place of Birth
Arcangelo		1877	Amato, Italy
Maria	Wife	1893	Amato, Italy
Carmelina	Daughter	1912	Winnipeg
Tony	Son	1913	Winnipeg
Peter	Son	1915	Winnipeg
Angelarosa	Daughter	1917	Winnipeg
Adelina	Daughter	1919	Winnipeg
Serafina	Daughter	1923	Amato, Italy
Virginia	Daughter	1923	Amato, Italy

ROOTS OF MY BECOMING

Top, Left to Right: Grandfather Arcangelo Scerbo, Grandmother Maria.
Bottom Left to right: Tony, Peter (sitting,) Carmelina (my mother), and Angelarosa, circa 1918

Crescendo to Becoming

My father Antonio Fiorentino and my mother Carmelina, (dressed as a pacchiana, the traditional dress of Calabria) on their wedding day in Amato, 1930

ROOTS OF MY BECOMING

Antonio Fiorentino, my father, was born in Amato, Italy, November 16, 1905, of parents Pietro Fiorentino and Carmela Guzzi who had three children: Uncle Onofrio, my Aunt Maria, and the youngest of the three, my father Antonio. My grandfather Pietro Fiorentino died suddenly quite young in 1914 leaving my grandmother a widow, and three young children as orphans, including my father who was barely nine years old.

It was my grandmother Carmela (see photo below), as a single parent, who was left to raise the three children by herself. This she did by working the land in the country very hard, especially in a place known as *Serravento*, located very near Amato and other locations that were much further from town.

My father loved music and started to take music lessons early in his life. His passion for music led him to study at the Conservatory of Music in Naples and had embarked in a music career that was well entrenched by the time we left Italy in 1949.

My father's specialty instrument in music was the *euphonium*, or baritone trombone, in which he became quite proficient. Not only did he become the "Maestro di Musica" i.e. the Band Conductor of the *"Giacomo Puccini Band"* in Amato, but also, he played for other large symphonic concert bands from other regions of Italy such as *Acque Della Fonti* in the region of *Puglie*, and in many an instance he would travel to far places to play "on tour" with these bands. As well, my father had also learned to be a shoemaker in his younger days, when it was the custom that every young boy had to learn a trade. But as long as I can remember, his passion was his music, and I have no recollection whatsoever of him as a shoemaker in Amato.

Zia Maria and Nonna Carmela 1949

Crescendo to Becoming

What I remember mostly through my childhood, was that my paternal grandmother Carmela had lost an eye through some kind of accident in the country, but not even this ever deterred her from working in any way. She was a very hardworking person, and she loved me and all my siblings immensely. She made sure that she always had something of a surprise for us children. I remember many an instance as a young child, that I would join her for lunch in front of the open fireplace in her home kitchen where she always seemed to cook my favorite recipes that I always thoroughly enjoyed with her. She sure had a way of making me feel special for she always seemed to enjoy my presence. After our arrival to Canada, I missed her more than I had thought I would, and I have long since realized how much she truly loved us all.

• •

"We are not what we know but what we are willing to learn."
—Mary Catherine Bateson

• •

GIACOMO PUCCINI BAND" OF AMATO, 1923 –CO-FOUNDED BY MY FATHER
Front Row: Giuseppe Anania, Amedeo Lucia, Francesco Cianflone, Alessandro Grande; *Second Row:* Gaetano Anania, Giuseppe Romeo, Gregorio Grande, Antonio Grande, Don Benigno Trapasso, Maestro di Musica Vincenzo Basile, Antonio Maruca, Tommaso Fiorentino, Pasquale Scerbo, Francesco Scerbo, Angelo Falvo; *Third Row:* Francesco Pingitore, Antonio Fiorentino of Alfonso, Romolo Loscerbo, Tommaso Gagliardi, Pasquale Fiorentino of Antonio, Giuseppe Mauro,

ROOTS OF MY BECOMING

Modesto Trapasso, Giuseppe Aiello, Basile Falvo, Francesco Loschiavo, Tommaso D'Amico, Giuseppe Fiorentino di Antonio; Fourth Row: Giuseppe Grande di Gregorio, Pasquale Cosentino, Antonio Cantafio, Giovan-Battista Mottola, Giacinto Graziano, Giuseppe Cantafio, Giuseppe Scarpino, Raffaele Cosentino di Giuseppe, Carmelo Rossi, Antonio Fiorentino (my father)

This is a sample of my father's handwritten music that he wrote for every member of the band for every instrument, and for all the pieces in the band's repertoire

My father's brother, uncle Onofrio Fiorentino (pictured below) immigrated to the United States from Amato, in the early 1920's and settled in Brooklyn, New York. Subsequently he became a source of help to many Amatesi that he himself sponsored, and many others that he helped either directly or indirectly. There are also many stories of his support to many people that he would go and meet upon their arrival at Ellis Island, New York, and often help them monetarily, in order that they could settle in North America. Uncle Onofrio also owned what must have been at least a ten-acre parcel of land very near Amato and in fact, a beautiful country setting that provided a principal source of food and survival for us as a family, and a place where I spent many days in the early years of my life.

My father once said to me that when you can't change the conditions, you're in, you must change the way you think about things.

Thinking back to Amato and my father's upbringing, it was amazing that under very adverse conditions my orphaned father did manage to make something of himself in what was then a very depressed region of the country. Amato was then a town where the vast majority of its approximately 2300 inhabitants were either illiterate or had grade one or two standing. My father, by contrast, was one of the most emancipated and educated

Photo on the left shows Uncle Onofrio (extreme right) and Aunt Anna on their Wedding Day in Brooklyn, New York, U.S

individuals in Amato. As part of his upbringing, he had enrolled and frequented the Conservatory of Music in Naples and there he learned to play all the wind music instruments found in a symphonic band.

Armed with this knowledge, he began teaching music to most young people in Amato, and in 1923 he and others founded what became the very popular *"Giacomo Puccini Band,"* of which eventually he became its director and conductor and performed in many festivals in Amato and those of nearby towns as well. At the age of twenty my father voluntarily joined the military forces for service in the Italian army. He first served one year and a half as obligatory service from January 1925 to August 1926, and then later after war had been declared, he served in Africa in Ethiopia, Eritrea and Abyssinia for four years, precisely from the thirty-first of October 1936 to the twenty-fifth of October 1939. In the army he was the director of the military marching band and taught many native young people where he was stationed, how to play a musical instrument.

Upon his official release from the military, he was given a *"congedo* i.e. a discharge which praised his *record "with exemplary good conduct"*. We were all happy that he was fortunate to survive the long and cruel conflict, but when finally, he came home to Amato, himself looking like a negro, he embarked like all other war survivors in yet another long and arduous battle: his and his family's battle for survival.

Immediately after the war in 1945, my father went in search of work in the reconstruction of *Monte Cassino* and took me, now nine years of age, with him. There he held two jobs simultaneously: construction worker in the daytime, and musician in the evenings and weekends when the symphonic band had a booking. I will never forget my stay with him in the cities of *Aquino*, in *Roccasecca*, and especially in *Monte Cassino* where every day there seemed to be a gory story in the newspapers of soldiers who had been buried alive under the rubble of the destruction of its historic Roman Catholic monastery. This, ironically, at the hands of the allied forces who believed falsely, that the huge monastery on top of the mountain, as the focal point of the region, was occupied and controlled by German forces. Because of the mistake, the U.S. saw to it that after the war, the great monastery was rebuilt to its original condition and status.

It must be remembered that during and immediately before and after World War II, conditions in Italy were terribly desperate. There was hardly any work anywhere in Italy, and survival became the number one preoccupation and focus of most people especially in southern Italy. Frankly, we as a family were not as bad as most others, for we hand several parcels of land to sustain us, and we had great support from my grandfather *et al* in Canada, and Uncle Onofrio in Brooklyn, New York in the United States. But even so, by 1947 I had finished attending the elementary school which went on only to grade five, inclusive, in Amato, and there was no way that I could be enrolled in a middle school which was located in the neighboring city of Catanzaro, and which was not universally free as was the elementary education. As the costs of schooling beyond grade five were prohibitive for most families to bear, it became necessary for me as well to discontinue school altogether with a grade five standing.

My father, however, has always had a great admiration for education and for learning above all else, and his intense desire and determination was that his children should and would receive a proper education. There was only one way to achieve this. He would have to subjugate his own personal goals, sacrifice everything including leaving his beloved Italy, and immigrate to Canada, which was my mother's birthplace, and where all my mother's family resided since 1930. The fact that mother was Canadian born helped immensely in facilitating and obtaining the immigration application or *"richiamo"* and passport required, and as a result, we were one of the very first families to be granted the authority to leave Italy after World War II. The date of our departure from Amato *"the loved place"* was New Year's Day, January 1, 1949, an unforgettable

Crescendo to Becoming

day marked by torrential rains, and from the day on, my father who was then 44 years of age, would never see his beloved Amato and Italy ever again.

* *

"The character of a community is determined by each of its members."
—Unknown

* *

"It's never too late to be who you might have been."
—George Eliot

* *

"The only person you are destined to become is the person you decided to be"
—Ralph Waldo Emerson

* *

4.
BECOMING ITALIAN: MY BIRTH AND EARLY YEARS IN ITALY

LIKE MY FATHER BEFORE ME, I was also born in Amato, Italy, specifically on February 20, 1936, and lived there until January 1, 1949, when on a month before my thirteenth birthday, my seven-member family left Italy and immigrated to Canada in search of a better opportunity for a better life.

Apparently, it was my mother that insisted on naming me Francesco as she made a vow to *San Francesco di Paola* (St. Francis of Paola) when she was pregnant carrying me. Because she often felt somewhat ill and uneasy during her pregnancy, she prayed and vowed to Saint Francesco that if He would protect me so that I would be born healthy and normal, she would name me *Francesco* in his honor. So, as was common in Italy, I was named after the most revered and venerated saint in Calabria, who incidentally, was, and is still, also the patron saint of our town of Amato.

I couldn't have picked a worse date and period of history to come into the world, for it was indeed a period of many terrible occurrences and experiences that had a great impact on me, and that I would never be able to forget. I was born in a time when the harsh effects of the great depression of the early 1930's were still being felt. Globally, it was probably the most deprived period of the twentieth century. If things were bad in Canada, and from all accounts of our relatives living there they were, things in Italy were even much worse. To make things even more intolerable, the years of depression of 1930 led directly into the greatest catastrophic period the world has ever seen: the Second World War, from 1939 to 1945.

In *Amato* we lived in a comparatively new three-storey house that had recently been built when my parents got married in 1930. Although it did

Crescendo to Becoming

not have all the modern facilities as are common now, it was nevertheless one of the better and newer homes in Amato in those days. It even boasted an indoor washroom, a rare reality then in Amato, but still lacked the fixtures to actually make it fully functional. Besides what is visible here in the photograph below, there was still a floor at ground level, which was used as a concert hall, a music studio and later as a barber shop run by the *Romeo Brothers,* the same three *Romeo Brothers* that were later established on Regent Avenue in Transcona, a suburb of Winnipeg, for well over 50 years.

Our house in Amato, 1936–1949. The memories I have growing up here are still quite lucid in my mind.

"Serravento" our beautiful country place, very close to Amato 1972). The boy in front is my ten-year-old son Tony.

"Serravento" in the forefront is very close to Amato (seen in background)

"Serravento" consisted of the two-storey building, the land, and the many olive and many fruit trees

"*Serravento*": The Terrestrial Paradise of My Youth

Serravento was, and still is, a beautiful piece of land, much more like an orchard and definitely not a farm as we know it in Canada. My guess is that it was about twelve acres in size and the building in the property consisted of a two-storey stone structure complete with a good-sized room on the ground floor that contained a built-in press used to press grapes that were used in the process of making wine. It was so handy, for it was located only about two kilometers from our house, if that, and less than a couple hundred feet from the outskirts of town.

For me, *Serravento* was truly a "terrestrial paradise", a place that contained many interesting things. There were many varieties of birds including eagles, swallows and canaries, and all kinds of lizards and snakes. As well, it contained probably about seventy olive trees, some dating back hundreds of years, many varieties of fig trees, prickly pears, apricots, cherries, mandarin and "nespoli" trees. Also, we had our own vineyard with both white and dark table and wine grapes. We usually cultivated some grain, and annually had a garden with most varieties of vegetables. Almost every year we raised our own pig there, and as it was a custom in Calabria, it was butchered annually in the month of February, a period known as the *Carnevale*. It was at this time that everyone made spicy Calabrese sausages, *salcicce* and *sopressate,* and as the word *"carnevale"* implies, everyone feasted on lots of meat for a period of two to three months. We also raised and maintained other animals such as a goat (mainly for milk), rabbits, chickens, and even guinea pigs for meat.

I will never forget the daily chores assigned to me, i.e. to bring water and food to *Serravento* and feed the animals: the pig, the goat, the rabbits, and chickens and the beautiful, multi-colored roosters. While this was no easy task for a child my age, it was a common practice of many young boys and girls, many of whom had to travel over much longer distances to their country locations. But after the chores were done, I often had lots of time to myself to explore the world around me, and then often an hour or so before supper, I had to be home without fail, in order to practice one hour on the clarinet, or my father in particular, would be very cross with me.

Now, I have so many great memories of *Serravento* for as a family, we had many good times there and some of the best days of our lives as a family were spent there together. Life there was simple then, but some very special picnic-like activities were held there, that were always happy family occasions. All these happy activities naturally took place there but mostly before the war years, and none during the German occupation, when the Germans literally took *Serravento* away from us, as they set up camp on most of it, took what they wanted, including our chickens, rabbits and other food staples. When they occupied the place, we had strict orders from my mother and relatives that it was off limits to all of us. After what seemed to me well over a year of occupation, the Germans finally left, and I remember distinctly that our poor *Serravento* was ransacked and looked as if it had been thoroughly beat up. Everything was left in shambles and everywhere there were fireplace grills dug into the soil, with "live" and spent ammunition, particularly hand grenades were left everywhere, especially in the hollow trunks of the older and thicker olive trees.

While my first three years of life were quite comparatively uneventful, all that and everything also as we knew it changed with the declaration of World War II in 1939. I was only five years old in 1941, but I remember the patriotic fervor of young children just barely older than I was, who were allowed to wear the beautiful uniforms of Mussolini's *"Barillas"* and I remember crying that I wanted one too. I remember that at the beginning, Mussolini was everyone's hero and the talk and the hope of the entire country, and all my family, relatives, and friends were no exemption. Everybody talked about him as if he were some kind of superhero and some kind of savior. The vision of the whole country was to return once again to the glorious times of the mighty Roman Empire.

As far as I can remember, the first activity in my life that I really got involved in, was with the church, no doubt because my grandmother Carmela was such a devout Catholic. At the age of about six, I became an altar boy and was assisting at Holy Mass at some pretty early hour every morning. It was something that I sometimes enjoyed and through it all, I learned to recite and respond to Holy Mass in Latin. I learned it by rote memory, but I knew very little what the words meant, and it wasn't until much later in my life that I finally figured out what the Latin words stood for. Today, I would give anything to hear Mass celebrated in Latin again, once more.

I also attended Catechism on Sundays in the sacristy located at the back of the church behind the alter, and learned by memory probably thirty of forty prayers, for it seemed to me that there must have been a prayer for each and every life occasion, for what one did or failed to do, and for each time of the day, week, month, and year.

As I remember, Sunday was always a special day in Amato. Everyone wore their cleanest and best clothes and going to church for Sunday was a "day of obligation" for us Catholics. Sundays were always happier times, and I can still remember the glorious, happy-sounding church bells before High Mass with their compelling sound, urging everyone to go to church. On special *Festa* days the bells played in such a manner as to engulf our soul in joyous celebration and their great, happy sounds could be heard and felt for miles into the mountains and the valleys downhill from the town.

Our beloved church in my hometown of Amato "Chiesa dell'Immacolata".

San Francesco di Paola, Patron Saint of Amato and the region of Calabria, has had a great influence on Calabresi

The greatest religious feast day or *Festa* of the year was that of *San Francesco di Paola* which traditionally used to be held in May, and which was later changed and is now held annually during the whole second week of August culminating with its climax on the second Sunday of August. The change, no doubt, was necessitated by the desire to accommodate the many *Amatesi* immigrant "tourists" that used to go to Amato from all over the world annually during the summer months of June, July and August.

Statue of l'Immacolata in the Church of Amato. Father Fred Olds from Winnipeg is admiring some of the art work in the church

The church's bells also set the tone for the day when someone died. On these sad occasions the bells would toll in a steady, monotonous manner, that definitely sounded and felt sad, and so appropriately reflecting the occasion. Upon hearing these sad bells, people would immediately ask: *"For whom do the bells toll today?"* It is also worthy of note that even today, whenever an *Amatese* person dies anywhere in the world, the bells of the church of Amato toll to announce the passing, and invariably this is followed by a regular funeral mass in the church of Amato, ordered by relatives or friends, to mark the event in honor of the deceased Amatese person.

When I was five years old my father began to give me music lessons on the clarinet. Actually, it was on the *"sestino"* as it was called, which. resembles a *"piccolo"*, and in fact is the smallest of the clarinet family and a wind instrument that is about a foot long. Then as I got older, my father introduced me

BECOMING ITALIAN: MY BIRTH AND EARLY YEARS IN ITALY

to the *"quartino"* a clarinet that is two-thirds the length size of the normal clarinet, and finally the regular clarinet that I started to play about a year after I arrived in Canada at age fourteen, when my fingers got long enough to be able to reach all its keys

My father had great dreams that one day I would perhaps be a very good musician. Regardless, learning a musical instrument did a great deal for the development of my self-esteem, for after about three years of fairly intensive and focused instruction, I was good enough to play with the big symphonic band in town, right on the big, illuminated stage built every year for the occasion of the *festa* of *San Francesco di Paola* the patron Saint of Amato. I could not have been more than eight or nine years old, and it was a huge, memorable occasion for me.

I can still remember the many eyes upon me as I played on that big stage, and the several children that came up to the stage close enough to me, to listen and see close-up if in fact, I was really playing or going only through the motions. It was such a unique event that many of my "paesani" i.e. people from my town, still remember the event and remind me of it whenever we reminisce about those times of my growing up in Amato. No question that my daring to be different and seek the limelight began very early in my life. And it was through music that I distinguished myself as being talented and very popular in Amato, and my positive self- concept was thus assured.

In 1942 at the age of six, I began attending elementary school right in Amato which was compulsory and universally-free to grade five inclusive. The instructional methods used in those days were quite primitive and antiquated, based for the most part on rote memory, and many of the teachers' approaches, if the truth be known, were psychologically and physically abusive by today's standards and thinking.

Instead of the provincially approved regulation strap that was used for corporal punishment by teachers in Canada, teachers in Italy used green flexible branches of willow trees, and for even more punitive punishment, they would order and force pupils to kneel on their knees over small pieces of stone pebbles that would cut into their knees, at the corner of the classroom. But regardless of the methods used, elementary school days for me were happy and rewarding, for I liked school and excelled academically even then.

Crescendo to Becoming

The highest reward for a person's toil is not what they get for it, but what they become by it."
—**John Ruskin**

Piazza in Amato, with the band stage and light decorations, circa 1948.

Piazza in Amato today (actually same location as photo to the left).

Even though we had many chores to do, we had much more unstructured time than kids do today. As we were only required to be in school from 9:00 a.m. to 1:00 p.m., the whole afternoon was spent doing a variety of activities including daily chores, play soccer and other games at the piazza with friends, music practice, and other play activities that varied according to the season we were in.

But by far the most striking and unforgettable images of my early years in Amato relate to the World War II that began in 1939 raging there in full force during the earliest years of my life. I remember so vividly still, the Germans' arrogance and their sense of superiority made visible even through their activities and through their authoritative posture and body language.

One day my mother had sent me to the communal water fountain called *"fontana italiani"* (see below) carrying a rather large glass pitcher in my hands, used to fetch some natural spring water for us, a chore which I was required to do almost every day. It so happened on one such an occasion, that when I reached the water fountain, there were German soldiers there with two

BECOMING ITALIAN: MY BIRTH AND EARLY YEARS IN ITALY

trucks parked on the roadway while they were filling their steel containers with water. I waited my turn for ten to fifteen minutes, and when I thought they had finished their task, and that the way was clear, I walked up to the fountain and began to fill my glass pitcher. As I was filling the glass container with water, a German soldier grabbed me by the forearm and literally tossed me into a puddle of muddy water some ten or fifteen feet away. The glass pitcher shattered in hundreds of pieces, and I actually received a cut on my arm. I began to cry and run-away home to my mother who quickly took me upstairs to the oven room, as if to hide me from danger, as she told me to be quiet and began to clean me up. That day I had learned to fear and dislike all Germans in the world!

Amato Elementary School (2005) the school I attended in the 1940s.

Amato's favorite public water Fountain, "fontana italiani".

There was nothing else said or done, but this incident had left me with a sense of hate toward the Germans in general, a hatred that only dissipated years later when I was in high school. I understood finally that it was the war that I hated most of all, and not the German people *per se*. These feelings were reinforced when I played soccer for the senior league team "Italia", particularly when we would play against a team of German players named "Germania" in Winnipeg.

It is interesting to note that there were more war children's casualties in my hometown immediately *after* the war than there were during the actual war. I remember a much more traumatic and scarier incident that occurred to me and some of my friends my age. Around 1945, after the Germans had left the area, children my age and older would go down the hillside toward the valley on homemade "wagons" or "cars" that as children we had built using ball bearings for wheels and other materials left there in the countryside by the German soldiers' occupation.

One day a group of seven or eight of us boys decided to go riding downhill on these so-called home-made cars. Further down the steep winding road, four- or five-kilometers past *"Serravento"* near a place called *"l'Acqua Santa"* we all stopped to explore the area near a very small creek and an adjacent retainer stone wall that prevented soil erosion into the roadway. There, nearby, we found in the trunks of several olive trees, very interesting-looking objects, that looked quite shiny and captivating. Not knowing that they were "live" grenades, we tried to open them up to see what was inside of them, but as we could not open them, we decided to take the grenades and hurl them against the little stone bridge to see if we could crack them open and thus satisfy our curiosity.

Luckily, after a while we became bored with this process, and four of us got back to our "car" and resumed our trip on the road downhill for a further ride. When we were about a couple hundred or so feet away, we heard an unbelievably loud explosion that startled and scared us all. We ran back to the source at the foot of the little retaining stone wall where we had left the others and found one of our friends, Eligio Falvo, lying on the ground, fully covered by blood and bleeding profusely all over his limp body. Immediately as if on cue, a man happened to be passing by going back to town, and hearing the explosion, ran over to see what was happening. He picked up Eligio and put him over his shoulder as if he were carrying a dead lamb and walked rapidly uphill toward town taking all the shortcut paths possible. All of us were following behind, actually believing that Eligio had died, and in great despair, we cried all the way to town. By the time we got to the "piazza" i.e. the town square, there were probably well over a hundred people quickly gathered there, eager to witness what was happening. Soon we reached doctor Priolo's house and office and he attended to Eligio, whom we were told was still alive but just barely, for he had lost so much blood, and he was full of "schegges", or pieces of jagged steel shrapnel that got lodged all over his body upon impact.

BECOMING ITALIAN: MY BIRTH AND EARLY YEARS IN ITALY

Incidentally, I last saw my friend Eligio in 2006 (some 60 years after the incident) whose body was still harboring several pieces of shrapnel which were left unremoved because of their dangerous location, and on his face, arms and legs were still visible the marks left by the unforgettable incident. Whenever I saw him again, invariably we always talked and recalled the remarkable incident that almost killed us all, but he especially, who had been so close to death. Actually, Eligio had what could be described as a normal life, had a rewarding career mainly with Northern Electric in Montreal, and raised a wonderful family. Sad to say, he passed away in Montreal in 2009 with serious illnesses unrelated to the incident here-in described. As long as I live, however, I shall never forget him.

Dr. Francesco Priolo, the active doctor during my youth in Amato, was well respected and loved by most Amatesi. Personally, I could never forget him either, for he not only saved Eligio Falvo's life (see above) but also saved my sister Maria's life when at the age of about two, she almost drowned on a large tub of water that my mother used to make soap and wash her laundry. We all imagined that the little girl went up to the large tub, saw her image in the water, and fell in headfirst, luckily with feet up resting on the tub's edge. This made it possible for us to spot her as we went by. I was the first to spot her, but we thought she had died, for she was totally blue. Luckily, Dr. Priolo happened to come by our house at that very moment and rushed into our house and somehow miraculously revived her and brought her back to life.

It's interesting to note that while Dr. Priolo saved several lives in Amato, he could not save his very own, dying of cancer at a very young age. It was learned later, when one read the lyric poems, he had written, that he knew for a while his fate, that he was dying, but kept it secret from everybody else and suffered alone, in silence. Thus, we learned of his anguish and torment that he endured prior to his passing.

Right after the war, as well, the most tragic accident occurred when one of my friends, my age, by the nickname of *"Pitarolu"* ventured to the countryside by himself, found olive tree

Dr. Francesco Priolo

trunks full of hand grenades, and not knowing what they were, he proceeded to fetch several of them, opened his shirt and filled it with as many grenades as he could place there. He then proceeded to make his way back towards town, and as he reached town, close to the medieval "historic tower" near the town's church, the grenades exploded, and my poor friend was blown to smithereens.

What I will never forget as well, were the German airplanes hovering close to our rooftops dropping their shrapnel among the people on the streets, and the people running desperately to take cover, while at the same time hurling curses against the Germans. Still vivid in my mind is my father's stubborn refusal to seek cover and refuge in an underground cave that the town of Amato had dug up, as a shelter location where the people could take cover when we were bombarded by enemy planes, especially during the night. I recall my father's reasoning comments that he would never concede to the Germans, and that if God had determined that he wanted us dead, then we would die in our home with some dignity, and not like animals in some cave.

* * *

"It's not what you are, but what you don't become that hurts."
—Oscar Levant

* * *

Teachers: how much you care about your students is often more important than how much you know.
—Frank Fiorentino

* * *

"We do make a difference – one way or the other. We are responsible for the impact of our lives. Whatever we do with whatever we have, we leave behind us a legacy for those who follow.
—Stephen Covey

* * *

5. BECOMING A PROUD CANADIAN CITIZEN

"Addio Italia Mia" (Oh! Canada!)

On January 1, 1949, the town of Amato was under a deluge of rain that we and all our friends and relatives still remember to this day. It was the day of our departure for "America", so-called for many people would or could not make the distinction between Canada and United States. For us, it was a day of ambivalent feelings, feelings based on heresy of people talking about what it meant to go to "America", and sad feelings of what it meant to leave our beloved homeland of Italy. So, we definitely had strong, conflicting feelings, feelings of joy of looking forward to a better future in "America", and sad because we all believed that we would never see our beloved Amato and our *bella Italia* ever again.

I Cruci" (the Calvary Crosses)

Crescendo to Becoming

As we said goodbye to all our relatives and friends, I remember my grandmother Carmela so sad looking, while trying to convince herself by telling and asking my father: *"We will see each other again...right?"* I am sure she knew very well that given her age and our economic reality, that would not be a realistic expectation. I can still imagine now the pain that she and my father must have experienced at that moment, realizing fully too well, that both of them would not see each other close up ever again, nor would she see her daughter-in-law and her grandchildren that she had loved so much and helped raise.

We were taken to the railroad station down in the valley close to the town of *Marcellinara* by horse and buggy. Om the way we passed the Calvary monument called "I Cruci" i.e. The Crosses, where - the procession from the church would go on Good Friday to reenact the Passion of Christ

Almost as if by instinct I ran right close up to it, touched the wall as if to kiss it, and said *"Addio Amato mio"* thinking that I would never see it again, made the sign of the cross, and left again to rejoin the group. By the time we arrived at the railroad station downhill to the valley at *Marcellinara,* we were all drenched with water and some of the new clothes that all of us were wearing for the first time began to discolor, including my brand-new charcoal-grey "heavy" overcoat that had been custom-tailored for me, as I was saying and crying the last good-byes to our friends and relatives.

Then, our train started to pull away heading West and then North at *St. Eufemia* toward Salerno. After seven or eight hours we reached the beautiful seaport of Napoli (Naples) and stared up where the ship that was anchored there was waiting for us as its passengers.

"THE SOBIESKI"

BECOMING A PROUD CANADIAN CITIZEN

With a lot of trepidation and ambivalent feelings, we finally boarded the "*Sobieski*", a Polish ship that apparently was the first ship to transport immigrant passengers from Europe to "America" after WW2.

The *Sobieski* was a relatively smaller ship as ships go, but one which regardless, to me seemed gigantic in size just the same, given my young age. The fare for the trip from Naples to Halifax was $ 215.00 Canadian dollars per adult, a considerable amount of money for those days (1949) and half that ($107.50) for children under twelve years of age. Therefore, the total cost for the family was $1199.00 a huge sum which would take us years to repay.

The ***Sobieski*** seemed fairly clean, but the sleeping quarters consisted of bunk beds, one on top of the other, and the second-class cabins that we occupied seemed quite cramped, even to my young eyes. For most of the trip my older sister Eleonora, my mother, and sometimes my father and younger sisters spent a lot of time in those quarters suffering from nausea and seasickness. I remember thinking that it was such a shame that they were unable to eat the food which was abundant and excellent as far as I and others who were well enough to eat it, were concerned.

Shortly after several hours on the beautiful Mediterranean Sea, we reached and stopped at the seaport city of *Genoa* in northern Italy. There, we had an opportunity to get off the ship and go exploring the area of the port where I remember seeing the huge statue of Cristoforo Colombo. My father met with some relatives from *Miglierina* (Amato's closest neighboring town) that had moved to Genoa in search of work, and soon after we were on our way toward *"The Rock"* or Fort of Gibraltar.

Gibraltar too, was quite memorable because we were greeted there by hundreds of people on small boats that came up close to the side of our ship to sell the passengers souvenirs and other trinkets. All this seemed like so much fun.

Crescendo to Becoming

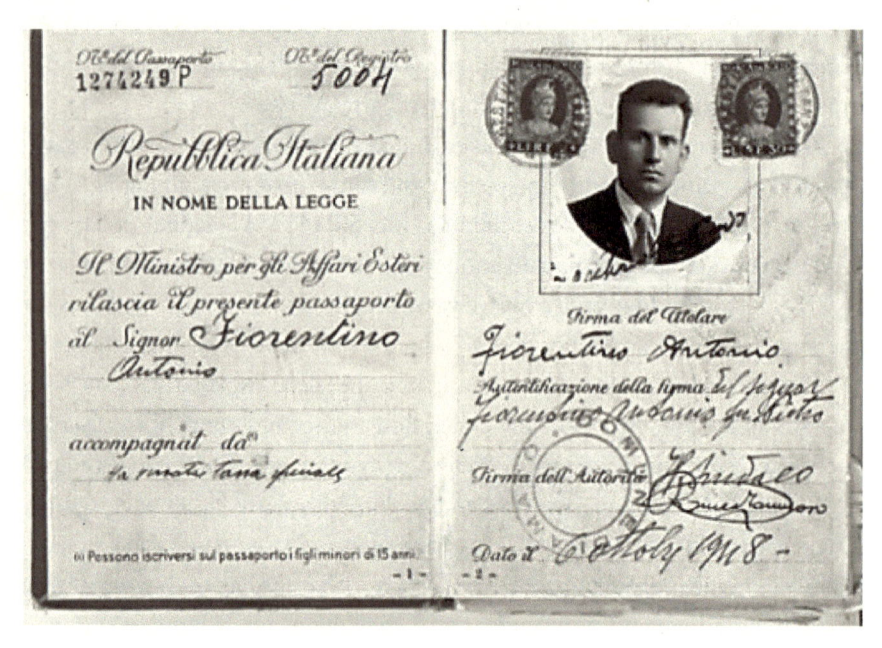

Father's Passport and Picture dated October 6, 1948

Passport Picture, 1948, taken two months prior to our departure from Italy for Canada
Back Row, Left to right: *Sister Maria, mother, and me*
Bottom Row: *Sister Delfina and brother Onofrio*

BECOMING A PROUD CANADIAN CITIZEN

After Gibraltar, however, conditions changed dramatically, and things got much more serious and threatening. I will never forget the ominous and frightening scenes as we crossed the Atlantic Ocean in January in the dead of winter. The ship would descend very deep down into the water which seemed to be unbelievably deep, and as the ship went down, the huge "mountains" of black-looking water rose up on both sides of the ship which seemed to engulf us into the bottom of the ocean. I remember being very concerned (afraid may be a better word) but I did not show it, as I kept looking at other adults around me, and they seemed to look at things as being "expected" and normal. The only relief we did have is that when the sea seemed a little calmer, we would go to the "bridge" in the very front of the ship, and looked down at how the water was being parted by the ship, and there you could sense more realistically the truer and faster speed of the ship. Having seen the movie *Titanic* a few years ago, I could really relate to the scenes where the young man would go right up to the front of the ship on the bridge, open his arms apart and make his body in the form of a cross, for I and my friends had done the very same thing some sixty years earlier.

As I stated before, for those that could make it to the dining room the food was great, and the portions were unbelievably large. Most of us had never seen steaks the size of the ones being served on the *"Sobieski"*. But what I remember most is that often the sea was so rough that our plates would slide off the tables if we somehow didn't hold onto them. Indeed, it was a very long couple of weeks until some people started to shout, *"land ahoy"* and we finally arrived with a great deal of anxious anticipation and disembarked in Halifax at the now-historically famous *Pier 21*, on January 17, 1949.

When we arrived at Halifax, we were all relieved and overjoyed by the fact that we had made it, and that we had overcome the perceived dangers of the high seas. But shortly after arriving and going through the "warehouse" called *Pier 21* my family was not very happy that officials there searched us thoroughly and in the process confiscated some genuine, wonderful homemade *capicollo", "soppressata" "salcicce"* sausages, and *"pecorino"* cheese, a couple of rare bottles of *"anice"* liquor, and other alcoholic bottles that my father had been so anxious to bring to our relatives in Canada as gifts. After we were "shepherded" through customs in the very crowded *Pier 21* warehouse-like

Crescendo to Becoming

facility, we were directed into a train waiting on the other side of the building opposite to where we disembarked, but now finally, on desired Canadian soil.

On that first long train ride in our new country, we began to experience the true and harsh conditions of Canada as they really were at that time. The inside of the train coach was rather cold, and its seats were all made of wood and not at all the comfortable seats we had experienced on the Italian trains. The bellows of dark smoke and soot that the train engines spewed and released made everything appear dark, black and very dirty.

I began to discern disappointment in my fathers' eyes, as we all began to wonder what we had done and where we had ended up. Regardless, we still looked forward to embracing our grandparents and relatives that most of us only knew through photographs.

"Pier 21", Halifax, the door facing the land (the Atlantic is behind the building)

Union Station (now Via Rail) on Main Street, Winnipeg (circa 1950)

After two days in the rough and uncomfortable train travelling through the Canadian Shield, through what seemed to be nothing but uninhabitable stone, bush and forest, we finally reached Montreal where we had almost three days stopover, enjoying the company of some of my mother' aunts and other relatives, and some *paesani* who had come from Amato years before.

Of course, Montreal changed our views about Canada, for Montreal was truly a magnificent city to our eyes and represented more realistically the idea of what we seemed to be looking for and expected in "America". It seemed to me that everything about Montreal was more to our liking, the smells, the foods, the city, St. Catherines the Main Street, St.Joseph's Oratory, the Notre Dame Church, and everything else that we saw there. Obviously, Montreal raised our hopes and our expectations of what we wanted to find in Winnipeg, but alas, Winnipeg was not Montreal, but something else altogether different!

The trip from Montreal was long, very long, and I remember how delighted we were when our *"commare"* Linda Cantafio and her husband Michele (the mother and father-in-law of my uncle Peter and aunt Serafina) and their son Joe came from Winnipeg to greet us at Capreol, Ontario. Apparently, as I learned later, these wonderful people came because they were the only ones that could afford it, for Michele had worked for the *Canadian National Railway* for many years and were entitled to a free pass from the company that they put to use to come and greet us. In any case, we were very happy to see them, and they told us many things about Winnipeg, and thus prepared us for the realities of what to expect in Winnipeg, our destination and our new home.

We arrived in Winnipeg, I believe on or about January 21, 1949, at the C.N.R. Station, what is today known as the *Union Station* on Main Street and Broadway. It was another moment in my life that I shall always remember.

The train station was bursting full of people, and it was wonderful to meet the large, extended Scerbo family that came to greet us there. At this wonderful moment we felt saved and lucky with incredible affection and support from all our relatives. Indeed, it became quite evident what grandfather meant when he often said: *"noi siamo ricchi di sangue--we are rich in blood"*.

I still remember the arrival in Winnipeg as if it were yesterday. At the train station I ran out of the front entrance doors on Main Street to check out the surroundings, and I literally felt myself shrink as it were, experiencing for the first time in my life, such unimaginable cold temperature which at first, I didn't even know how to handle, for my body had never experienced such a strange sensation before. I didn't know what it really was, but my instincts told me it wasn't good for me, and very quickly I ran again to the warmth inside the station. One of my uncles, Frank Maruca (aunt Angelarosa's husband) was the only one who owned a beautiful automobile as we used to call them, and he drove us from the railroad station to our new address at Stradbroke and Osborne where my grandparents lived in a large two-storey side-by-side duplex. I could not believe that it was possible for cars to run so smoothly in such a cold, harsh climate. But the car was warm and comfortable, and indeed the whole ride was "cool" for in Italy it was only the rich that could afford to own a car like my uncle Frank had.

What the passport picture on page thirty-seven above doesn't show was my older sister Eleonora, the oldest of the five children, for she already had her own passport, nor does it show Musetta, who was born in Canada later in 1951. As well, the picture doesn't show the fact that mother was pregnant with child, carrying a baby boy which died at birth shortly after our arrival in Winnipeg.

Still, my father was a proud man, and quickly became extremely disillusioned about Canada. In truth, upon arrival to Canada, my father felt lost. He thought of Canada as being still quite primitive, a land being void of culture, music, art, and so on. The only personal satisfaction he would really have in his life in Canada, was to see all his children (except for Eleonora the oldest) enrolled and making good progress in school. I know for certain that he was extremely pleased and proud that of all the children from Amato in Winnipeg (coming in significant numbers at that point in time) I was the only teenager that was registered and attending school at a time, when Italian people preferred to have their children find work in the local factories in order to earn some money.

It was my father that insisted in no uncertain terms, that I would go to school as long as possible, to the highest level possible. Because of his unrelenting insistence, I had no choice but to continue going to school, including secondary education at the university level. Thanks to his insistence, I stayed in school and achieved my three degrees and a *Professional Certificate in Education*, and this, at a time when very few people graduated with degrees in the field of education. For example, in 1963, in a staff of about 450 professional teachers, I was one of only two people with a Master's Degree in Education in the whole Transcona-Springfield School Division, when most teachers had barely class 1, i.e. a grade 11 equivalent standing.

But although my father insisted that I stay in school, the financial and other responsibility to allow it, in fact rested solely with me. Luckily, I had the desire and determination to accept the challenge and seize the opportunity, but more than anything I wanted to make my dad happy, for my father's nostalgic feelings for his native Italy were all pervasive. Indeed, he was consumed by it. In order to cope with it, he began to write poetry in both the Italian language, and the dialect of Calabria, and thus he found a most appropriate escape mechanism and medium to deal with his anguish, and at times, depression. He missed Italy immensely and so he began to write about both people and places of his beloved *Amato,* and of his beloved and unforgettable *"Patria"* i.e. homeland.

After we arrived in Winnipeg, for a period of three or four days, I stayed put at home, with my family to meet and receive many friends that came to visit us, to welcome us to Canada. As well, I would go to spend some time with grandfather and *uncle* Peter in their *"Perfect Shoemaker"* shop located at street level, right smack in middle of what is now the west side of the Osborne Village. There I would watch what seemed to me to be an incredible endless number of cars, streetcars and electricity-driven trolley buses going by, sights that were all too new and very interesting to me.

A few short days after our arrival, I was taken to *Gladstone School,* the nearest school to where we lived, to register. This school was then located right on the corner of Osborne and Corydon (now referred to as "Confusion Corner" on the diagonal where the northern point of Pembina Highway ends. Once at school, I was given an I.Q. test which I must have failed miserably for the test was all in English, (except for the arithmetic questions) and I had no functional knowledge of the English language whatsoever. In any case, based probably on the test results, I was placed in grade one with children who were all six years old, and therefore half my age, for I was almost thirteen in three weeks' time, that is on February twentieth. But more on this later.

Front Row: Nonno Arcangelo and Nonna Maria
Back Row Mrs. and Mrs. Linda Cantafio who came to meet us on the train in Capreol Ontario

But the most traumatic experience that occurred very soon after our arrival in Winnipeg arose as soon as my grandmother Maria found out that my mother was pregnant with child, and because of this, she became downright angry and belligerent, first with my mother and days later with my father. My father, who was a proud and passionate man argued vociferously

Crescendo to Becoming

with my grandmother, finally telling her in no uncertain terms, that she had no business intruding into his personal life and affairs that were solely his and my mother's responsibility. He argued often and loudly, pointing out that she, herself, had brought seven children into the world, and that she should not interfere where his own family composition was concerned. But my grandmother was adamant and so angry that the animosity quickly exploded into a major irreversible family conflict which quickly and effectively, devastated my father's relationship with my grandmother, and soon with the rest of our relatives.

It was so bad, in fact, that things escalated to intolerable levels, and my poor mother found herself in the middle, in a "no man's land", relative to my kind grandfather, and with all her brothers and sisters, (my uncles and aunts). As a result, we quickly found ourselves on the "outside looking in", and found ourselves strictly on our own, in a strange new land, and at this point, without any real means of survival. This situation became a frightening nightmare and the acrimony lasted for many years, and so devastating to all of us, that it not only added immensely to the serious insecurities, doubts and frustrations of our family members, but also to the family's fragile ability to cope and survive in the challenging new world.

The whole mess caused a great deal of havoc for us all, particularly my mother, and my parents never ever really recovered totally from the harsh blow. To make things even worse, another serious problem, at our very beginning in Canada, was the fact that father had no work, even though a job had been guaranteed to him by some fake farmer, to satisfy the conditions of the application which allowed us to come to Winnipeg. The money my father had brought from Italy from the sale of our house was given to my grandfather upon our arrival to help defray the current expenses, and as a result my father was penniless. He somehow managed by borrowing some money from friends and had to buy some groceries on credit from some Italian grocers that knew my father from Italy.

As the days advanced, I even felt frustrations and tensions growing due no doubt, to the feelings of helplessness on the part of everyone, especially my mother who had developed health issues, and father, who was now often in a constant state of anger and who sometimes even threatened to go back to Italy. In such a scenario, finding work for my father became a critical issue,

BECOMING A PROUD CANADIAN CITIZEN

and we, the two of us, (I was 13 years old) began to look for a job, but that proved to be more difficult than we could have imagined, not only because my father was not able to communicate due to the language barrier, but also by the fact that he lacked even the necessary basic skills in almost everything where work might have been available.

The only job that might be available to him was that of a laborer. Finally, purely by chance, we ventured into a construction site on Westminster Avenue not far from the Misericordia Hospital, where a new apartment building was beginning to be built, and there, as a laborer, my father had his first job working with a wheelbarrow. Several months later, however, he was hired at the *Canadian National Railway* in Transcona, and indeed this was truly a godsend. Even so, I will never forget how painful the first few years in Canada were overall for our entire family, but the energy of my youth helped me cope and overcome many problems. At age thirteen, I found my first job, part-time, delivering groceries for a grocery store on Notre Dame near Sherbrooke. Later, at age fourteen, I found a more substantial job washing cars at Russell Motors located at 730 Portage Avenue, (where Gordon Bell Field of Dreams now stands) and my financial contributions to my father helped immensely, no doubt, to alleviate the daily tight money crunch at home.

However, the arguments at home were a daily occurrence, and our lives were continually disrupted, and this too, impacted negatively on my schooling. During the first two years in Canada, we moved no less than four times. We moved to Lipton Street and Portage Avenue on the top third storey, a suite in the attic belonging to a kind Luigi and Caterina Aiello who were an immense help to us in those critical early days. I recall that in the winter the attic apartment was quite cold, and, in the summer, it was unbearably hot. While on Lipton Street I had to attend *Laura Secord School* on Wolseley some walking distance away.

Then, a few months later, we rented a second floor of a house on McDermot Street close to Sherbrook Street, a deal negotiated by well-known Italian realtor Rose Champlone, and a place very close to where the *Holy Rosary Church* used to be, where *Cancer Care Manitoba* now stands, and there I was required to register at *Montcalm School* on nearby Tecumseh Street. I remember this school so well because there I became a School Patrol Boy and

Crescendo to Becoming

met my friend Ray Knowles who was the leader "captain" of the group, and who I have never forgotten since. Then, eventually, we finally bought a very modest, old one-level house at 726 Toronto Street between Wellington and Notre Dame avenues, and that brought me to *Hugh John Macdonald Junior High School* which gave me a new start on things, and where I experienced some new-found interests.

After a couple of years there, I finally reached *Daniel McIntyre Collegiate Institute,* a high school, which gave me a great deal of new-found energy, motivation, and satisfaction. Thank God for *"Daniel Mac"* for it changed my life forever. Both schools, but particularly *"Daniel Mac"* proved to be critical in my development and growth and in my life generally, for it was there that I met two great teachers that had a super positive impact on my life. It was these two teachers that truly motivated and empowered me to achieve greater things and gave me considerable personal fulfillment. But more on these later.

Only one year after our arrival in Winnipeg, in 1950, there was quite a significant flood which forced many of the Italians living in Fort Rouge and other locations to move to higher ground with friends and relatives such as in Transcona. As if that weren't enough, in 1950 there was also an outbreak of polio, and many children were affected by this dreaded disease. At this point, my father in particular, felt very insecure in this new land to say the least, and longed more and more for his beautiful, native country of Italy. It was at this point that we all wandered whether we had made a huge mistake coming to Canada.

We all seemed to find a way to escape from the sad and atrocious reality that was now our new home. For me, going to school was a way to escape the pain, for my older sister Eleonora, it was to hurry up and get married as soon as possible. But for my mother, she did not seem capable of escaping the harsh reality that we found ourselves in, and she began to suffer many illnesses including some psychosomatic ones that were very difficult to diagnose and most difficult to cure. As for my father, he found his escape mechanism in a new pastime which gave him remarkable *raison de vivre,* and that was writing poetry, both in the Italian language and in the Calabrese dialect, and so out of these devastating conditions, a poet was born, and he wrote incessantly and tirelessly at every spare moment he had, even during his coffee breaks at work. He wrote of his beloved country, places where he grew up, and wrote something about most of the people of Amato. Amazingly, it was through this beautiful expressive medium, that my father was able to cope, for he had found a meaningful new way of expressing his lyrical and nostalgic feelings of anxiety, feelings that often became so poignant as to border on melancholy.

Antonio and Carmelina Fiorentino's (my) Family:

Name	Relation To Me	D.O.B.	Birthplace
Antonio	Father	16/09/1905	Amato, Italy
Carmelina	Mother	29/07/1912	Winnipeg
Eleonora	Sister	23/12/1931	Amato, Italy
Francesco	(me)	20/02/1936	Amato, Italy
Delfina	Sister	16/03/1941	Amato, Italy
Maria	Sister	26/04/1944	Amato, Italy
Onofrio	Brother	15/02/1946	Amato, Italy
Musetta	Sister	04/10/1951	Winnipeg

Antonio Fiorentino (my father)

My Father and Mother, Antonio and Carmelina Fiorentino, circa 1954 on the back porch at the Alexander Avenue residence

Crescendo to Becoming

In front entrance of our house at Alexander Avenue near Keewatin in Weston
Front Row, Left to Right: *sisters Musetta and Delfina, my Mother Carmelina, Brother Onofrio and sister Maria* **Second Row:** *second cousin Connie Fiorentino, father Antonio Fiorentino*
Back Row: *Giuseppina and Antonio Fiorentino (father's cousins)*

As mentioned above, we somehow managed to buy our first house located on Toronto Street, a one-storey bungalow that needed a lot of work, and a house that had a 8' by 8' mud hole under the kitchen for a so-called basement intended only to allow access to the water pipes which often would freeze up in the coldest months of winter, and which too often, I personally would have to thaw out with boiling water, when I arrived home from school.

As part of the heating system the house had a smelly and dangerous oil-burning heater in the middle of the living room that exhausted through a dangerous 8-inch exposed pipe-like metal heating duct to the ceiling. The doors of the bedrooms had to be kept open day and night so that some of the heat would hopefully reach the bedrooms, but which in fact were always very cold in the winter (and very hot in the summer). As well there was an efficient wood-burning stove in the kitchen which produced a lot of heat in that area itself, but very little of it found its way into one of the adjoining bedrooms. But in the months of January and February we could invariably expect and in fact have about an inch thick of ice along the corners of the bedroom walls, and the windows would often be a totally solid mass of ice, usually one to two inches in thickness.

BECOMING A PROUD CANADIAN CITIZEN

A couple of years later, we bought a three-storey house located on Alexander Avenue very near Keewatin in the Weston area of Winnipeg, and then in 1958 we finally had progressed into buying a beautiful bungalow at 1181 Burrows Avenue just west of McPhillips, the same house that I was living in when I got married in 1960.

Left to Right: Jimmy Maruca, Maria Rossi, Carmela Scerbo, my sister Eleonora Maruca, her husband John Maruca, and his mother Angelina Maruca

The Holy Rosary Church

Since its inception a hundred years ago, in 1923, the *Holy Rosary Church* has been the cradle, the heartbeat, and nerve center of the Italian community in Winnipeg. From the time we arrived in Winnipeg in 1949, I remember Father Cimichella, Father Furlan being very active in the early 1950's, and since 1995 to the present time, (summer, 2024) the popular Father Sam Argenziano, that made the *Holy Rosary Church* "the glue" that bonded and linked together the Italians in Winnipeg in a relevant and meaningful way.

Throughout these years, first and foremost, I can remember the ever-present Father Fiore who was always in the middle of the action with his

Crescendo to Becoming

guidance, in all things Italian. I can also remember Peter Maruca who was involved with the church's choir from the early 1950's to near 2010. They both certainly are deserving of all the accolades they have received from the community for their dedication, commitment, and perseverance. It was the Holy Rosary Church and its leaders that gave us not only a sense of spiritual harmony with God, but also a social and cultural connection and sustenance with of our homeland which we have all craved.

I don't think that anyone could deny that the *Holy Rosary Church*, from the very beginning, and certainly during the past one hundred years, has been a veritable pillar of strength and support for the members of the Italian Community in Winnipeg. If not for the *Holy Rosary Church*, I am sure, that many of our people including members of my own family, would have found life in the new land even more unbearable, particularly in their early years in Canada.

It must be acknowledged, therefore, that the *Holy Rosary Church* has contributed significantly to the quality of our very life, and that its role in helping us define who we really are collectively as a people, will never be surpassed. In a mere personal way, I recall that in the early 1950's, the *Holy Rosary Church* on several occasions sent my family for a couple of weeks on an almost all-paid holiday to *Camp Morton*, a wonderful catholic beach property just north of Gimli. For my siblings and me, this summer holiday was a true respite, and the highlight of our lives during those very difficult early years in Canada.

It was simply a wonderful outing and just what the young family needed. *Camp Morton* was a super place for swimming, relaxation, and prayer. Beside the wonderful regular chapel, there was an open grotto on the plateau at the water's edge, game facilities, open stages, flower gardens, barbeque pits, and other facilities to keep the participants and visitors happily engaged and interested. For the family, *Camp Morton* was a super place, and for me personally, it was like a gift from heaven.

BECOMING A PROUD CANADIAN CITIZEN

Summer holidays for Delfina, Musetta Maria and Onofrio at Camp Morton

Sister Musetta and Brother Onofrio at Camp Morton

Father Domenico Fiore *pictured on the left, provided over the years not only the spiritual leadership that we needed, but also helped provide the vision, the mission, and motivation for us to become the best that we could be. In short, he has been and is still, our hero and thus deserving of all the accolades he has received since his retirement in Ottawa.*

NOTE: The paragraphs below is part of a speech I delivered on the evening in 2004, when Father Fiore received the **Eccellenza Award** from the Italian Community of Winnipeg

"Father Fiore! In the name of absolutely everyone in this Italian community that you know so intimately well, I would like to say this: we love you with all our hearts because from the moment we got to know you, you have demonstrated your unconditional love towards us. We give infinite thanks for everything you have done, for everything you have been for us, and infinite thanks for having been our priest, our brother, and our friend."

Crescendo to Becoming

"Blessed are those that can give without remembering and receive without forgetting.,"
—**Author Unknown**

A PROUD CANADIAN CITIZEN BY CHOICE, 1961

Becoming a Canadian citizen was not as simple as people may think. Certainly, it is not as easy as being born one. It took me no less than 12 years to become Canadian, partly because there were many difficult issues that were more pressing at that time. The number one priority was survival itself and all other concerns seemed insignificant by comparison. All our efforts, at the beginning, therefore, were directed toward that end. .. . We must remember that my father was in no way convinced that Canada was the place where he wanted to stay. Every day here in Canada, during the first twelve years or so, my father was somewhat depressed and dreamt incessantly and nostalgically about his *bella Italia.* Thank God, he found that writing about Italy and its people provided for him a fulfilling escape, and writing became a passion that gave him a real reason for being. Finally in 1961, after my father went to a few sessions of night school to learn some rudimentary facts about Canada, both my father and I went to Citizen Court and received our respective, official Certificate of Canadian Citizenship. Amazingly, I remember the occasion as a very proud day in our lives.

More specifically, I became a Canadian citizen on the twenty–seven day of February 1961 and I must add that I did so, of my own volition. I was 25 years old, married just seven months earlier, and I considered it a very special event in my life. As it was a requirement then that to be a teacher in Canada, one had to be a Canadian citizen, the decision was a "no brainer". Actually, I had decided to seek Canadian citizenship well before this date, but I never seemed to have the time to go through the process. It must be said that I had absolutely no qualms about becoming a Canadian citizen, even though I was always very proud of my Italian roots and heritage. It was my view then, as it is still my view now, that being both Italian and Canadian, is having the best of both worlds.

BECOMING A PROUD CANADIAN CITIZEN

*My Canadian Citizenship Card and Certificate issued 1961,
12 years after coming to Canada.*

• •

"I honestly think that it is better to be a failure at something you love, than to be a success at something you hate."
—George Burns

• •

"We are not what we know, but what we are willing to learn."
—Mary Catherine Bateson

• •

"Life is not the way it's supposed to be. It's the way it is. The way you cope with it is what makes the difference."
—Virginia Satir

• •

"It is the nature of man to rise to greatness if greatness is expected of him."
—John Steinbeck

• •

6.
BECOMING A STUDENT, A MUSICIAN, AND A YOUNG ATHLETE

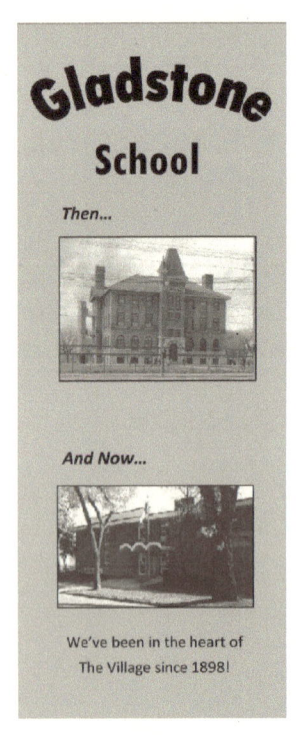

Gladstone School

Then...

And Now...

We've been in the heart of The Village since 1898!

WE BECOME WHO WE ARE as a result of many factors. Some are of our own choosing, and some are not. The seeds of me becoming a student, a musician, and an athlete were all activities rooted in my early years in Italy.

Like most children, I became a student by going to school in Italy beginning in grade one, (there was no kindergarten) an obligatory activity demanded by the state from grade one to grade five inclusive. While in Italy in grades 1 to 5, I was always the top student in my class, but in Canada it was the opposite. For many reasons, I did not have a very good beginning in school in Canada. School authorities' decision to place me in grade one with the children half my age, was inappropriate and dysfunctional, and resulted in many physical altercations with the other pupils who could not resist to bully and ridicule me due to my inability to speak the English language. Every word I uttered became a reason for boisterous laughter for my class. It seemed that with every attempt I made, someone would invariably laugh at me, and as a result, I would lash out physically in retaliation, for at this stage I was physically much bigger and stronger than the remainder of the pupils in my class (although this advantage did not last long).

BECOMING A STUDENT, A MUSICIAN, AND A YOUNG ATHLETE

But thank God, shortly after I began school, I got lucky. **Mrs. G. I. Keith**, the principal of *Gladstone School* at that time, invariably kept me in her office. Although she would let me go out for recess, (the Public Schools Act prohibited the taking away of the recess period from children), she accommodated me so that I even had my own desk there, and God bless her, she saw to it that I covered all the primary readers and storybooks under her close supervision and scrutiny. Her "individualized instruction" and attention, together with some of the supports she threw my way, were exactly what I needed at that time. There was a lot of scholastic progress made that first year, and this gave me a great deal of confidence and provided a great boost to my self-esteem. I have never forgotten her initiative and I took the opportunity to thank her many times in her retirement years well into her nineties, until she died. She would rank as one of four great teachers that made a huge difference in my growth and development and for that reason I will never forget her.

Another teacher that I will never forget was at *Hugh John MacDonald Junior High School* by the name of **Mr. Leavens**, a rather dogmatic and traditional teacher who really cared about his students, and who went out of his way to get to really know all the students in his classroom.

Mr. Leavens' Grade 7 class picture at Hugh John MacDonald, 1952. I am the first student in the Middle Row, left to right.

It was my luck, that I was placed in his classroom and that he was also my homeroom teacher. When he learned that I had never skated on ice, he brought me a pair of used ice skates and gave them to me outright as a gift. He encouraged me to join the school soccer team, whose coach was a new young gentleman just starting out as a teacher by the name of Mr. Richard Muchmore. It was Mr. Muchmore that made me realize the love that I had for sports. Then in the spring, I became the pitcher of the school's softball team. Because I was quite good at both activities, my interest at school became quite high. However, the process of becoming a musician began by me taking lessons on the clarinet at the early age of six, strictly to satisfy my father I might add, himself a musician of note, and probably to satisfy his dream to have a son become a great musician in Italy

I believe it was when I was in grade eight at *Hugh John MacDonald Junior High School* that Mr. Leavens learned that I had also been a clarinet player for a few years in Italy. I had given up playing the clarinet in Canada simply because I didn't have an appropriate instrument, for it needed many repairs which we could not afford, and because I had outgrown the size of the "quartino", which was now too small for me. I learned later on, that it had been the same Mr. Leavens that had talked to Mr. Glen Pierce about me, the music teacher at *Daniel McIntyre Collegiate,* the school which I was due to attend the following school year, and a school that would have a tremendous impact in my life.

In any case, one day Mr. Pierce reached out to me at *Hugh John MacDonald*. I was summoned to the principal's office where I met Mr. Pierce for the very first time. He had come give me not one, but two clarinets (one was a B flat and the other an A flat). He told me to take them home and start practicing once again in preparation for the day next Fall, when I would be attending *Daniel McIntyre Collegiate Institute*. However, when my father got home that evening, he found me practicing hard on the clarinet. Thinking that he too would be happy, I was caught totally by surprise at his unexpected reaction. Very angrily, he asked me where I had "bought" the instruments, and there was no way that I could convince him that a teacher from another school, a teacher that I did not even know, had given me the two clarinets on loan, "with no strings attached". My father was furious and more than a little irate and hollered at me that he had no money to pay for a musical instrument, let alone two. He let me know in no uncertain terms, that I had to return the instruments where I got them, first thing the very next day, no ifs, and or buts.

So next day I did as I was told, and returned the two clarinets to Mr. Patterson, the principal. I explained to him, the best way I could, in my

BECOMING A STUDENT, A MUSICIAN, AND A YOUNG ATHLETE

broken English, that my father did not want me to have the instruments. "My father no want clarinets ...no have money" I said, as he kept on trying to convince me to keep them. Finally, I asked him: "Give me letter, please, to explain to my father", and this he did do, explaining that I was loaned the musical instruments legitimately at no cost. But even with the letter as "proof", it still needed a great deal of arguing, until I was able to convince my father, but only with my mother's intervention and total support. We were finally able to convince him, that Mr. Pierce, a music teacher from *Daniel McIntyre Collegiate*, was preparing me for next school year, for he wanted me to take part in the music program of the school. And so began the love affair I have always had with **Mr. Glen Pierce**, who died in 2015 at the ripe old age of 103, and with whom my wife and I kept in touch, from time to time, to the very time of his passing. My association with Glen Pierce has been super great. At *Daniel McIntyre Collegiate* in the mid 1950's, Mr. Pierce made a soloist and a star out of me. I became a very popular individual mainly because of my participation and excelling in music through the motivation, mentorship, and guidance of Mr. Glen Pierce.

But the dream to become an athlete was mine and mine alone. As a child, this really meant becoming a soccer "hero", the same as those of the Italian national soccer team that won the first world title in 1934, and whose names of the players we all knew in Italy, even as children at the age of four or five. Also, at *Daniel McIntyre Collegiate*, in my next school year I met **Mr. John Potter**, another giant of a teacher as far as I am concerned. Mr. Potter was my history teacher, my Physical Education teacher, my teacher advisor, my football coach, and later my general mentor and supporter. Lucky for me, he took a very keen interest in everything I was doing at that time. In particular, he liked the way I could play the clarinet.

• •

"Be careful what you plant now; it will determine what you will reap later."
—Unknown

• •

Crescendo to Becoming

Glen Pierce   John Potter

These two teachers were my heroes at Daniel Mac and in my life.

Glen Pierce and John Potter were two of the greatest influences in my life. More than anyone else they genuinely cared about what would become of me. They genuinely believed in me, and they took a chance on me, challenging me with some great responsibilities, and their great expectations of me demonstrated that they really had faith in me.

Both will always be my heroes. I hope that in some small way, that I too, was able to transfer to my students, those qualities they taught me. I know I tried to deliver some of the same principles and methods that they demonstrated, and I do know that I was satisfied that I was able to reach many of my students, thanks to them.

Above all else, Mr. Potter was such a natural motivator who easily inspired those that really got to know him, to achieve great things to the best of their ability and beyond. He had an uncanny way of empowering young people and changing their beliefs from "I can't" to "I can"! (This is what I believe that teaching is all about.) He made me believe in myself and even convinced me that I could play high school football, and as a result, I actually made the team! Truly, I would have done anything to please him, for he believed in me so much. Interestingly, in addition to football, I became an all-star in high school soccer, and competed in track and field, in softball, and in bowling.

My Homeroom Class at Daniel McIntyre Collegiate, 1953
(I am second from the right on the back, top row)

While at *Daniel McIntyre Collegiate*, I excelled in music and was recognized for "outstanding achievement". By 1955 I had performed with my clarinet in most of the Gilbert and Sullivan operettas including in Daniel McIntyre productions of *H.M.S. Pinafore, The Mikado, The Pirates of Penzance, The Gondoliers, Iolanthe, and The Yeoman of the Guard.* These I performed not only at Daniel McIntyre but in other Winnipeg high schools who sought my help in the production of their own Gilbert and Sullivan operettas. Moreover, by 1955 I had become a soloist with the Manitoba Senior Schools' Orchestra in each of the two last years that I was a member of the orchestra, we went on a tour throughout the province of Manitoba that lasted some 12 days each year, if my memory serves me correctly.

Crescendo to Becoming

On the last year of high school, I was the orchestra's popular soloist performing Mozart's original *"Clarinet Concerto in A Major"* in its entirety which consisted of three movements: A*llegro, Adagio, Rondo Allegro*. The orchestra Conductor was Mr. Glen Pierce (who else?), and the Assistant Conductor was Miss Frances Port. I remember clearly that our final performance was at the Winnipeg Auditorium, (today the Winnipeg Archives Building) the greatest and biggest venue in Winnipeg in those days, with well over 2000 in attendance. Also, I entered and competed at the great Winnipeg Music Festival of those years and won the competition for my section with very high scores. This led me to meet Walter Kauffman, the conductor of the *Winnipeg Symphony Orchestra* who told me that I was good enough for the orchestra but that there were no openings, as the orchestra had already two capable, relatively young clarinetists on its staff. He advised me to go to Toronto and talk with the administrator of the *Royal Conservatory of Music*, which I did, but very quickly I came to the conclusion that the cost would be prohibitive and well beyond what I or my family could afford. In any case my performances as a soloist of Mozart's *"Clarinet Concerto in A Major"* constituted the highlight and the pinnacle of my classical music "career" and its still hard to imagine why Mr. Pierce would take such a chance on me with such a demanding piece of music. I now know his answer quite well as he said: *"It's simple. I knew that you could do it"*. For all my music achievements at *Daniel McIntyre Collegiate* I received the Gold Pin, and the certificate below *"emblematic of major achievement in musical activities"*

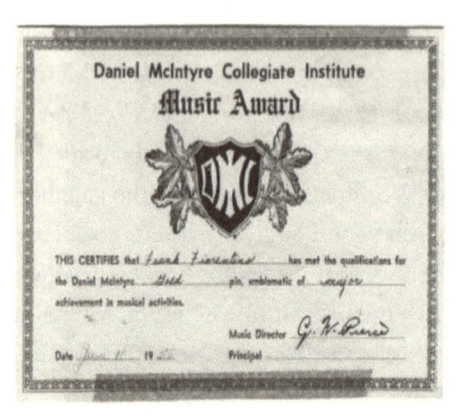

My DMCI Music Award, June 6, 1956   *Glen Pierce, Music Conductor*

BECOMING A STUDENT, A MUSICIAN, AND A YOUNG ATHLETE

*"You must begin to think of yourself as **becoming** a person you want to be."*
—**David Viscott**

One of Gilbert and Sullivan operettas, "The Yeoman of the Guard" produced by Daniel McIntyre Collegiate at the Winnipeg Playhouse (now Pantages). The conductor is Glen Pierce, and I (a member of the orchestra) am sitting in the front row immediately to the right of, and facing Mr. Pierce

There is no question that music was a significant part of my life from 1942 when I began learning to play the clarinet in Italy, until 1963, when I abandoned my musical "career" in favor of redirecting all my energies to focus totally on my growing family, and on my professional career in education, both which were beginning to get established. But there is no doubt that it was *Daniel McIntyre Collegiate* that provided me with the opportunity to express my considerable talents followed by the unbelievable recognition that came with it.

Actually, music was not the only interest I had in which I excelled during my high school years. Sports was the other area, and at *Daniel McIntyre Collegiate,* sports were the area that seemed to develop boys into young men of character, and I think that I was no exception and typical of that fact.!

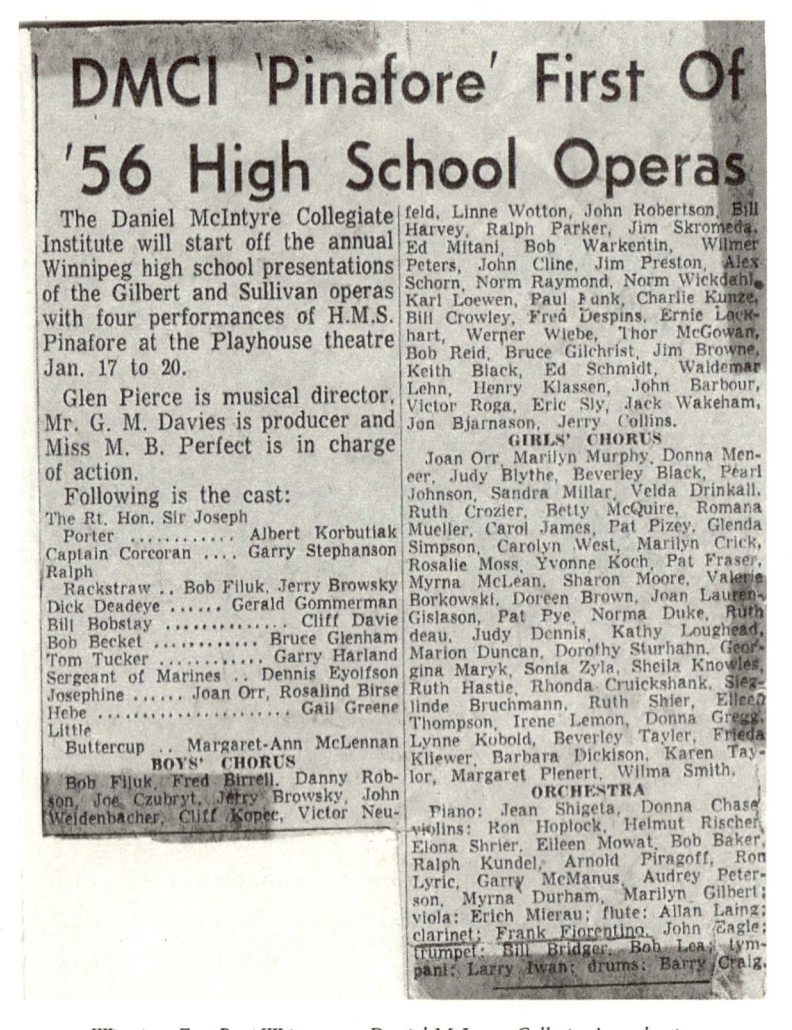

DMCI 'Pinafore' First Of '56 High School Operas

The Daniel McIntyre Collegiate Institute will start off the annual Winnipeg high school presentations of the Gilbert and Sullivan operas with four performances of H.M.S. Pinafore at the Playhouse theatre Jan. 17 to 20.

Glen Pierce is musical director, Mr. G. M. Davies is producer and Miss M. B. Perfect is in charge of action.

Following is the cast:

The Rt. Hon. Sir Joseph Porter .... Albert Korbutiak
Captain Corcoran .... Garry Stephanson
Ralph Rackstraw .. Bob Filuk, Jerry Browsky
Dick Deadeye ...... Gerald Gommerman
Bill Bobstay .... Cliff Davie
Bob Becket .... Bruce Glenham
Tom Tucker .... Garry Harland
Sergeant of Marines .. Dennis Eyolfson
Josephine ...... Joan Orr, Rosalind Birse
Hebe .... Gail Greene
Little Buttercup .. Margaret-Ann McLennan

BOYS' CHORUS

Bob Filuk, Fred Birrell, Danny Robson, Joe Czubryt, Jerry Browsky, John Weidenbacher, Cliff Kopec, Victor Neufeld, Linne Wotton, John Robertson, Bill Harvey, Ralph Parker, Jim Skromeda, Ed Mitani, Bob Warkentin, Wilmer Peters, John Cline, Jim Preston, Alex Schorn, Norm Raymond, Norm Wickdahl, Karl Loewen, Paul Funk, Charlie Kunze, Bill Crowley, Fred Despins, Ernie Lockhart, Werner Wiebe, Thor McGowan, Bob Reid, Bruce Gilchrist, Jim Browne, Keith Black, Ed Schmidt, Waldemar Lehn, Henry Klassen, John Barbour, Victor Roga, Eric Sly, Jack Wakeham, Jon Bjarnason, Jerry Collins.

GIRLS' CHORUS

Joan Orr, Marilyn Murphy, Donna Meneer, Judy Blythe, Beverley Black, Pearl Johnson, Sandra Millar, Velda Drinkall, Ruth Crozier, Betty McQuire, Romana Mueller, Carol James, Pat Pizey, Glenda Simpson, Carolyn West, Marilyn Crick, Rosalie Moss, Yvonne Koch, Pat Fraser, Myrna McLean, Sharon Moore, Valerie Borkowski, Doreen Brown, Joan Lauren Gislason, Pat Pye, Norma Duke, Ruth deau, Judy Dennis, Kathy Loughead, Marion Duncan, Dorothy Sturhahn, Georgina Maryk, Sonia Zyla, Sheila Knowles, Ruth Hastie, Rhonda Cruickshank, Sieglinde Bruchmann, Ruth Shier, Eileen Thompson, Irene Lemon, Donna Gregg, Lynne Kobold, Beverley Tayler, Frieda Kliewer, Barbara Dickison, Karen Taylor, Margaret Plenert, Wilma Smith.

ORCHESTRA

Piano: Jean Shigeta, Donna Chase; violins: Ron Hoplock, Helmut Rischer, Elona Shrier, Eileen Mowat, Bob Baker, Ralph Kundel, Arnold Piragoff, Ron Lyric, Garry McManus, Audrey Peterson, Myrna Durham, Marilyn Gilbert; viola: Erich Mierau; flute: Allan Laing; clarinet: Frank Fiorentino, John Eagle; trumpet: Bill Bridger, Bob Lea; tympani: Larry Iwan; drums: Barry Craig.

Winnipeg Free Press Write-up on Daniel McIntyre Collegiate's production of Gilbert and Sullivan's H.M,S, Pinafore

Yes, both music and sports did wonders for my self-esteem, developing in me a real sense of worth, and creating in me a great belief in myself. But more on this important part of my life later.

BECOMING A STUDENT, A MUSICIAN, AND A YOUNG ATHLETE

ECHOES OF SPRING CONCERT, 2006 **Left to Right:** *Stephen Leung, Mrs. Daisy Pierce, Frank Fiorentino, Mr. Glen Pierce and Agnes Leung*

The Daniel McIntyre Collegiate Orchestra, 1953. I'm the clarinet player, front row, fourth from the left, and left of Mr. Pierce.

Crescendo to Becoming

∙ ∙

"A caring teacher hands children their passport to the future."
—**Jenlane Gee**

∙ ∙

MANITOBA SCHOOLS' ORCHESTRA

Senior Section

Annual Concert

Y.M.H.A. HALL
WINNIPEG

THURSDAY, APRIL 28, 1955
At 8:30 p.m.

CONDUCTOR:
Glen Pierce, *assisted by* Frances Port

AUSPICES
Manitoba Provincial Government—Dept. of Education
Winnipeg School Board   Winnipeg Free Press
Winnipeg Tribune   Men's Musical Club
CBW, Manitoba

BECOMING A STUDENT, A MUSICIAN, AND A YOUNG ATHLETE

PERSONNEL
MANITOBA SCHOOLS' ORCHESTRA
Senior Section

FIRST VIOLINS:
Ronald Hoplock (Concert Master)
Patricia Pats
John Bachynsky
Robert Baker
Albert Korbutiak
Wally Neufeld
Violet Maelstrom
Eileen Mowatt
Carole Woodward
Gail Penstone
Garry McManus
Ronald Lyric
Ralph Kundel
Roy Yrau

SECOND VIOLINS:
Beatrice Payne
Sylvia Ashley
Beryle Plews

Margaret Small
John Smaizys
Dolores Krusiak
Claire Hartley
Leona Bingham
Gladys Maloney
Audrey Peterson
Marilyn Gilbert

VIOLAS:
Koren Kozub
Manfred Legrehn
Sandra Wesley

CELLOS:
Paul Ross
Janet Cameron

BASS:
Peter Garnuk

FLUTE:
Jacques la Fleche

CLARINETS:
Frank Fiorentino
John Eagle
Jim Lorimer

OBOE:
Jack Close

ALTO SAXOPHONES:
Melvin Naser
Vivian Reiter

TRUMPET:
Hins Wretting
Bob Frankin

DRUMS AND TYMPANI:
Larry Iwan
Barry Craig

PIANO:
Maureen Allen
Margaret McDonald

Committee

Honorary President..HON. W. C. MILLER
(Minister of Education, Province of Manitoba)
Chairman..C. K. ROGERS
(Department of Education)
Secretary..H. J. BENNINGEN
(Winnipeg Public School Board)
MRS. N. PATRICK..Winnipeg Public School Board
G. T. MACDONELL..Winnipeg Public School Board
MISS M. HORNER..Winnipeg Public School Board
MISS ETHEL KINLEY..Women's Committee, Winnipeg Symphony
W. S. CUMMING..Men's Musical Club
T. M. TAYLOR..CBW, Manitoba
S. R. MALEY..Winnipeg Tribune
MISS SHEILA MCILWRAITH............................Winnipeg Free Press
G. E. SNIDER..Winnipeg Schools
MISS E. M. KNAPP..Winnipeg Schools
MISS MARJORIE COLPITTS..............................Winnipeg Schools
GLEN PIERCE
MISS FRANCES PORT..} Conductors of Orchestras
ARTHUR BUSS

• •

"We do make a difference – one way or the other. We are responsible for the impact of our lives. Whatever, we do with whatever we have, we leave behind us a legacy for those who follow."
—Stephen Covey

• •

Teachers: how much you care about your students is often more important than how much you know.
—Frank Fiorentino

• •

Crescendo to Becoming

Write ups in the Winnipeg Free Press about my musical performances, 195

As if my involvement in music in high school weren't enough, during the same years I was attending Daniel, I was also a member of the *Winnipeg Sea Cadet Band* which I enjoyed as well, and which gave me more involvement in music but in a totally different setting. As a marching band we performed at a variety of concerts, and annually played in the famous *Eaton's Santa Claus Parades,* even though inevitably it was usually quite cold for it took place on or about 15 of November every year. In any case it was an enjoyable event just the same. It's also interesting to remember that while a member of the Sea Cadets I was able to rise to the rank of *"Leading Seaman",* another achievement of which I am still proud.

BECOMING A STUDENT, A MUSICIAN, AND A YOUNG ATHLETE

THE H.M.S. CHIPPAWA SEA CADET BAND OF WINNIPEG, circa 1954. I am seated on the first row, immediately right of the band conductor, ninth from the left.

Left to right: Ferruccio Moscarda, Dennis Zambruk, Ron Gregg, Me, Casey Bialek, and Ray Balan. *I am the leader standing up.*

Also, in the 1950's, while still at *Daniel McIntyre Collegiate*, but outside of school, I formed a ballroom dancing orchestras: the *"Amati 5"* which later became the *"Combo Italiano"* when Angelo Ferla, a relatively newcomer from Italy, joined us both as a drummer and as a singer. The *"Amati 5"* was composed originally of five musicians, as the name itself implies, but on occasion it was composed of six members, but eventually settled on four musicians for most jobs.

Crescendo to Becoming

The **Combo Italiano** had a comparatively large repertoire of Italian and Latin American music in Winnipeg, and fast became quite popular, and soon had three to four year-long engagements in night clubs such as the *"Normandy"* on Sherbrook Street just south of Portage Avenue, the *Rainbow Dance Gardens* on Smith and St. Mary's near Eaton's, and in the new *"Monterey Dance Pavilion"* which became my personally favorite place located in Headingly just west of Winnipeg. In addition to those "fixed" locations, we played at many Italian and other community events and weddings. Coupled with other part-time jobs I had at *Russell Motors Lt.*, at 730 Portage Avenue, and later at *Eastern Sales Ltd.* at 1305 North Main Street, for several years my income was greater than my father's, who worked as a laborer at the C.N.R. in the Transcona shops.

*"Reunion" 50 years later, of the Amati 5 Dance Band in 2004 at the Centro Caboto Centre. **Left to Right**: Me, Denis Zambruk, Denis' Cousin, Ferruccio Moscarda, and Casey Bialek*

It was with the income that I derived from music that I was able to pay for my university education and to support our family as my highest priority, while actually leading a fairly good quality lifestyle myself. Soon after, our family moved to McDermott Avenue, and my older sister Eleonora got married in the early 1950's. I recall that she could hardly wait to get married for she even tried to elope in the dead of winter and my father had to run outside without wearing proper shoes, in order to physically stop her and her boyfriend from doing so.

I think that she wanted to escape the situation she was in so much that she rebelled at the fact that she believed she would have to be partly responsible for helping raise the family. Soon after this episode, she married the same young man with my parents' blessing, and so the commitment to help out the family fell solely upon me, now barely at age 15, I was in fact the oldest in the family. This I did so very willingly for at least 10 years, until 1960, when

BECOMING A STUDENT, A MUSICIAN, AND A YOUNG ATHLETE

I too got married at age 24. And even though I started teaching in 1959 at Dominion City, Manitoba, I still had to borrow money and go into debt for about $2,000. to get married a year later on August 20, 1960. I did this so willingly, knowing that my future would be secure, as my resolve to become a teacher was now solid.

Sports

When I reflect upon the life I have had, I can say with certainty that my considerable participation in sports as a young man gave me an opportunity to shape and develop my values, and to grow in character as to become the principled, ethical person that I eventually I believe I became. Regarding sports, in Italy a boy grows up playing the game of soccer at every turn, every day. Soccer was, and is still in Italy and in the world, the "beautiful game" and the number one sport of choice for many reasons.

At the time of my childhood in southern Italy, there was no other sport for the young. In Italy, soccer was, and still is everything, and it starts to capture the imagination of boys at a very early age. It was also the case with me in *Amato*, even though children my age had to play with a ball made of leftover cloth materials that we found as scrap in the town's tailor shops. I also remember that at age seven or eight each individual on our "team" contributed a few *liras* to by a small eight-inch diameter rubber ball, but after playing with it a couple of times, it was lost in the thick ravine that run deep under the piazza into the deep creviced water creek downhill. Thinking back now, it was still a good experience, but nothing could compare with the incredible excitement we had when we finally were able to play with a regular soccer ball. In any case I was quite adapt at catching the ball, a skill that I began to develop quite early in my life, playing often the position of goalie. However, in high school I made the team as a striker as we had a super goalie by the name of John Gowerluck. We actually had strong teams, teams that won the provincial championships two years out of the four in which I played.

Although I enjoyed taking part in several sports in high school such as soccer, track and field, baseball, bowling, and inter-class competitions in volleyball and basketball, the one which gave me the greatest personal satisfaction was not soccer, but football. For me, the greatest moment in sport

Crescendo to Becoming

in high school was when I was able to make the football team for it meant the world to me, and as a result, I felt that there wasn't anything I couldn't achieve after that. There is no doubt that it was football that empowered me and that did wonders for my self-esteem.

During my four years at *"Daniel Mac"* from 1953 to 1956 Mr. John Potter was the coach of the "Maroons" football team. *Daniel Mac* had already a strong tradition of winning previously with coach Andrew Currie before John Potter. Every young man at *Daniel Mac* seemed to want to play football, and the competition to make the team was fierce. So, I too decided to go out and crack the team in my grade eleven year. I made the team all right, but just barely I think, and so I did not get a chance to play very regularly, for I was a "second stringer". But in my next year I made the team as a halfback but was used mainly to receive and run back punts. You see, I had "sure hands" and had remarkable skill in catching the ball, even if the ball was such an odd shape, and not the round ball I was accustomed to growing up in Italy and Canada. Being one of the smallest players on the team, I had good speed but not much power. Astonishingly, I was not the smallest member of the team, for that distinction went to Billy Colpitts, number 44, who was an all-star halfback and for sure one of the best players on the team.

Senior Soccer Team at Daniel McIntyre Collegiate Institute. I am sitting on the first row, immediately right of the super goalie John Gowerluk holding the soccer ball in his hands, (who incidentally died a relatively short time after).

BECOMING A STUDENT, A MUSICIAN, AND A YOUNG ATHLETE

Being a member of the famous *"Daniel Mac Maroons"* became an empowering status symbol for all members of the team and especially for me. Everyone in school seemed to respect and look up to the *Maroons* who were held in very high esteem indeed. It was interesting to note that Mr. Glen Pierce, the music teacher, went after the robust football players and recruited them as members of his musicals and choirs. For me this was a positive factor, for I was a natural tenor and Glen Pierce made sure I was an integral part of the wonderful music program that he directed.

So, it was through actively participating in the three activities of student, musician, and athlete during my teenage years, that I could prove to myself that I could do things other kids could do, and the fact that I could not speak English that well didn't seem to be that important. The ability to compete in these three areas did wonders for my confidence and my self-esteem. And whatever ability in these areas I did have, helped a great deal to persuade me to stay in school, and that has made all the difference in my life.

The Daniel McIntyre Football Team, 1955. I was in the third row, third from the left, the second person to the right of Mr. Potter, wearing No. 2. Incidentally, Billy Colpitts, the smallest member of the team, is immediately below me wearing no. 44.

Dannies Crowned Champs

By CHUCK McOUAT

That football trophy room at Daniel McIntyre must look somewhat like Fibber McGee's closet by now.

It was a well-worn plot which buried Saturday afternoon at Winnipeg Stadium as the Maroons made great use of a fast-starting backfield to defeat the fighting Panthers of Gordon Bell 27-15 and win their High School Football league sudden-death final.

This was hardly a new experience for the Dannies who now have won the championship every year since 1947 with the exception of last season when they lost the final to St. John's Tech. Count 'em up and you'll find seven trophies, enough to fill a trophy room. The big question is who will open the door to put this years' addition into storage? You know what McGee has to go through.

. . .

TWO IMPORTANT factors highlighted the game which was played in near zero temperatures on a slippery field.

Firstly, the speed of the Daniel backs; three of their four touchdowns came on long breakaway runs of 90, 85 and 41 yards.

Secondly, the great line play of the Panthers.

Only three times in the game did the Maroons threaten the Panther goal-line. Once, Billy Colpitts kicked a 26-yard field goal and another time, in the dying minutes of play, Paul Vivian smashed over for the final touchdown, his first of the year.

On all other occasions, Gordon controlled play. However, they didn't have the speed in their backfield and when Colpitts, Keith Simms or Keith Webster broke through the secondary, they were away.

That's the story in brief form. It was speed against power and on that slippery field, speed was bound to be the winner.

. . .

It was 6-5 for Daniel after the first quarter and 15-5 at the intermission. Gordon pulled to within a converted touchdown later in the half, at 21-15, but with minutes remaining on the clock, threw three incomplete passes from their own six-yard line. Daniel took over with two plays left and Vivian bulled over on the final play of the game for the extra points. Colpitts converted for his 12th point of the night and Daniel had another title.

. . .

Fullback Keith Simms broke away from the Daniel 15-yard line with just minutes gone in the first quarter and the Maroons were in front for good. Milt Pearson and John Hiley gave chase, but never came within 10 yards of the speedster. Colpitts converted.

The Panthers trudged back late in the quarter with John T. Brown climaxing a 90-yard downfield march with a 24-yard burst around the right end. Pearson's pass to Kemp for the convert was knocked down by Brian Palmer.

Colpitts fumbled to start the second half and Gene Kobzar recovered for Gordon on the 55. However, they went nowhere and kicked to the Daniel 20-yard line. Colpitts more than made up for his miscue on the ensuing play, breaking clear on a quick opener and showing his heels to the Panthers for an 11-5 lead. He then converted.

Colpitts' 26-yard field goal just before the half made it 15-5. Billy had earlier attempted a 31-yard boot which hit the crossbar dead in the middle.

Brown, who played his finest game of the year for Gordon both offensively and defensively, recovered a Daniel fumble on the Maroons' 16-yard line midway through the third quarter to set the stage for the next Panther scoring play. Warren Barnard carried three players on his back in churning up the remaining yardage and it was 15-10. Pearson's convert attempt was wide.

. . .

Later Gordon started on another march, but lost a third down gamble on the Daniel 45. Gurney ran to the Panther 41 and then shook Webster loose on another quick opener for the touchdown. Colpitts converted and it was 21-10. But the Panthers were far from dead.

John Hiley reached high to intercept a Gurney throw on the Panther 34 yard line. Kemp carried to the 43 and then took off around the end to the Daniel 34. Fred Pritchard bulled to the 14, Barnard picked up a first to the two-yard line and then Kemp pushed over for the score. Pritchard tried to run the convert and was stopped.

. . .

SPLITTING T'S: Both clubs ran from the split T, but the Panthers used a multiple offence, changing T and then spread formation at will.

It was a rough, tough ball game with both clubs playing it to the hilt . . . Jim Foubister, Arn Taylor, John Kendle and the rest of the Panthers should receive a special award for effort. They were supposed to be dead a couple of weeks ago . . . Some corpse! Simms, Colpitts, Vivian, Gerald Anderson, Jack Bruzell, Stan Gaidy, Len Olipnek and a host of others were stickouts in the winning cause . . . Barnard, John Willis, Kemp, gritty Ray Ash, Milt Pearson, John Willis, Trev Stinson and Brown all gave it the works for Gordon.

Gordon out first-downed the Maroons, but it was pretty even along the ground, due mostly to those long Daniel dashes . . . Passing was at a minimum as were fumbles when you take into consideration the conditions under which the boys were forced to play . . .

The Maroons now meet Dauphin Collegiate Saturday afternoon for the Manitoba high school championship. Dauphin won the Manitoba schools rugby football league. It is hoped the game can be played in Winnipeg Stadium, but nothing has been decided to date.

The Winnipeg Free Press, Monday, November 14, 1955

Family Debt Consolidation

While conditions at school were great, conditions at home were going from bad to worse. Everyone, from the youngest to the oldest member of the family, seemed to be in a life's struggle. It was just too tough, if not almost impossible, to raise such a large family on the inadequate laborer's income that was being generated by my father. I recall that there was an office at the Legislative Building which was there for the purpose of helping families and others "consolidate" all their debts into one, and this provincial office would determine how much it was feasible and realistic to pay monthly out of the

BECOMING A STUDENT, A MUSICIAN, AND A YOUNG ATHLETE

income coming in. From this one payment they would distribute a portion to each of the debtors that we owned money to, and thus some "breathing room" was created for families like us in such a tight financial situation. This proved very beneficial to our family to say the least, and as a matter of fact, we had to reconsolidate our debts one more time a few years later that I can remember. I was the one, of course, that was the spokesperson for my father, and although I found it somewhat humiliating to have to take this action, I was never-the-less glad that there were such avenues for help.

One thing was certain, my father was determined, as was I, to repay every penny of every debt, and although it took an inordinate amount of time, eventually we were able to do just that. I'll never forget all the blessings I received from both my mother and my father during these early years in Canada for helping the family financially actually for well over a period of over ten years, until 1960.

Guido and Gregorio Cantafio's Double Wedding, 1955 **Left top Right:** *Alfredo Cantafio, Franco Rossi, Joe Fiorentino, Guido Cantafio, Gregorio Cantafio, Dominic D'Amico, me, (Frank Fiorentino), Gabriele D'Amico, and Raymon Cosentino*

I worked really hard especially from 1955 to 1959, in order to be able to purchase and maintain this dream car (a 1952 Chevrolet Convertible) that I owned for about two years. Then, because of other more important priorities

Crescendo to Becoming

in my life, I chose to trade it in for a new Vauxhall, a very efficient small car that would take me reliably to Dominion City (near the Emerson and the Canada-U.S. border) where I was to assume my first teaching job in September 1959. But of all the cars I have owned in my life this one still ranks as my most favorite.

1955 to 1966 were the years when there was a strong consolidation movement for my family and in my own life, including a period of planning and decision-making that laid the foundation for my future. It was during these young adulthood years, that the determination of who, and what I was going to become, really took hold. As it turned out, the decisions made or not made during this period would have tremendous impact on me with repercussions on the rest of my life. It was the period of my life when I really selected my priorities and goals in life and began to work toward them. It was through having a sense of vision and mission, commitment, hard work, determination and courage that shaped what was to happen in the immediate years ahead and which set the stage for future years.

After graduating from high school, I continued to be active in soccer and softball at the community level, particularly in soccer. As part of this involvement, I became a founding member of the *Italian Canadian Club,* the organization that sponsored the *Italia Soccer Club,* and I became an active soccer player as the first team's goalie for some nine years, culminating with winning our first provincial Winnipeg senior soccer championship in 1959. Some evidence of those years and soccer teams I played with follows on the next page.

BECOMING A STUDENT, A MUSICIAN, AND A YOUNG ATHLETE

First Italia Soccer Team in Winnipeg, circa 1958–59. (I was on injury reserve)

"Italia" Soccer Team Champions, Won 10 Games and Lost Only Two (1958)

Bickering Mars Soccer Match

By SCOTTY HARPER

Everybody wanted to be referees or telling what the harassed gent should do Monday night when the Flying Dutchmen whacked the Italians 3-1 in the first round of the John Queen cup.

We saw more gesticulating and finger-pointing at a soccer arbitrator at Alexander park than we've seen in covering soccer for years.

But Tony Sylvano evidently went a little too far in his gestures or told referee Sep Demetzer that he was a good scout, with the result that Tony was despatched to the sidelines for keeps.

The Dutchers and the Italians put up a good fight (not from a fistic standpoint, for it was a clean game) but too often the players huddled together like a bunch of grapes. Wherever the ball was there you'd find about six players with nobody on the extreme wing.

The bright spot of the game was the undersized goalie of the Italians with a movie name, Franco Florentino. True he was beaten three times, but Franco stole the show. His display was terrific in the first half when the Flying Dutchmen, with the aid of the strong breeze, laid down a barrage of shots. His daring dives at the feet of the Dutchmen were a marvel. How he escaped getting a boot in the face was just one of those things.

Bill Boonstra scored the Dutchers' first goal in the first half and brother Johnny Boonstra got their second goal in the second half. Johnny hit the crossbar with a wicked drive, and then caught the rebound to head the ball into the net.

Rens De Koning smacked home the Dutchmen's final goal with a line drive from point-blank range.

Frank Onselmu scored for the Italians.

Referee Demetzer awarded the Dutchmen a free kick inside the penalty area, which led to more gesticulating. They scored from the free kick, but it was called back for some infringement. In the second attempt the Italians managed to scramble the ball out of danger.

Thursday night Luxton Royals meet Ukrainians in the John Queen cup.

A Winnipeg Free Press account of one of our soccer games

Work

Shortly after we arrived in Canada, I began to look for work so that I could have some of the things that boys my age had, such as a wagon, a sled, a bicycle, and eventually a car at age 16. So, at age 14, I had my first part-time job delivering prescription drugs and all kinds of items for *Sair's Drug Store* on Notre Dame Avenue not far from McDermott Avenue and later Toronto Street where we were living at the time. After that, I delivered groceries for a grocery store (using a boys' wagon) still on Notre Dame Avenue just east of Sherbrook Street.

BECOMING A STUDENT, A MUSICIAN, AND A YOUNG ATHLETE

But at age fifteen my "real" job was working at a service station at *Russell Motors* located at 730 Portage Avenue that belonged to a gentleman by the name of Jimmy Russell who, as I recall, was also the president of the Winnipeg Blue Bombers Football Club. Here I began a job by washing cars, and then advanced to doing car lubes, oil changes, oil filters, tire repairs, gasoline sales (i.e. pumping gas) and everything else that went on in street corner service stations in the 1950's. It was here that I learned to drive a car, so that by age 16 to the very day, I was ready to pass the provincial test, and thus qualify and receive my driver's license. Upon reaching that age, I bought my first car, a Model "T" Ford, a car that had to be physically cranked in order to start the motor. After a couple months of that, I bought a 1939 Plymouth, and later my dream car, the beautiful 1952 Chevrolet shown on page 76.

Although I had a great experiences at *Russell Motors*, under Doug Murray, the man in charge of the service station, who often left me in charge of running the service station on weekends, I decided to leave it in 1957, to go and work at a new car dealership relocating on Main Street from Beausejour, Manitoba, by the name of *Eastern Sales Ltd.* I was immediately hired there and one of my first duties was to drive most of the vehicles from the Beausejour location via Lockport, to 1305 Main Street in Winnipeg.

Eastern Sales was a vibrant and exciting forward-looking family business belonging to Mr. Andrew Rewucki, and his two sons Joe and Edward. Relatively short after the opening in Winnipeg, Edward left Winnipeg and opened a new dealership in Calgary and Joe remained the President of the Winnipeg dealership.

At Eastern Sales I met the owner Andrew Rewucki, a serious-looking older man in his 60's, who looked and acted like a "survivor" from old Ukraine, but an honest man of character and integrity. I recall that when I "graduated" to car sales, that Mr. Andrew Rewucki would almost always prefer to approve a sale for a lesser profit than lose the deal altogether. Such was his philosophy.

But what I remember most, as if it were yesterday, was the unforgettable meeting I had with Mr. Andrew Rewucki, when it quickly became evident that not only did he know things about me, but that he was genuinely interested in my well-being and my future. At a private meeting with him, he told me that he knew that I was a good boy, a good worker, and an honest young man. Then, he proceeded to ask me what my plans for the future were at university, and I responded that I was hopefully going to become a teacher. Hearing this, he quickly and assertively interjected to say that I should know that there is no money in teaching, and that perhaps I should reconsider. As I hesitated to say anything, he said that if I reconsidered and go into dentistry, he was prepared to pay for the university registration costs for the duration of the 4-year program. Of course, I couldn't believe what I had heard, that a man who hardly knew me, had made me this great offer. And although I did not accept the very generous offer, I have always had a great deal of appreciation and respect not only for Mr. Andrew Rewucki, but for all of his family and for *Eastern Sales* as well.

My Undergraduate University Years

When I graduated from *Daniel McIntyre Collegiate*, I wasn't really sure which of the three universities in Manitoba I should attend, nor did I know if there was any difference between them. So, I decided that I would attend all three of them consecutively and spend one year in each one, to see for myself if there were any discernible differences. Beginning in the fall of 1956 I registered at United College, known today as the University of Winnipeg. Being in downtown Winnipeg, its location was very handy for me since I had a part-time job at Russell Motors, a car dealership just down the street west on Portage Avenue and Chestnut Street, where today Broadway meets Portage Avenue. Unless I had a booking with my dance band, I would report to the Russell Motors service station on late Friday afternoon and often I would work straight to Sunday, when I would finally go home and collapse asleep until Monday morning or afternoon.

One of the things that sticks out in front of my memory is one day in the Fall of 1956. I had just parked my car in the parking lot behind United College about 12:30 p.m., while I was listening to the car radio that was describing *"Sputnik"*, Russia's first rocket into space. I was so disappointed to hear that Russia had beaten "us" (America and the western world) in the race into space. This gigantic "coup" was a hard pill to swallow, and it was not until John F. Kennedy announced shortly afterwords his commitment to the space program, that we felt better about where the West was headed in the space exploration race.

BECOMING A STUDENT, A MUSICIAN, AND A YOUNG ATHLETE

For my second year (1957–1958) I registered and attended the newly-built *St. Paul's College* that was just opening up at the University of Manitoba campus for the first time. Most of the professors at St. Paul's were very learned *Jesuits*, highly respected for centuries for their dedication to their chosen teaching field. While there, I also played with my dance band for the *Newman Club* at their social activities and thus got to know a more complete picture of life at St. Paul's. Really, I enjoyed the year a great deal and when it was over, I was glad I had "experienced" St. Paul's.

For the third year of my B.A. program, I registered and attended the University of Manitoba proper and took a variety of courses from several departments and colleges. By comparison, I found the University of Manitoba much more impersonal and not as cohesive and friendly as either United College or St. Paul's.

Faculty of Education

Frank Fiorentino's "Education"
- *Bachelor of Arts.1961.*
- *Professional Certificate of Ed.,1961*
- *Bachelor of Education, 1963*
- *Master of Education, 1965*

In the summer of the fourth year, (1958–1959) I enrolled into the Faculty of Education at the University of Manitoba whose facilities consisted of a series of "sheds" which were located about two blocks south of the Faculty of Education, and which were unbearably hot and uncomfortable in the summer months. At the time of registra-tion, I also signed an agreement with the Province of Manitoba that specified that the cost of the registration fees would be forgiven, if I agreed to seek employment and teach in the rural areas of the province for at least two years upon graduation. This was a provincial incentive program to encourage teachers to teach in the rural areas of the province where the shortage of teachers was most acute. At the conclusion of Faculty of Education and only after a few days off that summer I found myself in my first teaching assignment at the secondary school of Dominion City, Manitoba, a small town near Emerson

Crescendo to Becoming

near the Manitoba-USA border. It was there that I launched my long career in education after only six weeks in the Faculty of Education. Then, after three summer sessions at the Faculty of Education of six weeks each, I finally obtained my *Permanent Professional Teaching Certificate.*

As the reader can readily see above, in the 1950's I was very involved in a variety of activities to the extent that often I have wondered how I was able to manage them all. However, my soccer playing days came to an abrupt end in 1961, one year after I was married, the result of a kidney injury in the field of play. But my dance band activities went on until 1964 when other more important identified priorities in my life just took over.

After I got married my new focus was raising a family, and so I put both music and sports and part-time work aside. As well, I began instead to focus my energies, which were substantial, mostly on furthering my studies, namely on my master's degree in education, and on my teaching career. These became my new interests and realities in my life. And as they say, the rest is history.

Frank Fiorentino's Diplomas and Degrees, Awards, etc.

7.
BECOMING A TEACHER, A PRINCIPAL, AND A SUPERINTENDENT OF EDUCATION

THE CREDIT FOR ME BECOMING a teacher goes predominantly to three people: my father and to two of my high school teachers, namely Mr. John Potter, and to a lesser degree, to Mr. Glen Pierce. My father, who taught music with passion and determination to most of the young boys of Amato, and to Mr. John Potter, my high school teacher and football coach, who helped me conclude that I could indeed become a teacher, if only I could believe that I could be, take ownership for the decision, and just "go for it".

During my last year at *Daniel McIntyre Collegiate* 1955-1956, Mr. Potter, lucky for me, was also appointed and assigned as my "teacher advisor", and it was in this capacity, that he called me aside in his office one day and proceeded to ask me questions regarding my plans for the future. He wanted to know if I had thought about what I wanted to become and/or wanted to do in the future after leaving *Daniel Mac*. I hung my head down and mumbled something under my breath, hardly discernible, something to the effect that I was hoping that someday I could become a teacher, but that I really thought that it would never be possible. Mr. Potter then asked me why I thought that, and I explained that I did not have a good grasp and command of the English language to be a teacher as yet, that I had a discernible, noticeable accent, and that my year-end marks on the Provincial Exams were usually too marginal to even think that I could become a teacher.

Quickly as if on cue, Mr. Potter got up, told me to remain seated and to wait there for a few minutes, and left the room. He came back about five minutes later with a gentleman by the Name of Mr. K-------- and proceeded to introduce us, one to the other. I'll never forget what happened next. Mr. Potter said: "Mr. K---, this is Frank Fiorentino, and he thinks he can never become a teacher because his English is not good enough. Then Mr. K---- shook my hand and began to talk. "Frank, my name is Mr. K---- and I have been in this country not even two years and I have been teaching at *Daniel McIntyre* since last September".

What became unmistakably clear is that Mr. K---'s English was far worse than mine, for he had such a thick accent that one could "cut it". When the interview was over, Mr. Potter asked if I had any other questions regarding teaching. I said no and told him that he had made the point obvious. "Frank," he said, "obviously if you don't go into teaching you will have to find another excuse". I know your English will be just fine and you will make a good teacher." Again, Mr. Potter reassured me that my English was good enough and that it would even get better if I focused on it. God bless him, he had proved to me beyond any doubt, that teaching was indeed possible if I really wanted it. It was at that particular moment, I remember it so vividly still, as if it were yesterday, that I made my decision to become a teacher, and I have never wavered from that choice ever since.

I believe that good teaching is the ability of the teacher to change the student's negative mind-set to a positive one, and Mr. Potter did just that. He had managed to change my belief from "I can't" to "Yes, I can!", and in so doing, he removed whatever resistance I had to my path to success. This ability to motivate and empower young people was his genius, for he was a master at it, and I was one of his luckiest students to learn and profit from it.

Further, it's interesting to note that Mr. Potter and I became life-long good friends. Actually, our paths crossed over and over for many years until he retired from education. As for me I did become a teacher, implementing many of the principles I learned from such teachers as Mrs. Keith, Mr. Leavens, Mr. Potter, and Mr. Pierce, and, not only did I become a teacher, but a vice principal, a principal, both at the junior high and high school levels, and then later on, an Assistant Superintendent of Education at the Transcona-Springfield School Division No. 12 at the same time that Mr. Potter was an Assistant Superintendent at River East School Division, a neighboring school jurisdiction. Ultimately and unbelievably, I became the

Superintendent of Education. Who could ever have imagined such a scenario and turn of events?

In any case, Mr. Potter and I not only became good friends, but we were professional colleagues for many years, and often we talked about our meeting at *Daniel Mac.* that changed the course of events for my own life, and the enabling power that teachers can have over their students. We even told the motivating story at the graduation ceremonies of our respective School Divisions, and I believe that many students profited from me telling "my story" of how I decided to become a teacher.

One of my Typical Graduation Speech

What follows is a typical graduation speech, one of many that I delivered at the Graduation Exercises of the three high schools of the Transcona-Springfield School Division No.12 either as a principal or as a member of senior administration over a period of 16 years. I include it here because it contains several statements which in fact describe my beliefs and philosophy about education and about life itself. You will also notice that my concept of "becoming" as contained in this book, was already well-engrained by the early 1970's.

Mr. Chairman, Ladies and Gentlemen, Graduates:

*"**Graduation is a celebration for all of us**. We are satisfied that the graduates have earned the right to this magic moment in their lives, but other stakeholders in the piece, such as the parents and relatives, teachers, trustees and members of the community at large, can rightly consider the occasion a significant and triumphant achievement. Symbolically it marks an end of an era, but in reality, it represents a promising beginning of another.*

*Graduates, after thirteen years in the "cradle" that we call "school", **you have attained your first major dream**. But just as you thought your schooling was coming to an end, you will discover today and tomorrow, that your education is a life-long process, and that **it is a journey and not a destination**.*

Crescendo to Becoming

Graduates, you have a great deal to be thankful for. You have accomplished much. You have learned, no doubt, that **you don't have to be stopped by things you don't know.** *The fact that you entered kindergarten with very little knowledge did not stop you from going this far. Every day we discover that human potential is far greater than we ever thought possible. As* **people developers**, *teachers believe in the great potential of human development and growth. So, free the energy that is within you, and know that* **there is no limit to the goals you can attain, the success you can achieve.** *The possibilities are as endless as your dreams.*

And what are dreams, if not a perception we have of the future? Some say the future is for those who are fast on their feet. I prefer to think that when you visualize your future you visualize yourself. The future is a perception of yourself, the result of the perception of the forces within you. The future, like our dreams, has no boundaries except those that we ourselves place in our minds. **You see, invariably we become as we perceive ourselves to be.**

The perceptions we have of ourselves may be more important than the reality. What we think of ourselves, our self-image, has a tremendous impact of who and what we can become. The great Gandhi realized this when he said: **"Man often becomes what he believes himself to be".**

In the final analysis there is no failure, except what comes from within us. But what have you to show for your thirteen years? Well, let's see:

You have acquired a language or two. You have discovered your ancestral heritage, your culture, your traditions, your roots. All of these provide you with a solid foundation and you are the richer for it.

You should have learned by now that **communication is the essential skill that will determine a great deal of your success in life.** *But the most critical ability you must cultivate is interpersonal relationships, i.e. the ability to have* *positive interaction with people, in other words, **friendships**, for blessed are they who have the gift of making friends, one of God's gifts. It involves above all the power of going out of oneself, and **appreciating whatever is noble and loving in another**.*

*Another requirement for success is **a positive attitude**. Negative people remember Columbus as the man who failed to discover a shorter route to India. Positive people think of Columbus as a daring explorer who opened up a whole new world.*

*Remember, when you dream, dream in bold terms. **It is in dreaming the greatest dreams, seeking the biggest goals, that we build the greatest tomorrows.** Dreaming to escape from reality is counterproductive and consumes all your energy in vain; dreaming to move forward by setting up goals that are achievable, manageable, progressive, and worthwhile. As Eugene P. Bertin said, **"The poorest man is not he who is without a cent, but he who is without a dream"***

In closing graduates, I wish to leave you with this biblical thought:

"All things are possible to the one who believes,
They are less difficult to the one who hopes,
They are relatively easy to the one who loves,
They are simple to anyone who does all three"

May God bless you and energize you with his spirit.

Carpe Diem. Thank you.

My First Year as Teacher at Dominion City, Manitoba, 1959–1960

My first year teaching in 1959 was quite unique and unforgettable. I was required to teach grades seven to twelve Social Studies (History and Geography), French, Music, and Physical Education. Interestingly all 37 students I taught occupied one classroom as follows: two rows of grade sevens, one row of grades eights, a few grade nines, fewer yet in grade ten, and fewer still in grades eleven, with the fewest number in grade twelve.

It was during my very first days of my teaching career that I quickly learned that in teaching, as in everything else, planning and preparation are critical. When I taught the grades sevens, the other students were required to work on their own, but often they would be listening to me anyway. I learned a great deal myself about individualized instruction that first year, and I learned about grouping and regrouping for instruction, and many other aspects of teaching and learning. Much satisfaction was derived from teaching Physical Education, Music and Choir, and I enjoyed my involvement with the school's extra-curricular program in a variety of areas such as sports and music and choir. Even with such demanding conditions, it is interesting to note that one of my grade nine students from this group, John Barsby, became a great scholar, and later became a brilliant teacher of Mathematics.

Because of my involvement with choir, in June of my first year in teaching, I met for the first time, up close, the Graduation Guest Speaker who was none other than Robert "Bobby" Bend, a highly respected "demagogue" who was not only a great speaker, but a man whom everyone knew as a former MLA, a Minister of Health and former Minister of Education with a previous Liberal Manitoba Provincial Government of Premier Campbell. Little did I know that this "super" person sitting next to me on the front row, would become my idol and mentor in five years' time, and a friend for the rest of his life.

I believe that 1959–1960 was the first year that the Dominion City School ever had a choir at the high school level. There were thirty-three students that were members of the choir, which was quite a high percentage of the total student body. Actually, the choir consisted of a fairly talented group of students who were disciplined enough to learn several pieces, particularly two beautiful pieces that we performed at the Graduation Exercises in June, 1960.

While in Dominion City I coached the Touch Football Team that won the championship in the high school league that included teams from schools at the Manitoban towns of St. Jean, Morris, Steinbach and Vita.

BECOMING A TEACHER, A PRINCIPAL, AND A SUPERINTENDENT OF EDUCATION

"A vision without action is but a dream; action without vision is a waste of time; but vision with action can change our lives".
—**M. Ignacio Tinajero, 1995 Texas Teacher of the year**

Dominion City School Choir, 1959–1960, with Me as the Choir Director

My very first Grad 12 Graduates at Dominion City School

My First Teaching Colleagues at Dominion City, Manitoba, 1959–1960

Crescendo to Becoming

But the one experience I will never forget is the one as "coach" of the *Dominion City Jets,* a very talented community hockey team made up for the most part, of junior-age players who were in my high school classes. As the team found itself without a coach, a delegation of players came to see and asked me to be their coach. What they really needed was a supervisor who would act as coach, for the team was so well-formatted that everyone already knew very well his role on the team. As coach, the only task I really had to perform was to change lines as often as I thought appropriate, knowing that whenever I wanted or needed a goal, I would put out the high-scoring line of Solnes, Thom, and Gruenke and invariably they would score a needed goal. Needless to say, the team won the district championship, and this accomplishment was done with a "coach" who could hardly even skate, and who basically applied whatever theories he knew about soccer to hockey and got away with it, thanks to the high talent of the team members!

At the Easter Break of 1960 (this was changed many years later to the Spring Break which now occurs the last week of March every year) I went home to Winnipeg and during the week I answered an ad seeking teachers in three school divisions in and around Winnipeg. As a result, I was offered a teaching position in the Transcona-Springfield School Division No 12 which I accepted, only because I was now engaged to Josephine Graziano, an Italian girl from my home town in Italy, who would be my wife in August 20, of that year, i.e. 1960, and who happened to live in what was then, the City of Transcona. . . . . Upon returning to Dominion City after the Easter Break, the Dominion City School Board quickly summoned me to its meeting right away to make me an offer for the position of principal, which I had to turn down, only because I was already committed by contract to another school jurisdiction. If nothing else, however, the offer did boost my ego as an affirmation that I had done a good job in my first year of teaching, and the success gave me a great deal of confidence, personal satisfaction and fulfillment.

The actual writeup in the 1959–1960 yearbook regarding the Football and Hockey Teams reads as follows:

BECOMING A TEACHER, A PRINCIPAL, AND A SUPERINTENDENT OF EDUCATION

The Football and Hockey Teams at the Dominion City School

It was rather a short season for both football and hockey in the High School this year. I am sure that those of us that were connected with those sports, along with the many enthusiastic supporters of the teams had an exciting, enjoyable season.

In "flag football" the boys did a tremendous job considering the very short time we had for practices. Their behavior in practices and the games was outstanding. Their sense of "fair play" was not short of superlative.

In hockey, where my experience is far from adequate, the boys showed a great deal of co-operation. I am sure that the fact we won every game we played was not due to the "coach", but rather to the promising young hockey players relative numerous in the school.

I hope the school will continue with many sports in the future and I wish "good luck" to all in the future.

The Coach, F. Fiorentino

Dominion City School "Touch" Football Team, 1959–1960, with me as Coach

Dominion City Jets Hockey Team, 1959–1960, with me as the "hockey" coach

Teaching at Transcona Collegiate, 1960-1966

In September of 1960, soon after Josie and I returned from our honeymoon in Banff and Lake Luise, I began my second year of teaching with my new employer, the Transcona-Springfield School Division No.12 at *Transcona Collegiate Institute* located then on Day Street, next door to *Central School* (in front of present-day *Ecole Centrale*), historically the first school in Transcona that had been built in 1913 in the year that Transcona received its city charter. I taught Grade 11 and Grade 12 French, and Grade 11 Canadian History. Invariably I had some bright classes composed of students who had plans to attend University, for in those days, a graduating high school student had to have French as a required pre-requisite subject in order to qualify for university entrance. In the main, therefore, I had good students who were bound for university, and therefore who simply were more motivated to learn.

The principal of the collegiate was Mr. Steven Quelch, a very traditional, and somewhat dogmatic gentleman who appreciated the game of soccer, and who had amassed a great collection of butterflies as a hobby, which he donated to *Arthur Day Junior High School* and later to the Transcona Historical Museum.

I shall never forget what happened to me soon after school opening of my first year at *Transcona Collegiate*. In teaching Grade 11 Canadian History class, I always liked to write the names of the people we were studying, and

BECOMING A TEACHER, A PRINCIPAL, AND A SUPERINTENDENT OF EDUCATION

accordingly as we began to investigate the early period of exploration of Canada, I wrote this: "*Cristoforo Colombo, 1492*". "*Giovanni Caboto, 1497*", Without saying anything to me, two of the brightest students in the class went to the principal's office and complained to Mr. Quelch that I was trivializing Canadian history by "Italianizing" the names of the explorers such as *Columbus* and Cabot and making them out to be Italian when the textbook referred to them as Spanish and English respectively.

More specifically, they reported to the principal that the textbook referred to "John Cabot" sailing out from Bristol for England. Immediately I was summoned by Mr. Quelch to his office and while I must have been shaking in my boots, (I was only 24 years old) he told me that a teacher of history must first and foremost "teach truth above all else". He asked me why I had changed the names of Columbus to Cristoforo Colombo and John Cabot to Giovanni Caboto", and I said that in fact, those were their real names because they were of Italian origin. Columbus was of Italian origin working for Queen Isabella of Spain in 1492, and Cabot was working for England in 1497.

Finally, not convinced of what I was saying, Mr. Quelch said that he would look into the matter more and let me know the result of his investigation by calling the dean of the History Department of the three Manitoba universities.

Two or three days later, Mr. Quelch called me down again to his office and asked me where I had learned history with such accurate detail. He told me that the Dean of the History Department wanted to know who the teacher was that knew so much historical and factual detail, and that indeed I was correct and that it was time that the textbooks of the day be scrapped, for they misrepresented the truth about history. In any case, Mr. Quelch shook my hand congratulating me on my teaching of the truth, and subsequently called the students in to explain and clarify to them the whole situation. Before I left his office, I could not resist commenting to Mr. Quelch that it was shameful that the textbook being used in grade eleven referred to, and always depicted the Indigenous people of North America as "savages".

In any case, during the next history class, the two boys apologized in front of the class and just to make a point of my victory, I seized the opportunity of this "teachable moment" and wrote at least a half dozen names of other Italian explorers on the black board such as Cristoforo Colombo, Giovanni Caboto, Giovanni da Verrazzano, Amerigo Vespucci, and others whose names now

Crescendo to Becoming

escape me. I asked the class if they had ever heard of **Amerigo Vespucci,** but no one had. I explained to the class that he was an Italian explorer who explored many of the coastlines of North America, and incidentally, **that's how America got its name.** Interestingly, nobody ever questioned any of my data again, and my reputation as a teacher and historian was certainly enhanced.

The following school year, in 1961, the new *Transcona Collegiate Institute* was built at 1305 Winona Street in Transcona, and it was a thrill to move into a brand-new school building with some of the latest innovations such as a large gymnasium, science labs, and ancillary spaces such as a medical room, and so on. From 1961 to 1966 when I left T.C.I. the classroom assigned to me was always Room No.307 on the third floor.

I was happy to accept more than my share and responsibility for a number of extra-curricular activities including that of coach of the Senior Soccer Team, a team that incidentally won the Suburban Conference Athletic Association (S.C.A.A.) championship twice, in the school year 1961–62 and again in 1963–64. In 1962–63 the team went undefeated the whole season and met Silver Heights in the sudden death game which resulted in a 1 – 1 tie. In the second sudden death game the team lost for the first time and lost also the opportunity for three consecutive championships.

Transcona Collegiate Institute Soccer Team, 1961-62
Back Row left to right: – *Frank Fiorentino (coach), Frank Torchia, Dan Dilay, Bill Vallis, Bob Balbas, Bill Paulson, Bill Rayner, Dave Tyson*
Front Row left to right: – *Tom Chernetz, Jim Harrison, Ermano Barone, Ray Shuel, Bob Marshall.*

BECOMING A TEACHER, A PRINCIPAL, AND A SUPERINTENDENT OF EDUCATION

Note: Caption Under Soccer in the Transcona Collegiate 1961-62 Yearbook Reads as Follows:

*"Ably coached by Mr. Fiorentino, T.C.I. soccer team rolled undefeated through its regular season games. The finals consisted of a sudden death game which resulted in a 1 – 1 tie with Silver Heights. A second game was necessary to determine the winner. This game, played at Silver Heights, was Transcona first loss. T.C.I.'s five **year** as suburban Soccer Champs had come to an end".*

Transcona Collegiate Senior Soccer Champions, 1962–63
Back Row, Left to Right: – Mr. Fiorentino (Coach), Tom Chernets, Bob Hinds, Dennis Morton, Gerrit Brakel, Bill Rayner,
Front Row, left to right: Gordon Kasian, Ermano Barone, Jim Ogsten, Tom Raske.

Note: **The Caption in the 1962-63 Yearbook, Under the .. Caption "SOCCER", Reads as Follows:**

"T.C.I. regained the suburban soccer crown this year after a short one-year lease to St. Vital. We had previously won the suburban soccer championship on five successive occasions. This

year's championship was won rather easily, as our team had only to dispose of West Kildonan Collegiate in a best-of-five series. Our team made no mistakes in taking the series in three straight games, thanks to our able coach and French teacher, Mr. Fiorentino, Italy's gift to T.C.I.

Back Row, Left to Right: *– John Hrynkow, Larry Goodchild, Robert McIvor, Zoltan Virag, Cameron Bowie, Nelson Groening* **Front Row, Left to Right:** *– Mr. Fiorentino, (coach), Werner Matysiak, Dave Edwards, Wayne Hawthorne, Mervin Deckert, Dave Rundle*

As the reader can see from the above pages, it's no secret that from the very beginning I found teaching a challenging but enjoyable and potentially rewarding undertaking, and it was due mainly to the fact that I intentionally tried to make the onerous task of teaching both enjoyable and relevant for my students.

I believe that students liked to come to my classes, for it was a place where an "inviting" process of education took place. I must say that my methods were somewhat different for those days, when a more traditional and rigid approach was the norm in most classrooms of the province.

The first 3 to 4 minutes of every class were devoted to discussing whatever students themselves wanted to discuss, provided that no names were mentioned, and that the language used by students was civil and appropriate for class-room consumption. The whole idea was to create a rapport that relaxed the class so that the students would be more ready and receptive to learning.

BECOMING A TEACHER, A PRINCIPAL, AND A SUPERINTENDENT OF EDUCATION

Invariably small talk would take place (just like adults) and students would always bring up topics related to sports, hockey or football, and whatever was "hot news" or controversial at the moment

At the end of the 3–4-minute period, I would call for order and attention and focus on work. Upon this signal, the classroom would usually be transformed into a task-oriented learning lab. I still remember how great I felt that I had such "power" or control over the class, and that the young people would respond so positively to my wishes and be ready and willing to be actively engaged in the learning process planned for them.

R. W. (BOBBY) BEND
Born in Poplar Point, Manitoba, a prominent sports figure in his own right, and a former member of the Manitoba Legislative Assembly, a Minister of Health and Minister of Education under the former Liberal Campbell Government of Manitoba.

R.W. "Bobby" Bend

It was in 1965 that another "giant" of a person, came into my sphere of interest, a person who would change and impact so positively and so greatly into my life. He would become a model, my mentor, and more importantly, a true friend for the rest of my life. His name was Robert W. "Bobby" Bend, yes, the very same person that I had met at Dominion City School Graduation Exercises in June 1960 at the end of my first year of teaching. He was the demagogue who had been a Member of the Manitoba Legislative Assembly, a Minister of Health, and a Minister of Education. It was my good fortune that in 1965 he was offered (and he accepted) the position to become the first Superintendent of the Transcona-Springfield School Division No.12, the result of the amalgamation of Transcona School District No. 39 (Elementary Schools) and the Transcona-Springfield School Division No.12 (secondary level schools) as he left the provincial position of Assistant to the Deputy Minister of Education in charge of Special Projects.

In 1965 we saw a provincial movement toward Consolidation and Amalgamation of many school Districts into fewer larger School Divisions throughout Manitoba, and with this came the position of *Superintendent of Education* that would, in essence, be the Chief Executive Officer (C.E.O.) of each and most local education jurisdictions. The position of Superintendent was designed to replace and eliminate the redundant position of *School Inspectors* in Manitoba. In this new scenario, Evaluation of the local Division would become a local requirement under the control of the superintendent, who would be accountable and obliged to report regularly and directly to the elected local School Board.

Months after Mr. Bend had become the superintendent, I made an appointment to meet with him. The purpose of the meeting was to share and discuss with him my plans for my career path which I had recently developed on my own as a general framework of intent. I shared with him my vision of Education and my career path goals along with my immediate goal which was to pursue my studies toward my master's degree in education in the field of Administration, with a minor in Guidance and Counseling. For many years after that, we both recalled how he was taken aback by complete surprise for no one had ever requested a meeting with him before for the

BECOMING A TEACHER, A PRINCIPAL, AND A SUPERINTENDENT OF EDUCATION

purpose of sharing with him his own professional career plans for the future. I explained to him my view, that *planning* as a process of preparation had always been important to me, and that I was a very strong believer and a proponent of the planning process, particularly in education as a process of setting and reaching goals and objectives that provide direction and purpose for instruction. *"We must know the direction toward where we want to go, if we really have any expectation of where we want to end up",* I boldly stated. We ended the meeting after he told me how he had found the occasion refreshing and informative and promised that he would place the information I had given him in my personal file, and that from time to time we could meet to update its contents and to review it. He recognized that most people spend very little time planning their own life, and therefore I was congratulated for being the exception to that rule.

It was only a year later after my self-initiated interview with Mr. Bend, in the Spring of 1966, that I found myself being interviewed for the position of Vice-principal of *John W. Gunn Junior High School*, a new school being built in the western section of the same lot consisting of a whole city block that contained *Transcona Collegiate* and *Radisson Elementary School*. I was successful in the bid and was promoted to that position effective August 1966 mainly due to the fact, I believe, that we, Mr. Bend and I, had established a level of professional and personal trust one for the other, not only for the short term, but for many years to come.

And so it was that in 1966 my six years at *Transcona Collegiate* as a teacher were culminated by a wonderful farewell: the dedication to me of that school's yearbook which I considered a tremendous honor then, as I still do today after so many years. I know for certain that the students of those six years appreciated my involvement and contribution not only in academics, but also in the school's extracurricular program. Indeed, some still remember the genuine effort I made teaching at night school and after school hours, to get students through the provincial French exam, so that they could pursue their university studies leading to their future lives' endeavors. (Note: In those days standing in Grade 12 French was required in order for students to qualify for university entrance.)

Mr. F. Fiorentino

In grateful acknowledgement of your unfailing interest in your students and the activities of Transcona Collegiate, we dedicate this book to you. We are sorry to lose an excellent French teacher and a good friend, but we know you will do well in your new vice-principalship. Merci beaucoup, et bonne chance!

Dedication of 1965–1966 Transcona Collegiate Yearbook to Me.

Officially my first administrative position was as vice principal of the new *John W. Gunn Junior High School* that opened its doors for the first time in September of 1966. It was a unique administrative arrangement whereby Mr. Fred Kasian would be principal of two schools, *Central Elementary School*, and *John W. Gunn Junior High School*. In the mornings he would be stationed at *Central Elementary School* and in the afternoons, he would be positioned at *John W. Gunn School*. Thus, the two newly appointed vice principals, i.e. Barry Kramble and me, were actually in charge in our respective schools on a half-day basis when Mr. Kasian was in one of the two schools. In other words, when Mr. Kasian was at *Central School* in the mornings, I was in charge of *John W. Gunn* and vice versa. Then the following year, in 1967 I was appointed principal of *Arthur Day Junior High School* located on Day Street next to the historic *Central School*.

BECOMING A TEACHER, A PRINCIPAL, AND A SUPERINTENDENT OF EDUCATION

The School District of Transcona No. 39

BOARD OF TRUSTEES 1966

H. C. HATCHER — Chairman
MRS. M. ANDREE   A. T. ORUM
H. SOSIAK   L. A. WALLACE

R. W. BEND, Superintendent of Education
D. G. WOOD, Business Administrator and Secretary-Treasurer
E. F. SOLOMCHUK, Assistant Business Administrator and Purchasing Agent

STAFF OF JOHN W. GUNN JUNIOR HIGH SCHOOL

N. F. KASIAN, B.Sc., B.Ed. — Principal
F. FIORENTINO, M.Ed. — Vice-Principal

BERRIE, Miss H.
BROWN, Miss V.
DOUGLAS, E. R., B.A.
DUECK, J., B.Sc.
FERMAN, A., B.A.
FIA, Miss P.
FROESE, Miss J.
GANESTSKY, W., B.A., B.Ed.
JAMES, K.
KATAZINSKI, R. J.
KATHKIN, Miss L., B.A.
KLASSEN, H.
KORCHAK, J. W.

KUBLICK, Wm.
LAI, B.
LEFTERUK, D.
McKAY, Miss K.
MOORE, Miss N., B.Sc. (Home Ec.)
PAULISHYN, W. F.
RICH, Miss J.
RIEDMUELLER, Mrs. D., B.A.
STAMLER, A.
STEPHEN, J.
TOWSE, Mrs. S.
WADDINGTON, Mrs. C., M.Sc. (Home Ec.)

ENEFER, Mrs. M., Principal's Secretary

LONGDEN, W., Custodian

My First Administrative Position in the Transcona-Springfield School Division No. 12 was as Vice-Principal of the new John W. Gunn Junior High School when it opened in September 1966

Crescendo to Becoming

During the summer of 1967, before school opening, Mr. Kasian and I were interviewing to fill a few teacher vacancies for September at both *Arthur Day* and *John Gunn* schools. It was during this time that I selected Vera Derenchuk as my Guidance Counsellor for the vacant position at *Arthur Day*.

In 1972 there was an opening for an Assistant Superintendent but as I wanted to be a principal for several years yet, I did not bother to apply for the position, even though I knew that I had considerable support at the School Board level. With my considerable support, and her "vaulting ambition" Vera who incidentally, had done her Master Thesis on the guidance and counseling programs for the Transcona-Springfield School Division, applied successfully for the position and advanced quite quickly through the ranks and by 1972 only five years after she started in the Division, she was appointed Superintendent of Education of the Transcona-Springfield School Division No. 12.

Because of the ever-increasing enrolments, a new *Arthur Day Junior High School* was being built which was to open officially the following year in September, 1968. As I had been appointed principal of the new school, I had an opportunity during the whole 1967–68 school year, to work closely with the school architects to provide input into the design of the various facilities within the school. The new undertaking was to be a "state of the art" junior high school, with facilities such as a 200-seater theatre (a first-time achievement for any Transcona-Springfield school) a circular "resource center" plunk in the middle of the school which housed a library, audio visual materials, a film library, and which included built-in study carrels, and a spanking new language lab. I was so excited and anxiously awaited the day that I would be there as its principal, but ironically my dream to be its first principal was not to materialize, for Mr. Bend and the School Board had other plans for me.

....

"If you treat an individual as if he were what he ought to be and could be, he will become what he ought to be and could be."
—**Wolfgang von Goethe**

....

"Always establish the best goals you can. Goals are the seeds of success – you become only what you plan. The quality of your harvest is a direct reflection of the quality of your seeds….your decisions!"
—***Unknown***

....

This was, and still is to this day, my philosophy as a teacher and educator and it is something that I have always tried to pass on to "people developers", i.e. to teachers, parents and others that live and work with children: *"Love children generously, simplify your teaching to enhance understanding, care deeply about everyone, and speak kindly to all."*
—**Frank Fiorentino**

....

Crescendo to Becoming

John W. Gunn Junior High First School Staff, 1966-1967
Back Row: (left to right): William Kublick, Ben Lai, Ed. Douglas, Henry Klassen, Adam Ferman, Al Stamler **Middle Row: *(left to right)*** – Jake Dueck, J. Korchak, Julie Rich, BobKatazinski, C. Waddington, W. Ganetsky, Don Lefteruk **Front Row: *(left to right)*** – V. Brown, H. Berrie, J. Froese, Frank Fiorentino, N. F. Kasian, M. Enefer, Pauline Fia, D. Riedmuller, l. Kathkin.

Arthur Day Junior High School Staff, 1967-1968
Back Row, Left to Right: Harold Partap, George Pelletier, Jack Pyra, Earl White, Cathy McKay, Vera Derenchuk, Mrs. Doan, Jim Stephen, Bob Lowen, and Peter Falk **Front Row, Left to Right:** ___?_ ____?__, Mrs. Brown, Mts. Dixon, Nestor Gylywoychuk, me, Frank Fiorentino, Eleonor Trenholm, June Menzies, Florence Harvey, and Claire St. Amant

Transcona-Springfield School Division No. 12

D. G. WOOD, SECRETARY-TREASURER
1305 Winona Street — Phone CAstle 2-3211
TRANSCONA 25, MANITOBA

April 7, 1967.

Mr. Frank Fiorentino, Vice-Principal,
John W. Gunn Jr. High,
351 Harold Avenue West,
Transcona 25, Manitoba.

Dear Mr. Fiorentino:

It is with great pleasure that I inform you that at last night's school board meeting, you were appointed Principal of the Arthur Day Junior High School, effective September 1, 1967.

It is probably unnecessary for me to say how completely I concur with the board's decision. I would like to extend to you, my sincere congratulations and I am looking forward to working with you in your new position.

Yours sincerely,

R.W. Bend

R.W. Bend,
Superintendent of Schools.

RWB/fc

Crescendo to Becoming

R. W. BEND
SUPERINTENDENT OF
SECONDARY SCHOOLS

D. G. WOOD
BUSINESS ADMINISTRATOR
AND SECRETARY-TREASURER

Transcona Springfield School Division No. 12

BOARD OF TRUSTEES:

CHAIRMAN:
S. MASLOVSKY

VICE-CHAIRMAN:
MRS. M. ANDREE

COMMITTEES:
FINANCE:
P. M. LIBA
MRS. M. ANDREE
M. M. KOWALCHUK
T. F. MILLS

STAFF AND POLICY:
L. A. WALLACE
MRS. M. ANDREE
H. C. HATCHER
T. F. MILLS

TRANSPORTATION
AND PROPERTY:
W. KRUCHAK
H. C. HATCHER
M. M. KOWALCHUK
H. J. VAAGS

SCHOOL BOARD OFFICE
1305 Winona Street — Transcona 25, Manitoba

Phone CAstle 2-3211

April 14, 1967.

Mr. Frank Fiorentino,
Vice-Principal,
John W. Gunn Junior High,
351 Harold Avenue West,
Transcona 25, Manitoba.

Dear Frank:

I was most pleased indeed to receive your letter regarding your recent appointment. I took the liberty of reading it to the school board. They expressed the wish that I acknowledge your letter and express to you, their appreciation for it.

Both the board and I feel that your work this year, as Vice-Principal of John W. Gunn Junior High School, has demonstrated beyond any shadow of doubt that your present abilities as an Administrator are more than evident. In addition, your potential convinces us that your future contribution to our division will be even greater than that of your past service.

Yours sincerely,

R. W. Bend

RWB/fc

R. W. Bend,
Superintendent
of Schools.

BECOMING A TEACHER, A PRINCIPAL, AND A SUPERINTENDENT OF EDUCATION

R. W. BEND
SUPERINTENDENT
OF EDUCATION

D. G. WOOD
BUSINESS ADMINISTRATOR
AND SECRETARY-TREASURER

Transcona-Springfield School Division No. 12

BOARD OF TRUSTEES:

CHAIRMAN
S. MASLOVSKY

VICE-CHAIRMAN
H. C. HATCHER

COMMITTEES:
FINANCE -
T. MALASHEWSKI
H. R. FISHER
W. PHILLIP

STAFF AND POLICY -
L. A. WALLACE
H. C. HATCHER
S. MASLOVSKY

TRANSPORTATION AND
PROPERTY -
W. KRUCHAK
MRS. M. ANDREE
H. JOHN VAAGS, JR.

SCHOOL BOARD OFFICE
650 Kildare Avenue East — Transcona 25, Manitoba

Phone CAstle 2-3211

November 17, 1967

Mr. F. Fiorentino,
Arthur Day Junior High School,
706 Day St.,
Transcona 25, Manitoba.

Dear Mr. Fiorentino:

It is with greatest of pleasure and satisfaction that I send you this letter. I know that I commented verbally to you with respect to your parent-teacher night. I was amazed to find the auditorium nearly full by 7:00 P.M. It was obvious from my observation during my brief visit that the evening was most exceptionally well organized. Since that time I have heard many comments - all favourable with respect to it.

I would like to pass on my congratulations to your staff and all those responsible.

In closing I would add this comment - "the whole program was further justification of my confidence in your ability as an administrator."

Yours sincerely,

R. W. Bend

R. W. Bend,
Superintendent
of Education.

RWB/s

R. W. BEND
SUPERINTENDENT
OF EDUCATION

D. G. WOOD
BUSINESS ADMINISTRATOR
AND SECRETARY-TREASURER

Transcona-Springfield School Division No. 12

BOARD OF TRUSTEES: SCHOOL BOARD OFFICE   Phone CAstle 2-3211

CHAIRMAN
S. MASLOVSKY

650 Kildare Avenue East — Transcona 25, Manitoba

VICE-CHAIRMAN
H. C. HATCHER

COMMITTEES:
BUSINESS-ADMINISTRATION
T. MALASHEWSKI
H. R. FISHER
V. KRUCHAK
H. J. VAAGS

EDUCATION-ADMINISTRATION
MRS. M. ANDREE
H. C. HATCHER
V. PHILLIP
L. A. WALLACE

May 27, 1968

Mr. F. Fiorentino,
Principal,
Arthur Day Junior High School,
706 Day Street,
Transcona 25, Manitoba.

Dear Mr. Fiorentino:

I am very pleased to inform you that at the last regular meeting of the Board you were appointed principal of Murdoch MacKay Collegiate, effective August 1, 1968.

I wish to offer my sincere congratulations to you on this appointment. I am looking forward very much to working with you in this new field of responsibility. I know that the pleasant relations that have existed between us in the past will be continued in the future as you continue to make an even greater contribution to the students in our division.

Yours sincerely,

R. W. Bend

R. W. Bend,
Superintendent of Education.

RWB/s

c.c. -- Mr. D. G. Wood

BECOMING A TEACHER, A PRINCIPAL, AND A SUPERINTENDENT OF EDUCATION

R. W. BEND
SUPERINTENDENT
OF SCHOOLS

E. F. SOLOMCHUK
BUSINESS ADMINISTRATOR
AND SECRETARY-TREASURER

Transcona-Springfield School Division No. 12

BOARD OF TRUSTEES:

CHAIRMAN
S. MASLOVSKY

VICE-CHAIRMAN
H. C. HATCHER

COMMITTEES:

BUSINESS-ADMINISTRATION
T. MALASHEWSKI
H. R. FISHER
W. KRUCHAK
H. J. VAAGS

EDUCATION-ADMINISTRATION
MRS. M. ANDREE
H. C. HATCHER
W. PHILLIP
L. A. WALLACE

SCHOOL BOARD OFFICE

650 Kildare Avenue East — Transcona 25, Manitoba

December 16, 1968

Phone CAstle 2-3211

Mr. F. Fiorentino, Principal,
Murdock MacKay Collegiate,
260 Redonda St.,
Transcona 25, Manitoba

Dear Mr. Fiorentino:

I would like to take this opportunity as the year draws to a close to express my appreciation to you as principal, as well as to all members of your staff, for the cooperation and help that I received.

Never in the history of education in this Province have the problems the principals and teachers face been so many and varied. No one person can ever come close to meeting the challenge that is presented by education today. However, I am certain that if all our resources, both in respect to personnel and physical facilities, are pooled our efforts will be crowned with success.

In closing I would like to express my personal hope that you and every member of your staff will enjoy the most wonderful holiday season ever.

At the last regular Board meeting it was requested that I express to all members of staff on behalf of the Board, appreciation for the services being rendered as well as the very best wishes for the coming holiday season. Finally Mrs. Call has asked to be associated with this letter.

Yours sincerely,

R. W. Bend,
Superintendent of Schools

RWB/j

Crescendo to Becoming

Principal of Murdoch MacKay Collegiate Institute (1968 – 1975)

In 1968 there was considerable chaos in the *Transcona-Springfield School Division,* particularly at the high school level. The main concern of the Division was that it needed a new principal at *Murdoch MacKay Collegiate* after its first principal, George Derenchuk and half of the school's staff of approximately thirty, resigned outright over arguments with the superintendent and the School Board, presumably over issues related to on-going shortage of school materials and equipment. It was in this scenario of revolt that I was approached by Superintendent "Bobby" Bend to consider the principalship of this high school, a school in trouble and in a bad state of affairs and disarray, to say the least.

I initially refused the offer on two different occasions, telling Mr. Bend that I was looking forward to being the principal of the exciting new *Arthur Day Junior High School*, for which I had considerable input into the design of its facilities. But Mr. Bend (and I assume also the School Board) had already decided that I would be the right person for that position, and he tried to convince me that I should take it on. I did a lot of thinking about the offer, for I knew that this was a great challenge, and that it would either "make me or break me".

To be honest, I wasn't even sure that I was ready to face such a challenge, as I even wondered whether I was apprehensive or even afraid to face the ominous task that I knew inevitably it would be. I concluded that it would be better to face such a challenge while I was relatively young than later in life. And so with some reluctance and a lot of trepidation, I finally agreed to the appointment but with two conditions: (1) that Mr. Bend would support the changes that likely would be necessary for me to implement in order to assume control of the school, and (2) that I, as Principal, would be involved directly, and actually have a major saying in the hiring of the new staff for the various positions left vacant by the 16 teachers that had left with its former principal. Mr. Bend's gave me his assurance that he would support both items, and that was good enough for me. And so I agreed to the appointment.

BECOMING A TEACHER, A PRINCIPAL, AND A SUPERINTENDENT OF EDUCATION

I knew up front that the school was a "rough" place, as the staff seemingly had lost control of the situation, and the students were becoming bonded into "gang-like" groups that would be a force to be reckoned with.

I will never forget that on June 30, 1968, when all the staff had left for the summer holidays, I and Miss Sheehan, my newly appointed vice principal, actually reported to work at Murdoch MacKay to begin to try and piece things together, and to begin making plans, and construct a timetable structure for September, which was only two short months away. Only a Guidance Counsellor by the name of Marvin Field came forward to offer me a great deal of information on the status of things in the school, and the names of the students expected to attend the school. What a great help he was to me and Miss Sheehan!

Miss Sheehan and I worked feverishly hard the whole summer to get things ready for school re-opening in September, and by then, we had pieced together information on every student that would be registered at the school. As most of the students in previous years had always been timetabled as groups, this meant that they moved through the grades together with their particular label of "University Entrance Students", "General Program Students", or "Commercial Program Students". I took the view that we had to find a better way to structure the groups, grades, and programs for the present situation was creating serious havoc with the system and a lot of effort was being wasted in maintaining order and discipline, instead of implementing and maintaining effective instruction and learning methods. Several teachers described the whole school situation at Murdoch as "gangbusters" and that did not sit too well with me. As administrators, we agreed that the school needed changes and changes there would be. We committed to undertake a mission to bring changes that would challenge many things that were traditionally part and parcel of high school life of that day.

Beginning with day one in September on the re-opening of school, we had planned an assembly with the total student population, which in itself represented quite "a risk" for I really didn't know how the students would react to me, the new administration, and to our new policies. In any case I wasn't about to change anything. So, I devised a seating plan in the gym for the total school population, designating to every classroom a specific row and designating specific seating arrangement for every member of staff, and for every member of the student body. Well, no teacher had ever seen such planning of details, and many teachers would tell me afterwards, that they had never seen such planning and detailed organization. The seating plan in the gym was well received by staff as a great idea. In private, I told them that it was called *"planning for success and survival"*. In any case, it was in such a setting that I described our philosophical base entitled "**The Young Adult Concept**" which I defined as ***"a theory in education which seeks to treat high school students as responsible, young adults, allowing them to be accountable to make certain decisions for themselves, as they grow into mature citizens"***. In accordance with this belief, we gradually relaxed certain rules and regulations in the school such as the abolition of the strap, the abolition of the paddle system, the detention, and the rigid dress code which, in any case, could not be enforced anyway. We also allowed students representation at staff meetings for the first time ever. In short, students would be accountable for their actions and were expected to act their age, i.e. as young adults that they were, taking responsibility for their own actions.

The second strategy that I undertook on the second and subsequent days at Murdoch was to actually call students individually to the office for the purpose of getting acquainted with them one-on-one, and to discuss and share our expectations of each other. The idea was that I wanted to meet and get to know each other, and to discuss our expectations of one another BEFORE they had issues or got into any trouble. I wanted them to meet me in a situation to get acquainted, when we were both relaxed and not in any defensive mode. So, I started by calling those students to the office almost at random, intermingled with "good" kids, so that no one could see any specific pattern in my calling them down to the office. But make no mistake about it. Before the first month of school was over, I had met with every student who had a negative history in the school, outlining expectations and consequences if they were to go outside the parameters outlined. I made it obvious that I kept notes on what we had discussed, and what had been agreed upon, and the documentation and record would be part of my personal live file on each student.

But while the outcome was not 100% positive, it helped greatly to revisit what had been agreed-upon, and as time went on, things slowly but definitely began to improve. I recall that we kept a record of each student's referral to

BECOMING A TEACHER, A PRINCIPAL, AND A SUPERINTENDENT OF EDUCATION

the office on pink slips and the first year we had a rather huge pile stacked up seven or eight inches high, numbering several hundred of them. But by the end of the fourth year, the number was visibly reduced to about fifty referrals for the year, if that, and reduced further to just a relatively few by 1975, when I was promoted to the Superintendent's Department and left *Murdoch MacKay Collegiate* after only seven, but unforgettable years, as its second principal.

• •

"Be who you are and say what you feel, because those who mind don't matter and those who matter don't mind."
—Theodore Seuss Giesel

• •

Crescendo to Becoming

OUTSTANDING STUDENTS OF MURDOCH MACKAY COLLEGIATE DURING MY TIME AS PRINCIPAL

1. **ANNETTE COULOMBE (TRIMBEE), became President and Vice-Chancellor of the University of Winnipeg, and has just recently become President of MacEwan University in Edmonton**

DR. ANNETTE TRIMBEE
President and Vice-Chancellor, University of Winnipeg

Upon assuming her new position as president of the University of Winnipeg, Dr. Trimbee gave the following interview:

1. Where did you grow up?

    I grew up in Transcona, as did my mom and dad. I am from a family of six kids and both of my parents were from families with eight kids. Even though there has been some drift to the West, I still have lots of relatives that call Winnipeg home. Both of my brothers and their families live here.

2. During your years in Alberta, what have you missed most about Winnipeg?

    The lakes! I have fond memories of incredible daytrips with my family and relatives to Grand Beach, Birds Hill Park, St. Malo and the Whiteshell.

3. What attracted you to want to come back to The University of Winnipeg?

I have a special place in my heart for UWinnipeg. I am a leader because of my experience here. UWinnipeg made it easy for me to decide to attend university. I was under no pressure to go to University, it was not a family tradition and as a middle child from a large family, I was really under no pressure at all for anything. UWinnipeg found me. I got a scholarship without even applying. Combined with a scholarship from the CNR, I didn't have to worry about money. It was easy to take a bus downtown, most of my classes were teeny and I had very caring professors including my first year Chemistry professor, Dr. Lawrence Swyers. There were fewer than 25 of us in his class and I sometimes thought we were handpicked to be his last class, special for him and very special for us. I graduated with a BSc in Biology and went on to do a PhD and post-doc with the dream of coming back to UWinnipeg to be a Biology professor.

UWinnipeg has a strong reputation that lives up to its brand as a unique and innovative downtown university that connects to community, cares about its students, is committed to academic excellence, has a focus on social justice and is turning out tomorrow's leaders.

UWinnipeg's commitment to serving Aboriginal students really appeals to me. Like many kids growing up in the 1960s in Winnipeg I was confused about my heritage. My parents both spoke French as their mother tongue but all of their siblings married partners who did not. They stopped speaking French at home before I was born. My grandmother on my dad's side was pretty clear that she was Metis and yet my dad said we were not. I understand my parents' choices but at the same time do wish times were different and my parents had continued to speak French at home and celebrated our Metis heritage. My Metis grandmother had a huge influence on me.

Students coming to university are not just coming for a credential and skills to go on to graduate school or get a job. They want to be inspired, they want to discover and grow their special talents whether they are a 17-year-old right out of high school or a 50-year-old going back to school. The decision to go to university is more than a practical one, it is a decision of the heart, especially for students that come from families were going to university is not yet a tradition and were going to university and distance you, geographically and otionally. UWinnipeg gets this and creates a community environment. Time spent at UWinnipeg is life changing.

4. Why did you leave academia?

I got the policy bug while doing a post-doc at the University of Alberta. As an aquatic ecologist, much of my time was spent collecting data in the field and in labs doing analysis. I got to know people in government for two reasons- they had tons of data, and they had grant money to fund research that was intended to inform public policy. I thought I should figure out what public policy was all about. So I ventured across the river for what I thought would be a short term stint and just really liked it. I liked the people, both civil servants and politicians. And I have had tremendous opportunities to shape public policy in a number of sectors.

5. Tell us about your family.

I am married to Kevin, who is an advanced care paramedic, and we have two adult children - a daughter and a son.

2. ZANE ZAZULA (ZALIS), Became an Outstanding, Caring High School Music Teacher

Of the many excellent students that attended the school, I must admit here that for some unknown reason, I did not "catch up" to Zane until he was in his Grade XI high school year. It was at that point that I learned of his appreciation of music, and his dreams and ambition. I related to him I think because of my own involvement and appreciation of music, and thus I sought him out to discuss with him his plans after he would leave Murdoch. I recall that we talked at length on two or three occasions about his goals and objectives, and I strongly recommended to him that he pursue his dreams by reminding him of my strong belief in *"carpe diem" (seize the opportunity).*

I recall that at the graduation ceremonies, as I handed him his well-earned Graduation Diploma, I stopped him and reminded him, then and there, not to forget to pursue his dream, a particular moment in my relations with him that he still remembers very well to this day! Zane went on to become an

BECOMING A TEACHER, A PRINCIPAL, AND A SUPERINTENDENT OF EDUCATION

outstanding high school music and band teacher, and has built a great reputation as being one of the best in the Province of Manitoba, if not Canada.

Zane has also composed a music score that has received some serious and meaningful acclaim. His composition of "**I Believe**", a remarkable work about the persecution of Jews in the *Holocaust*, has met with considerable success. It premiered in Winnipeg as it was performed by the Winnipeg Symphony Orchestra and was an unqualified success. It has remarkable potential for growth in today's world, particularly with the fact that the Museum for Human Rights is being built right here in Winnipeg. So, we wait for its full impact upon the world's music scene. Bravo, Zane!

Zane Zalis (2012) former student at Murdoch MacKay Collegiate

Zane is now retired from teaching at Miles Macdonnell Collegiate in Winnipeg. But before retiring, he was chosen to receive two very notable awards: (1) the Queen's Diamond Jubilee Medal, which is designed to honor Canadians and recognize them for their contributions to the country, and (2) The Prime Minister's Award for Teaching Excellence Certificate of Achievement

3. TERRY DUGUID, became a Member of Parliament in the Canadian Government

With a diverse background including civic government, business, and environmental leadership, Terry Duguid is well-prepared, and honored, to serve his constituents in Winnipeg South

Terry Duguid

Terry has a lifelong interest in science and its role in the betterment of society. He earned first-class honors in obtaining his Bachelor of Science degree in Biology, and his Master of Environmental Design degree (Environmental Science) focused on tackling the crucial issues of water quality, ozone depletion and acid rain.

Throughout his career, Terry has had an abiding commitment to public service. In 1997 he founded Sustainable Developments International, a firm specializing in environmental management, sustainable development, transportation and international affairs consulting. In 2000, he was named Chairman of the Manitoba Clean Environment Commission, and in 2004 he became President and CEO of the International Centre for Infectious Diseases, a research facility he helped to create. In addition to his professional career, Terry has devoted considerable time and effort contributing to his community, including serving as Executive Director of the Manitoba Climate Change Task Force in 2001, Chair of the Nature Task Force in 2003, and as a Member of the Manitoba Emissions Trading Task Force in 2004. Terry has a wife and two daughters.

4. PAUL MOREAU became a Superintendent of Education in Transcona and in Winnipeg.

Most of my school years were spent in East Transcona, attending high school at Murdoch MacKay in 1965 to 1969. Murdoch MacKay had a special place in the Moreau family as all 6 children graduated from the Collegiate.

My program of studies was the University Entrance Program. Upon graduation, I attended the University of Manitoba, completing a Bachelor of Arts and a Bachelor of Education.

My first teaching position was in 1975 with TSSD teaching Grade 6 at Harold Hatcher School, a new elementary school on Redonda. After 3.5 years, I was promoted to the position of Teaching Principal at Hazelridge School in the Springfield area.

The significance of this move is that it launched my career as an educational administrator. In subsequent years, I was appointed to positions which included Vice Principal, Acting Principal and Principal. This included the following schools: Hazelridge; Radisson; Oakbank; Wayoata; and Arthur Day. I continued to attend the University of Manitoba, Faculty of Education, completing a *Master's Degree In Educational Administration* in 1984.

Crescendo to Becoming

My final assignments in the Division were my appointment as Assistant Superintendent, Human Resources and then Superintendent of Education, both in 1998. I left the Division in 2000 after 27 years to pursue other educational opportunities.

I was appointed Superintendent of Education, Assiniboine South School Division. After a short tenure, amalgamation of some school divisions in Manitoba became a reality. At that point, I became Superintendent of the newly amalgamated Pembina Trails School Division. This included the former Assiniboine South and Fort Garry School Divisions. Leading and building a new administrative team led to the establishment of a progressive and dynamic school division. This transitional period, albeit challenging at times, was a highlight of my educational career.

Upon retirement in 2007, my wife and I continued being involved in the pursuit of educational learning opportunities in international settings. Together we spent several years teaching and providing professional development in China and Brazil.

Louise and I have now been married since 1975. We are proud parents of 3 wonderful sons and their loving partners along with 7 amazing grandchildren who all believe in the power of lifelong learning.

· ·

"He who teaches others teaches himself"
—Anonymous

· ·

"Your life becomes the thing you have decided it shall be."
—Raymond Charles Barker

· ·

Your Beliefs become your Thoughts, Your Thoughts become your Words Y our Words become your Actions, Your Actions become your Habits, Your Habits become your Values, and Your Values become your Destiny."
—Mahatma Gandhi

· ·

BECOMING A TEACHER, A PRINCIPAL, AND A SUPERINTENDENT OF EDUCATION

5. JOHN (Cooch) COUTURE, became a "special" Canadian with pride and passion for CFL Football and Grey Cups

Winnipeg Blue Bomber fan John Couture, a.k.a. the Grey Cup Pope, is attending his 49th Grey Cup week.

John's claim to fame is the fact that he is probably the number one super fan of Canadian football. He has likely attended close to fifty Grey Cup games in person, more than any other individual in Canada. He has been written and reported in many newspapers in Canada during the Grey Cup week regardless of the teams who are actually playing in the game itself. The pins and other paraphernalia that he has accumulated over the years is itself remarkable as you can see some attached to his Blue Bomber jersey in the photo above. It's amazing how anyone can find a unique path to distinguish oneself!

Principal's Message

May I express to you, Jackie, my sincere thanks and appreciation for your kind invitation to contribute a message in this edition of the yearbook.

As I reflect on this past school year, I recall vividly the many apprehensions and expectations I had even before school opening last fall. You too will recall, no doubt, the hectic days of September, and our student assembly which gave me the opportunity to speak to all of you of these apprehensions and expectations.

It was at this event that I pronounced for the first time, that our school was embarking on what we called the "Young Adult Concept" in education, namely, a theory which seeks to treat high school students as responsible young adults, allowing them to make certain decisions for themselves as they are growing into mature citizens. In accordance with this belief, we gradually relaxed certain rules and regulations in the school such as the abolition of the strap, the paddle system, the detention, the rigid dress code. We also allowed student representation at staff meetings for the first time in our school.

The school year 1968-69 has been a year accentuated by animated discussions of change — not only by the students in the hallways, but also by our teachers in their staffroom. There is a genuine concern to ameliorate the learning situation, and to do away with obsolete rules and regulations. There seems to be considerable agreement between high school students and teachers however, that legislation alone, or the changing or modification of rules, will not improve or increase the human learning relationships unless the individual student is both ready and willing to learn.

The great debate at school has been whether or not young adults are mature enough to assume responsibility for their own actions. I personally like to believe that they are, and if they are not, they should be given the opportunity to practice handling this responsibility in as many ways as possible.

The main controversy stems from the following problem: "Are students willing to learn?" There is a great difference between "wanting" and "willing."

To want is to desire, to have; but "willing" may be defined as "the push of discomfort and pull of hope." For example, while it is true that most young people "want" to pass, not all of them are "willing" to put forth the required effort to achieve it. It is my sincere belief that most of us have an abundance of the "pull of hope", but lack the determination and awareness necessary to face up to the "push of discomfort", which the difficult task of learning requires. A mature, responsible person has developed enough self-discipline to be able to balance the two, a prerequisite for those that wish to succeed.

It is my sincere belief that the students of M.M.C.I. and the graduates in particular, have discovered a "state of equilibrium", which will contribute vitally to your future ambitions.

May I say how much I have appreciated being associated with you, this past year, and I look forward to an even more rewarding and enjoyable year in 1969-70.

BECOMING A TEACHER, A PRINCIPAL, AND A SUPERINTENDENT OF EDUCATION

PRINCIPAL'S MESSSAGE

May I express my thanks and appreciation to you, Dave, for the very superlative manner in which you and your staff have carried out your duties and responsibilities in producing this excellent Manitoba Centennial Edition of our yearbook. I am grateful once again, to have this privilege of contributing this brief message. This past school year should be remembered as the year when we tried in our small way to make education of the learning process more human. We are trying to establish that learning is an individual matter, always personal, a process to develop every child's heritage which consists in part of initiative, curiosity and inventiveness. We are making a modest beginning to bring about changes to meet the needs of the students. We are striving to change a curriculum and an approach which are subject-oriented, and make them child-enriched or child-centered. We have insituted the self- scheduling classes within out Modular Timetable to give our "Young Adult Concept" more meaning. We have tried to give the student the opportunity to make realistic decisions and assume responsibility for the consequences. All of these things we have tried in the hope that the students be treated more like human beings, because we believe in the supreme worth of every individual above all else.

My sincere wish is that all of you have profitted from all this as we, as educators have. In my opinion, your morale and spirit in the school have never been better. It was indeed gratifying to see that our library has been frequented by students to the extent that it never has been in the past (as was our coffee area during S.S. time).

May I say once again how proud I am to have been associated with the teachers and students this past year. And for those who are graduating this year, I hope that you will look back in retrospect and feel satisfied, as I am, that you were involved more than ever before, that you had opportunities to show your initiative, curiosity and inventiveness. You leave those that will follow a great challenge to equal your efforts and achievements. Carpe Diem! ! !

F. Fiorentino

3

Murdoch Mackay Collegiate to present its first musical - Fiddler on the Roof

The past two months have been a flurry of activity at Murdoch MacKay Collegiate as studnets prepare for their performance of **Fiddler on the Roof**, to be held in the Murdoch MacKay Collegiate auditorium from March 12 - 15.

The play is about a poor dairy man, Tevye, played by Ken Lawson, his wife, Golde, played by Anne Torchia, and their five daughters. The setting is a small Russian village, Anatevka, on the eve of the Russian Revolutionary period. It tells of the strong Jewish traditions that unite the people and how the youth rebel against the traditions. Each of Tevye's daughters wants a husband, but not the one the village matchmaker, Yente, chooses. Tevye finds himself bending further and further away from tradition to give in to his daughters. If he bends any further, (as he sees it) he will break, and the traditions of his people will fall. It is a simple story, but full of emotion, excitement, and action. The complicated score contains such beautiful songs as "Sabbeth Prayer", "Sunrise, Sunset," "Do You Love Me?" and "Tradition." Choreography helps to convey the emotions of the characters, and the spirited Russian dancers add zest to the play.

This is Murdoch's first musical. "It's about time we had something like this," commented Mr. D. Heindl, choreographer. "It's a good way to celebrate our tenth anniversary, and a good way to put school spirit back in. I hope it brings back a lot of former students."

There is a lot of involvement in **Fiddler on the Roof** by both students and teachers. At least seventy-five people are involved in some way - whether it be acting, chorus, choreography, backstage work, etc.

Mr. F. Fiorentino, the Principal, said, "I think it's going to be the best entertainment in this division. The kids involved are putting in a lot of time and effort."

"The cast is making relatively good progress," added Mr. J. Minarik, Vice-Principal. "All systems are go as of now."

For added effect, the three-level stage will extend sixteen feet into the audience. Unique staging will make use of the entire area through dancing, dramatic scenes, and choral arrangements.

Cyril Keatan, who worked on the choreography of Sarah Sommer's Chai Folk Ensemble's production of "Fiddler" will be helping Mr. Heindl with the dancing in Murdoch's production. Pauline Broderick and Diana Laczko are also working on the choreography.

Diane, who worked on wardrobe for Manitoba Theatre Center's production of "The Dybbuk," is working on costumes along with Mrs. R. Mason, the Home Economics teacher.

Miss J. Lewandosky and Keith Perry have been doing a lot of work with the singers in the chorus; and Rob Strome and Patricia Mochnacz with the dramatic end of the production. They have been putting in an estimated fifteen hours a week - with excellent results.

There will be evening performances on March 14, 15, and 16 at 8:00 p.m. There will also be matinees on March 12 and 13 at 12:30 p.m. For more information about tickets, please phone Mr. Rob Strome at 222-3325 or 474-2855.

Everyone seems to agree on two points: it's a lot of hard work; and it-s going to be great!

Fiddler on the Roof is a play by Debbie Chorney.

Five daughters can create trying experiences for any father - but if the father is Tevye, a father steeped in Jewish tradition (played by Ken Lawson in Murdoch MacKay Collegiate's first musical) the frustrations are multiplied. From left to right are Pauline Broderick (Tzeitel), Kathy Breen (Hodel), Diane Laczko (Chava), Penny Berg (Shprintze), Tannis Hykawy (Bielke), Ken Lawson (Tevye) and Anna Torchia (Golde, his wife).

BECOMING A TEACHER, A PRINCIPAL, AND A SUPERINTENDENT OF EDUCATION

Principal's Message

Once again I am pleased to take this opportunity to express my gratitude and appreciation to Laurette, Betty, and Shereen, co-editors of this Yearbook, for their diligent effort, co-operation, and the efficient way they managed to produce this excellent 1971 edition.

We were indeed very pleased to see that more students than ever before supported this edition of the Yearbook. However, we are still quite concerned over the fact that a publication such as this is reaching amounts in expenditure that are almost prohibitive for a school our size to meet. It has become imperative, therefore, that we seek new ways of financing such a venture, or that we consider other alternatives to a publication of this nature.

As you are all well aware, our school is still searching for ways to improve the quality of teaching and learning. We are constantly seeking ways not only to make learning more relevant and meaningful, but also to make our school a more "humane" institution. To this end we have proposed the Trimester System. We sincerely hope that students, parents, and teachers will give their undivided commitment to this proposed plan, so that ultimately we can improve the education process for the student. Our basic goal is to provide a program with varied strategies and environments for learning through which all students regardless of differences in individual talents and interests, may proceed with gains.

May I also take this opportunity to say farewell to our graduates. I'm sure that you will take with you some fond memories of the days you spent at Murdoch MacKay. We wish you success and happiness in all your future endeavours."CArpe Diem!"

F. Fiorentino

Crescendo to Becoming

TO
MR. FIORENTINO:

For his untiring efforts to make Murdoch MacKay what it is today.

Yearbook at Murdoch Mackay Collegiate Dedicated to me, upon leaving the school in 1975, was well appreciated.

MY AREAS OF INVOLVEMENT/INNOVATIONS AS PRINCIPAL OF MURDOCH MACKAY COLLEGIATE, 1968–1975

1. The first thing I set out to do was to **"humanize" the education process** in the high school setting, by recognizing the supreme worth of all human beings, and accordingly treating young people with the utmost respect. Humiliation of any sort would not be acceptable nor tolerated. Our focus would be on the positive and on students' strengths.

2. Beginning my first day at Murdoch Mackay in September 1968, we introduced and implemented what I called **"The Young Adult Concept"** which focused on the principle of "Freedom with Responsibility". I believed then, as I believe now, that in order for young people to develop responsibility they have to be placed in a position of responsibility and let them make decisions that reflect their responsibility-taking. Similarly, with "freedom", students need to learn how to handle freedom by actually being given opportunities to handle it and learn from it. In other words, the theory placed responsibility squarely on the students' shoulders and expected that high school students would act and be responsible for their own actions. In such an environment everyone was to be held accountable for his or her own behavior.

3. Accordingly, and because of our new direction, we **abandoned all forms of physical and corporal punishment.** At the very first assembly that was held in early September 1968, we literally threw away the regulation size strap approved by the provincial department of education and abandoned *"the paddle"* which was required when students had to leave the classroom and visibly carry with them the "paddle" to let everyone know he or she had been given permission to go to the washroom. No doubt this had been implemented well before my time in order to cutdown the number of students that one would find in the corridors, but to me the implementation of the "paddle" made the solution worse that the problem, for it was humiliating and ridiculous to say the least, so I abandoned the whole policy of the paddle early in the very first year.

Crescendo to Becoming

4. In my second year at Murdoch Mackay Collegiate I designed and implemented an **Individualized Modular Flexible Timetable System** designed specifically to provide teachers the amount of time allowed for the subject taught in a variety of time modules of 20 minutes each. Instead of a teacher having 40 minutes every day (or 240 minutes total over a 6-day cycle) to teach a given subject such as Math or English, the teacher was given the option to request this time in a variety of lengths in multiples of 20 minutes modules. For example, the teacher could request the 240 in a variety of lengths of time to match the methods and subject that he/she wanted for each period, as per example below:

Previous (Usual) Method	New Method
Day 1 = 40 minutes,	20 minutes
Day 2 = 40 "	40 "
Day 3 = 40 "	60 "
Day 4 = 40 "	20 "
Day 5 = 40 "	40 "
Day 6 = 40 "	60 "
Total: 240 minutes	240 minutes

The strength of individualized timetabling is that one makes a structure for each individual student rather than for groups as such. The individual's timetable is custom made to meet the student's unique needs and particular strengths. As well, the administrator can also dictate and control who and how many students will be in a particular group, therefore, controlling the "chemistry" of each and every class. In this way the homogeneous aspect of the bonded or "gang-like" groups is eliminated.

5. In my third year at Murdoch Mackay Collegiate I designed and implemented for the first time in Manitoba, a Semester System Structure beginning with a 3-term system called **Trimester System,** which was quite revolutionary for its day. In this time structure the school year was divided into three equal, self-contained terms, whereby the students would attempt to complete one-third of the year's requirements in three

and a third months and go on to the next third with a corresponding third of the annual subjects. In fact, a trimester term was a mini school year. The Trimester System was very popular with students and teachers and in no time, about 20 high schools in the province copied and implemented our trimester system.

6. After a couple of years on the trimester, we changed to a **Semester System,** that is a two-term system, whereby the students worked on half of their course load for half a school year. In this scenario, the student worked on three or four courses on each of the terms, rather than the usual six to eight courses all at once. Thus, the system became less stressful for students as the traditional, previous systems that forced students to work on six to eight subjects daily, and such a task became often too onerous and stressful for many students. In the traditional setting for example, if each teacher were to assign half-hour homework on each subject, the poor student could have four hours homework each night, a situation which was quite heavy and unreasonable for most students. It sounds somewhat bizarre, but in fact this was often the case. It's interesting to note that the Semester System in some form is still today, in operation in the vast majority of high schools across Canada and other countries.

   Given the reality today that of necessity many students hold a part-time job usually in the evenings and weekends, the Semester System allows for this reality and thus the students are able to pursue both school and some employment, which is also an important learning experience.

7. The introduction of a music program consisting mainly of Operettas and Musicals into the high school extracurricular program was one of the most satisfying activities that I implemented for I have always thought of music as a "humanizing" influence on the system of education. As I was principal at Murdoch Mackay Collegiate for seven years, 1968 to 1975, and during the last three years, the school produced a musical and most of the staff were involved in the production in one way or another. The three major musicals produced were: **Fiddler on the Roof, South Pacific,** and **The Sound of Music.**

Crescendo to Becoming

8. We implemented the first School Initiated Courses (S.I.C.s), i.e. programs and courses **developed by students themselves** that met the requirements of the Department of Education and the school, that were "tailor-made" specifically to meet the specific needs and high interests of the students. The SICS had to be planned for at least 110 hours duration and included such things as sports, music, other languages, and variety of specialty areas of interest to students themselves.

9. We also implemented several School Initiated Programs (S.I.P.'s), i.e. programs and courses **developed by the school** to meet specific needs and/or high interest of the students in the particular school and district. At Murdoch MacKay Collegiate we developed such S.I.P.'s as Career Quest, Introductory Calculus, Student Leadership, Psychology, and Journalism, which incidentally included the publishing of a quarterly (three times a year) of a full-fledged school newspaper called **The Tartan Examiner** as part of a Journalism Course.

10. I chaired almost every committee of the School Division's School Principals' Council pertaining to secondary level education and was the Chairperson of the School Division's School Principals' Council itself, (1969-1970.

11. I was a member of the Provincial Committee on the Implementation of the revised High School Program in 1973 and a member of the Provincial CORE Committee (1974).

12. I introduced a Noon-Hour Chat Room to allow students to meet and talk with me as principal of the school on any topic of concern and/or interest of the student.

13. I met and spoke to every student who had scored and achieved marginal status at exams with the idea of trying to have the student improve in his studies (much like Mr. Kasian used to do)

14. Allowed girls to wear blue jeans in school for the first time as an alternative to wearing miniskirts which were in vogue in 1968–1973.

15. Allowed female teachers to wear pant suits in school for the first time.

BECOMING A TEACHER, A PRINCIPAL, AND A SUPERINTENDENT OF EDUCATION

Of course, my years as a school administrator brought me much closer to Bobby Bend, and that gave me a great deal of personal satisfaction. As a school administrator I was required to attend the Principals' Council a minimum of once a month to discuss matters and policies related to Divisional and /or school administration.

Promotion to Administrative Assistant to the Superintendent, 1975

The School Board wanted an Assistant Superintendent as a back up the Superintendent, but Superintendent Vera Derenchuk wanted the title to correspond in parallel fashion to the existing Administrative Assistant (Elementary) side. Regardless of the title as such, the position was to be a member of Senior Administration directly reporting and responsible to the Superintendent of Education, and as such, I was to be involved in all planning and decision-making activities of the Superintendent's Department.

Promotion to Assistant Superintendent, 1977

From the beginning of my involvement with senior administration, it was the position of the School Board to establish a new position in the growing school division, namely the position of Assistant Superintendent, a clearcut back-up position, that would be easily understood to take charge in the absence of the Superintendent and accordingly, two years after the first appointment, they voted to change my title to Assistant Superintendent. This helped to clarify the role responsibility and the order of command for all staff and community of the school division.

As Assistant Superintendent however, my role changed very little, if any. I was still a member of the Senior Administration Team, directly involved in all aspects of the operation of the School Division, with overall more specific responsibility for Personnel and Student Services. Also, I was responsible for the planning and projections of enrollments and staffing including planning for school facilities based on on-going enrolment projections, also my responsibility.

Crescendo to Becoming

. . . .

"To accomplish great things, we must not only act, but also dream; not only plan, but also believe."
—Anatole France

. . . .

* If you plant honesty, you will reap trust
* If you plant goodness, you will reap friends
* If you plant humility, you will reap greatness
* If you plant perseverance, you will reap contentment
* If you plant consideration, you will reap perspective
* If you plant hard work, you will reap success
* If you plant forgiveness, you will reap reconciliation.
—Unknown

. . . .

R. F. B. CRAMER
SUPERINTENDENT
OF SCHOOLS

E. F. SOLOMCHUK
BUSINESS ADMINISTRATOR
AND SECRETARY-TREASURER

Transcona-Springfield School Division No. 12
SCHOOL BOARD OFFICE
650 KILDARE AVENUE EAST — TRANSCONA 25, MANITOBA   PHONE 222-3211

BOARD OF TRUSTEES:

CHAIRMAN
  T. MALASHEWSKI

VICE-CHAIRMAN
  G. E. MARSHALL

COMMITTEES:

BUSINESS-ADMINISTRATION
  H. J. VAAGS
  W. R. GRAPENTINE
  W. KRUCHAK
  H. SOSIAK

EDUCATION-ADMINISTRATION
  S. MASLOVSKY
  MRS. M. ANDREE
  G. E. MARSHALL
  MRS. D. PEELER

February 2, 1971

Mr. F. Fiorentino, Principal
Murdoch MacKay Collegiate
260 Redonda Street
Transcona 25 Manitoba

Dear Mr. Fiorentino:

I would like to thank you for taking an active role in the public meeting held Wednesday, January 27th to discuss CORE and its implications for education.

I have heard many good comments about the way in which the meeting was run, and about the informed participation by teachers of the division. I appreciate your giving of your time. I only regret that I was unable to attend, due to a Board Meeting on budget.

Thank you again for your assistance.

Yours sincerely,

R. Cramer
Superintendent of Schools

RC/fp

Crescendo to Becoming

VERA M. DERENCHUK, B.A., M.Ed., A.M.M., L.R.S.M.
SUPERINTENDENT OF SCHOOLS

TODD M. BARANI
SECRETARY-TREASURER

TRANSCONA-SPRINGFIELD SCHOOL DIVISION NO. 12
SCHOOL BOARD OFFICE
118 REGENT AVENUE EAST — TRANSCONA, MANITOBA
R2C 0C1

PHONE 222-7851

BOARD OF TRUSTEES:

CHAIRMAN
H. J. VAAGS

VICE-CHAIRMAN
G. E. MARSHALL

MRS. M. ANDREE
M. BUYACHOK
J. J. ILCHYSHYN
W. KRUCHAK
S. MASLOVSKY
J. F. B. QUAIL
W. STOYKO

July 9, 1975

Mr. Frank Fiorentino,
340 Victoria Avenue West,
Transcona Manitoba.

Dear Frank:

I am very happy to confirm your appointment as Administrative Assistant to the Superintendent effective August 15, 1975. Your salary is $25,600. with a travelling allowance of $700. per annum. As you are aware, your position is on a twelve-month basis with three weeks vacation.

I have appreciated working with you in the past, but I look forward to working with you even more as part of the team at Central Office.

Sincerely,

Vera M. Derenchuk

Vera M. Derenchuk,
Superintendent of Schools.

VMD/fr

BECOMING A TEACHER, A PRINCIPAL, AND A SUPERINTENDENT OF EDUCATION

Career Preparation Argyle High School, 30 Argyle Street, Winnipeg, Manitoba R3B 0H4 Telephone 943-8
Counsellor: Gary McEwen,
Sponsored by: Winnipeg School Division & Canada Manp

July 14, 1975

Mr. F.P. Fiorentino
Administrative Assistant (Designate)
to the Superintendent of Schools
Transcona-Springfield School Division #12
340 Victoria Ave. West
Winnipeg, Manitoba

Dear Frank:

      Congratulations ! Just learned today of your new appointment. May I add further Frank that the Division has chosen a pretty nice guy to boot! Now that phrase doesn't sound right Frank - they picked a hell-of-a-nice guy! No doubt MMCI will miss their head knock but the Division will I am sure be the stronger for it. Vera, Peggy and yourself will make a pretty fine triumvirate at the Administrative level Frank. My sincere best wishes to you in your new capacity. A pleasant summer to you Frank and every success in the approaching term.

      Please find enclosed a brochure on Argyle and on the Outreach Program Frank(can't miss this opportunity to spread a little propaganda). If I can be of any assistance regarding these programs, I would look forward to discussing them with you.

Yours fraternally,

Gary R. McEwen

cc. Vera Derenchuk
    Peggy Hunt

TRANSCONA - SPRINGFIELD TEACHERS' ASSOCIATION
TRANSCONA, MANITOBA

RECEIVED DEC 1 1977
TRANSCONA - SPRINGFIELD SCHOOL

c/o 260 Redonda Street
WINNIPEG, Manitob
R2C 1L6

November 28, 1977

Mr. Frank Fiorentino
Assistant Superintendent
Transcona-Springfield School Division No. 12
760 Kildare Avenue East
WINNIPEG, Manitoba

Dear Mr. Fiorentino:

The Executive of the T.S.T.A. joins with me in extending congratulations to you on your appointment to the newly established position of Assistant Superintendent in the Transcona-Springfield School Division.

We are confident that your years as an experienced teacher administrator and Administrative Assistant qualify you for the position and that you will execute your responsibiliti at the highest professional level possible.

Rest assured that the Executive is prepared to meet with you on educational matters and others affecting the welfar of teachers in our Division with the aim of continuing improved relations between the Superintendent's Department and the local Association.

Yours truly

A. Hosein, President
Transcona-Springfield Teachers' Association

BECOMING A TEACHER, A PRINCIPAL, AND A SUPERINTENDENT OF EDUCATION

W. DERENCHUK, B.A., M.ED., A.M.M., L.R.S.M.
SUPERINTENDENT OF SCHOOLS

TODD M. BARANIUK
SECRETARY-TREASURER

TRANSCONA-SPRINGFIELD SCHOOL DIVISION NO. 12

SCHOOL BOARD OFFICE
760 KILDARE AVENUE EAST - TRANSCONA, MANITOBA
R2C 3Z4
PHONE 224-1271

October 26, 1977

Mr. George Marshall, Chairman
Board of Trustees,
Transcona-Springfield School Division.

Dear Mr. Chairman,

I take this opportunity to express my appreciation to you and to the members of the Board of Trustees for the recent change of title to Assistant Superintendent. I see this action by the Board as an expression of confidence in my performance in the past eighteen years of service to this Division as teacher, principal and administrative assistant to the Superintendent. For your confidence in me I am truly grateful.

I see this as an appropriate time to reaffirm my pledge to you and members of the Board (both former and present members) for my continued loyal service. Rest assured that I shall do my utmost to discharge my responsibilities to the benefit of every child in our care. As always, the child shall remain central in my thinking, and the intrinsic motivation and inspiration for my actions.

I wish you to know that I consider it an honour and a privilege to work in this Division. Over the past eighteen years, this Division has grown substantially and with this rapid growth it was perhaps inevitable as a result that some "growing pains" were experienced along the way. More remarkable though, have been all the many improvements and accomplishments that have taken place over the year - accomplishments relating to quality education, diversification of programs, outstanding facilities, and quality of instruction.

I am indeed happy to be a member of a very efficient and harmonious administrative team at Central Office. I have always admired the dedication and responsiveness of members of this team to be of "service to those in the field". Above all, I am particularly

... 2

- 2 -

delighted to work under the leadership of Mrs. Vera Derenchuk whom I consider to be one of the best educational leaders that this province has ever produced.

Thank you again for the trust in me. I look forward to working together with the Board and Administration in providing the main thrust toward our common and noble goal - the education of the young.

Educationally yours,

Frank Fiorentino,
Assistant Superintendent.

FF/fr

Crescendo to Becoming

* * *

"Once we believe in ourselves, we can risk curiosity, wonder, spontaneous delight, or any experience that reveals the human spirit."
—**E.E. Cummings**

* * *

June 8, 1979

Dear Frank,

As you know, I have always enjoyed working with you and have always regarded you as a friend. I hope we can continue to develop and grow in this friendship and possibly become business associates! Who knows?

Anyway, I'd like to say thanks to you for all you have meant to me over the past years. Your steadfastness and willingness to trust were great supports to me.

I wish you all the best in your present role and in the superintendency after Vera retires. I trust the Board will recognize what they have in you.

Thanks again for everything and I look forward to a continuing friendship.

Sincerely,
Oscar

BECOMING A TEACHER, A PRINCIPAL, AND A SUPERINTENDENT OF EDUCATION

W.M. JEREMCHUK, B.A., M.ED., A.M.M., L.R.S.M.
SUPERINTENDENT OF EDUCATION

TODD M. BARANIUK
SECRETARY-TREASURER

TRANSCONA-SPRINGFIELD SCHOOL DIVISION NO. 12
SCHOOL BOARD OFFICE
760 KILDARE AVENUE EAST - TRANSCONA, MANITOBA
R2C 3Z4
PHONE 224-1271

February 20, 1987

OUR FILE NO: _____

Mr. Gordon Newton
Past President
Manitoba Association of School Superintendents
900 St. Mary's Road
St. Vital, Manitoba.

Dear Mr. Newton:

I am delighted that the Manitoba Association of School Superintendents has nominated R.W. "Bobby" Bend as a candidate for the J.M. Brown Award for service to education in Manitoba.

I am writing this letter in support of the nominated candidate for I feel obligated to express my personal views which I believe are typical and representative of the views held by many people who have worked or known Bobby during his long and distinguished career in education.

I consider Bobby Bend one of the fathers of education in Manitoba. He represents a pioneer and a noble force in the development of public, free and universal education in this province. Few people, indeed, have equalled the impact and influence of Bobby Bend on the education scene in Manitoba.

Bobby Bend's record of service to children, whether as a teacher, principal, Superintendent, or Minister of Education, I am sure is well known and speaks for itself. Suffice to say that for a period of over forty years, Bobby Bend's sphere of influence has been felt at every level of the public school system throughout the whole province. For example, no one gave more unselfishly toward the consolidation of school districts and divisions in the movement to form unitary school divisions in 1967. He is a complete educator who can truly say that in his remarkable career he has "touched all the bases".

But the true measure of the man, I feel, has been his intense care and love for people. His trademark has been his tenacious fight for the "underdog". He has been and remains to be a true champion of "the little guy", particularly the child, the under-privileged, the handicapped, and the deprived.

- 2 -

Equality of educational opportunity has been advanced in our community to the degree it is today, because guys like Bobby Bend not only believed in the principle, but because he actually practiced what he preached. His message about his ardent and unshaken faith in the supreme worth of every individual has been heard loud and clear during the last four decades. He has never undermined the human potential inherent in all people. With these strong convictions, Bobby Bend has provided the intrinsic motivation, the challenge and the confidence to many an aspiring young teacher, including the undersigned. I can personally attest to this fact, particularly during the four years he worked in Transcona-Springfield School Division as the Division's first Superintendent. It was an honour and privilege for me to have been touched by this great leader and caring, loving person.

I, for one, and representative of many, feel grateful for the invaluable contributions Bobby Bend has made to Manitoba generally, and to education in particular. He has served us all with dignity, with love, and with distinction.

I know no other person at this time, as an educational leader and as a man of humanistic principles who would be a more meritorious recipient of the J.M. Brown Award than R.W. "Bobby" Bend.

Respectfully submitted,

Frank Fiorentino,
Assistant Superintendent,
Transcona-Springfield School Division.

FF/f

Interlake School Division, No. 21

337 Main St.
P.O. Box 549
Stonewall, Man. R0C 2Z0

PHONE 467-2492
PHONE 467-8485

March 3/81

Dear Frank,

It has not been very often in my life that I have been totally unable to put in words my feelings in regard to any incident that might take place in any given day. However, the receipt of the copy of the wonderful testimonial that you gave on my behalf has left me in that position. I have tried several times to put my thoughts in words since receiving your letter and have failed so far. As a result I have committed the sin of tardiness when I should have acted with much more despatch.

Over the years I have collected a few souvenirs that relate to very significant things that have happened to me. Your letter becomes a top member of that group of treasures capable always of bringing back many beautiful memories.

In all the various positions I have held there is no professional or personal relationship that compares with ours

BECOMING A TEACHER, A PRINCIPAL, AND A SUPERINTENDENT OF EDUCATION

R. W. BEND
UPERINTENDENT OF SCHOOLS
PHONE 467-2492

R. R. EICHLER
SECRETARY-TREASURER
PHONE 467-8485

Interlake School Division, No. 21

337 Main St.
P.O. Box 549
Stonewall, Man. R0C 2Z0

The method in which you handled the responsibilities I entrusted you with shall never be forgotten. Because in the success you have enjoyed I, too, have had satisfaction in knowing that I had picked the right man.

Whether I happen to receive the award is purely secondary to the pleasure your letter has given me. I know that I haven't made a very good job of telling you how I feel as you know I am not a very demonstrative person. But I'll close by saying that of all the men I have met you rank at the very top.

Please remember me to your good wife and I close by wishing you & yours the best of everything from one who will always be in your corner.

Sincerely,
Bob Bend

Crescendo to Becoming

My Testimonial Speech to Bobby Bend on Occasion of his Retirement, June 1981

Good Evening Ladies and Gentlemen,

I wish to express my pleasure and appreciation to the organizers of this memorable occasion for the invitation and opportunity afforded me to be in Bobby Bend's corner tonight for the man who's been in my corner over the last twenty years.

I feel honored this evening to give this testimonial and express my personal views which I believe are typical and representative of the views held by many people who have worked with or known Bobby Bend during his long and distinguished career in education.

Bobby Bend has often referred to me in an intimate kind of way as a "young fellow". In the same sincere way, I wish to refer to Bobby Bend as a "father", yes, a father, for I truly consider him to be one of the fathers of education in the Province of Manitoba. He represents a pioneer and a noble force in the development of public, free and universal education in this province. Few people, indeed, have equaled the impact and influence of Bobby Bend on the Education scene in Manitoba.

For almost half a century, Bobby Bend's sphere of influence has been felt at every level of the public school system. Bobby Bend's 50-year record in the public domain generally, and the 44-year service to the children of Manitoba in particular, where as a teacher, principal, Superintendent or Minister of Education, needs no elaboration.

He is a complete educator who can truly say that in his remarkable career he has "touched all the bases". Speaking of touching all the bases, I'm reminded that Bobby Bend is well-known in these parts for his reputation as a baseball umpire.) People are still trying to forget some of the calls he made some 30 years ago.)

Some 15 years ago, Bobby was Transcona-Springfield's School Division's first Superintendent of Education. He told me then that one of the best qualities for a school principal to have is to be able to call (umpire) a fair and impartial baseball game. He spoke with such conviction of this, that I actually believed him.

However, I shall never allow him to forget that I lost a Whist Tournament which he organized for the Manitoba Association of School Superintendents. As I remember it, it was a very close game and I saw my way clear to winning the tournament as the last condition of the tournament was that we could add to our

142

BECOMING A TEACHER, A PRINCIPAL, AND A SUPERINTENDENT OF EDUCATION

total score as many points as we had letters in our names. So, I took the total score, and added no less than 35 points, which represented all the numbers of letters in my name and presented the score card to Mr. Bend. I have never seen him jump so high! He took me to task right there and then asked me sarcastically if I had included the names of all the members of my family including all my ancestors. When I told him that my official name is Francesco Pietro Arcangelo Fiorentino-- well! When he heard that, he almost went into convulsions. He demanded proof. He asked me if I was born – and I said yes! He asked me for proof. I told him that I would send him a copy of my birth certificate, but he wanted and demanded proof right there and then. He gave me some other political excuses, and boy was he good at that. Needless to say, I lost the argument, and I lost the tournament. When I got home, I made a Photostat of my birth certificate and sent it to him by registered mail. He sent me a reply of apology, giving me all kinds of lavish praises. This is my last attempt tonight at trying to get a public admission and retraction from Bobby Bend, the politician.

But more seriously folks, the true measure of this man, I feel, has been his intense care and love for people. His trademark has been his tenacious fight for the "underdog", a champion of "the little guy", little guys like me, who would not be here tonight, had it not been for the confidence he has shown in me over the years. I am living proof of his ardent unshaken faith and belief in the supreme worth of every individual. He has never undermined the human potential inherent in all people.

With this living philosophy Bobby Bend has provided the intrinsic motivation to many an aspiring young man. It has been an honour and a privilege to have been touched by this great leader and such a caring loving person.

In short, he is the epitome and the living symbol embodied in the words of Alfred Martin which read as follows:

"That which constitutes the supreme worth of life is not wealth, not ease, not fame–not even happiness,…but Service".

Mr. Bend, on behalf of the Manitoba Association of School Superintendents, on behalf of all your friends and colleagues in the Transcona-Springfield School Division, on behalf of all "young fellows" in this province, I wish to extend to you and Mrs. Bend and all members of your family, our sincere wish that you all may enjoy excellent health and happiness in what we hope will truly be a golden period of your life.

Thank you and good evening.

Crescendo to Becoming

The 25th Anniversary of Murdoch MacKay School Reunion, Winnipeg Convention Centre, 1988

On the occasion of the Murdoch MacKay's 25th Anniversary I delivered the following speech quoted here in its entirety:

Thank you, Paul (Moreau), Good Evening Ladies and Gentlemen:

Rodgers and Hammerstein in The King and I, put it this way:

"It's a true and ancient saying.
And a very special thought.
That if you become a teacher,
By your pupils you'll be taught.

It seems it's been forever
Since the first time we met,
We shared some days together
That we cannot forget.

There was work and there was laughter.
There were tears and triumphs, too;
Success and Disasters,
But somehow, we came through.

Yes, we worked to make things last,
And yes, you had to strive.
But God, your blood ran hot and fast,
And, Boy, were you alive!"

It's inevitable that on an occasion such as this, that your mind turns back nostalgically to the days back at school, and the feeling of endearment we experienced is unmistakable and so real. I think that you can appreciate the overwhelming impact that this reunion is having on me, as I think back to the two thousand or so students that dominated my life, for an unforgettable seven years as principal of Murdoch MacKay.

As I was doing some reminiscing, I just figured out what were probably the two most common announcements that I made over the intercom, during my seven years at Murdoch. No doubt one was this: *"Good morning, will John Couture and Bruce Diack please report to the office."* You see, Couture and Diack were quite a dynamic duo, and as such interfaced with the office on a regular basis. Anyway, I wanted to make these announcements once more, in the hope that it would transport some of you back again, to your days at Murdoch Mackay.

But going back to John Couture for a moment, I like to tell you that three weeks ago, I had the pleasure of being on television with John, on a show promoting this reunion, I learned that "Cooch" is still very much into collecting things. Nowadays he goes annually to every Grey Cup game and has collected all sorts of buttons and memorabilia of the annual event and Canadian football. When he was at Murdoch, he was really involved into collecting different things: …like pink slips.

In terms of world events 1968 was both the worst and the best of times. It was the year that saw the great Martin Luther King and Robert Kennedy assassinated and it seemed that youth were rebelling against all traditional thought. But it was also the time when the Apollo Mission circled the moon and the banner cry for youth became "Make Love, Not War."

Murdoch Mackay Collegiate was a microcosm, a veritable miniature world in itself. We saw in our school the advent of long hair, the proliferation of blue jeans, the flower children, and heard the rock and roll music of *Elvis* and the *Beetles* at our dances. We implemented the *Young Adult Concept*, abolished the strap, and threw away the "paddle". For years before that, no student could go to the washroom unless he had the wooden paddle with him. The intent of having the paddle, was to let everyone who saw you in the hallway know that you were going to the washroom, and that indeed, you had received permission from the teacher to do so. (We've come a long way on that one.)

So, not all times at Murdoch were good times, but neither were they all bad. Rather it was like life itself, with its bad and good times. For me however, the unpleasant fades back into the background, and that which was good and worthwhile, emerges more clearly into focus.

But how do I really remember thee,... well, ... let me count some of the ways. I remember you in the classrooms, and always wanting to be leaning on the particular heat registers in the hallway. I remember you, hiding with your sweetheart under the staircases, with the intent of doing a little smooching. I remember you in the gymnasium, in the library, in the hut, and on the stage. I remember you in the plains of Crocus Park, on the "Murdoch Mountain", and at and in the river known as the Floodway. And yes, I do remember you in my office.

And I remember the scholars, the athletes, the sweethearts, the singers, the musicians, the actors and actresses, the motor cyclists, the NGCs, and the graduates. And yes, I do remember the ever exuberant *"greasers"*. And yes, I wish I could forget, what some of you no doubt like to remember, ...those Freshie Days.

I do, still, have but one regret though. The school flag went missing in 1973 and someone still has it. It was the only time that my detective work failed to bring results. So, if you still have it, I'll let you keep it, ...but I sure like to know who it was that got away with it!

I remember also the academic excellence, the school newspaper **"*Tartan Examiner*"** with its popular column called *"Frankly Speaking"* where students wrote in to receive nothing but objective (??) answers on any topic. I remember the many innovations in the classrooms, the dedicated staff, sports championships, and the four musical productions.

Never will I forget *"Fiddler on the Roof"*, *"South Pacific"*, and *"The Sound of Music"*. Nor will I forget that when I became the principal, it was Trustee Mary Andree, who inspired me with her challenge to bring some form of music at the high school level. Imagine how proud I was when the Saturday night (last) performance of *"Fiddler"*, our very first musical, was dedicated to Mrs. Andree. Those of you who lived through it all will never forget the feeling of personal satisfaction and achievement, and the tears of fulfillment that we shared when it was over.

We were brought together to learn and grow and in the process of working and playing together we formed bonds that drew us closer and closer together. In closing, I wish to acknowledge that "The greatest love a person can have is friendship". May I toast that friendship, which became the distinct trademark of the Murdoch MacKay students and staff am prouder still tonight, to know that you are still… my friends.

For what you have been, …and are tonight, …you have my love.

Maythe road rise up to meet you,
May the wind be always at your back,
May the sunshine warm upon your face,
And until the end of time,
May God hold you all,…in the palm of His hand.

Thank you for the memories…

Carpe Diem.

Front Cover Page of the book: From Slate to Computer

Contents

Part One — The Story of Schools

A Town is Born — 1910	1
Cook's Creek School — 1873	13
North Springfield School — 1877	15
South Springfield School — 1879	21
Dugald School District No. 80 — 1879	25
Prairie Grove School — 1882	31
Suthwyn School No. 530 — 1882	33
Cornwall School S.D. No. 1129 — 1903	37
South Transcona Schools — 1911	41
Hazelridge School — 1912	47
Anola Elementary School — 1912	53
Transcona Central School — 1913	57
Westview Elementary School — 1953	127
Transcona's First Collegiate — 1956	133
Radisson Elementary School — 1957	135
Nostalgia	139
The Manitoba Public Schools Act — 1959	153
Regent Park Elementary School — 1959	157
Wayoata Elementary School — 1959	163
Transcona Collegiate Institute — 1961	171
Oakbank Complex:	
Springfield Collegiate Institute — 1961	177
Oakbank Elementary School — 1965	183
Springfield Junior High School — 1969	189
Murdoch MacKay Collegiate — 1963	193
Margaret Underhill Elementary School — 1965	205
The First Superintendent of Education	
R.W. "Bobby" Bend — 1965-1969	211
John W. Gunn Junior High School — 1966	217
Centennial Year Project — 1967	223
New Arthur Day Junior High School — 1969	225
Harold Hatcher Elementary School — 1975	229
Park Circle School — 1977	235
Bernie Wolfe Community School — 1977	241

Crescendo to Becoming

viii   **History Committee**

Mary Andree   Frank Fiorentino   Aleck Robson

Sam Maslovsky   Paul Martin   Linda Hughes

Randy Evans   Wyn Fraser   Vic Woyna

Transcona-Springfield School Division No. 12 History Book Committee responsible for overseeing the writing the history of the School Division From Slate to Computer, *published in 1983*

BECOMING A TEACHER, A PRINCIPAL, AND A SUPERINTENDENT OF EDUCATION

Manitoba Association of School Superintendents

President:
Rex Williams

Executive Director:
Donna Phillips
Phone: 956-2891

Past-President:
George Buchholz

1st. Vice-President:
Walter Melnyk

2nd. Vice-President:
Gerry Dougall

Treasurer:
John Ilavsky

Committee Chairmen:
Peter Blahey
George Buchholz
Cec Cox
Ken Halldorson
Norm Isler
Al Yaskiw

October 2, 1984

George Marshall
Vice-Chairman
Transcona-Springfield School Boar
760 Kildare Avenue East
WINNIPEG, Man. R2C 3Z4

Dear George:

As you know, Frank Fiorentino served last year on the Executive of the Manitoba Association of School Superintendents.

The Manitoba Association of School Superintendents plays an important leadership role in the pursuit of excellence in Manitoba education.

The Association is appreciative of the contribution Frank Fiorentino made toward the realization of this goal.

Yours sincerely,

Donna Phillips
Executive Director

DCP/np

RECEIVED
OCT-4 1984
TRANSCONA-SPRINGFIELD SCHOOL
BOARD OFFICE

Suite 200 — 477 Webb Place, Winnipeg, Manitoba R3B 2P2

Crescendo to Becoming

Transcona-Springfield Trustees and Administration

Trustees

Rev. Msg. Michael Buyachok
Ward 2
1974 - present

Mary Andree
Ward 1   1962 - 1977
Chairman (1986)   1980 - present

Jean Chanowski
Ward 4
1977 - present

Elaine Gregg
Ward 5
1984 - present

Jim Ilchyshyn
Ward 3
1974 - present

Paul Martin
Ward 1
1952 - 1953
1983 - present

George Marshall
Ward 2
1969 - 1971
1973 - present

Wally Stoyko
Ward 1
1971 to present

Karen Watson
Ward 2
1983 - present

Administration

Vera M. Derenchuk
Superintendent

Frank Fiorentino
Assistant Superintendent

Peggy Hunt
Administrative Assistant

Todd Baraniuk
Secretary-Treasurer

Bruce Cairns
Assistant Secretary-Treasurer

As Reported in 1986 in "1911 Transcona, Celebrating 75 Years of Community", Page 5,

152

BECOMING A TEACHER, A PRINCIPAL, AND A SUPERINTENDENT OF EDUCATION

*Transcona-Springfield School Division No. 12
Logo that I created, circa 1980*

Crescendo to Becoming

Transcona-Springfield School Board Offices built in 1975 at Kildare Avenue and Redonda Street where I spent 16 years (1975–1991)

Senior Administration of the Transcona-Springfield School Division No. 12, (1980)
Front row, left to right: Peggy Hunt, Vera Derenchuk
Back row, left to right: Todd Baraniuk and Me

BECOMING A TEACHER, A PRINCIPAL, AND A SUPERINTENDENT OF EDUCATION

SENIOR ADMINISTRATION:
Back Row: Todd Baraniuk, Bruce Cairns, Frank Fiorentino,
Front Row: Peggy Hunt, and Vera Derenchuk

TRANSCONA-SPRINGFIELD SCHOOL DIVISION NO. 12 SCHOOL BOARD
AND SENIOR ADMINISTRATION, (1980)
Front Row: left to right: Pat Watson (Trustee), Elaine Boriskewitch (Trustee), Karen Watson (Trustee), Vera Derenchuk (Superintendent of Education) *Back row, left to right:* Todd Baraniuk (Secretary-Treasurer), Peggy Hunt (Administrative Assistant), George Marshall (Trustee), Ron Low (Trustee), Jean Chanowski (Trustee), Fr. Michael Buyachok (Trustee), Mary Andree (Trustee), Wally Stoyko (Trustee), and me, Frank Fiorentino (Assistant Superintendent)

MY AREAS OF ACHIEVEMENT AND/OR INVOLVEMENT AS ASSISTANT SUPERINTENDENT OF EDUCATION IN THE TRANSCONA-SPRINGFIELD SCHOOL DIVISION NO. 12, 1975–1991

The executive branch of the Transcona-Springfield School Division No. 12 was in essence a **Senior Administrative (Education) Team**, and consisted of the superintendent of education, the assistant superintendent, and the administrative assistant (elementary). In addition to senior administration there were the three consultants: early years, middle years, and senior years, and the four coordinators, namely music, physical education, work education, and industrial arts/vocational. Further to that, we always involved principals and those in the field as appropriate, in the planning, designing, formulation, development, implementation, administration and monitoring of anything and everything of importance. As assistant superintendent I was involved in almost everything, including the following:

1. The development and maintenance of A **Master Plan of Education**, encompassing the planning process, formulation and delivery of quality educational programming and services to Transcona-Springfield School Division comprising of 8,300 students, 1000+ staff that included approximately 530 teachers, and 220 support staff comprised of clerical, paraprofessionals, and library clerks, 57 bus drivers, 77 custodial and maintenance personnel as well as non-union staff.

2. The Master Plan of Education was a cyclic process consisting of planning through a system-wide setting of goals and objectives, specific job targets, reviewing progress reports, adjustments, evaluations, year-end review and report, followed by the re-setting of goals and objectives again for the following year.

3. Implementation of the **Management by Objectives** (MBO's) and Education by Objectives system for the 20 years as a member of senior administration as the Division's major planning and communication instrument.

4. Implementation of a Division-wide **annual budget** input process to rationalize and justify a budget of approximately $ 42,000,000. (1990-1991) including projections, formulation, and administration. The meticulous annual budget preparations included the compilation of a 300 page **budget rationale** document complete with appendices, which described all programs and projects to be undertaken and the related budgetary allocations. For 20 years, this process demanded a commitment to a tremendous effort and time well beyond regular hours, i.e. working evenings, Saturdays and Sundays during the months of November and December without ever receiving any additional compensation or time off in lieu.

5. An **annual comprehensive staffing strategy**/plan/formula for the deployment of all personnel in the Division—a staff of well over 1000 people.

6. Participated as an active resource person and member of the **Board's Negotiations Team** with no less than five bargaining units: teachers, custodians, bus drivers, paraprofessionals and library clerks.

7. Annual **in-service and professional development planning and programming** for all staff: teachers, administration, clerical, paraprofessionals, transportation, and maintenance.

8. The transformation **and re-organization of the five junior high schools into middle years schools** involving the implementation, staffing deployment and programming as concepts specific to the middle years school.

9. Research, plan and draft letter of intent, proposals for Board approval, and subsequent submission to the public schools finance board of the department of education from 1975 to 1991, for **the construction, additions, or renovations** including the following projects:

   a. Arthur Day Junior High (Grades7-9) – construction of new school 740,000 s.f.
   b. Bernie Wolfe Community School (K–9) 5,387 s.f.
   c. Central School (K–6) -- renovations
   d. Ecole Centrale (K–6) --new construction/renovations 79,000 s.f.

Crescendo to Becoming

    e. Regent Park (K–8) -- mainly renovations, 39,574 s.f.
    f. Dugald School (K–6)-- addition and renovations, 11,480 s.f.
    g. Murdoch MacKay Collegiate (9–12) -- additions and renovations -- 95,000 s.f.
    h. Oak Bank Elementary School (K–6) -- addition 40,000 s.f.
    i. Springfield Collegiate (9–12) --addition and renovations 81,000 s.f.
    j. Joseph Teres School (K–6) --construction of new school 51,000.s.f.
    k. Anola Elementary School (K–6) -- addition 9,500 s.f.
    l. Arthur Day School (5-8) -- addition 3,400 s.f.
    m. College Pierre Elliott Trudeau (9–12) -- construction of new school, --44,000 s.f.

10. Draft and prepare report for the **Reorganization of Central School and Central/ Ecole Centrale** and other schools in Transcona in 1983.

11. Research, prepare and draft **Report of Hazelridge School** with the view of possible school closure in two years' time.

12. Assist and input in the briefs to the **High School Review Panel** for the school division, for the Manitoba Association of School Superintendents (MASS) and for the inter-reorganizational High School Program Review committee of the Department of Education.

13. Prepare and conduct **workshops** for administrators, school staff, clerical staff, bus drivers, caretakers and paraprofessionals.

14. Assisted in the design, development and implementation of the performance-based staff evaluation comprehensive approach called **"Performance Planning, Coaching, Observation, and Assessment (PPOCA)** – first for teachers, and subsequently for all other employee groups based on support and coaching to encourage professional and personal growth.

15. The development and the implementation of the **Master Plan for Curriculum Implementation and Curriculum Implementation Model for Schools** for all subject areas, K-12.

16. The Formulation and Implementation of the **Education Continuum, K-17**, which established minimum teaching standards and expectations in all subjects and all grades.

17. Assume major responsibility for the initiation and implementation of a process for the development of Board/ Divisional Policies and compilation of the **first Policy Manual**. Drafted at least 90% of policies and with input into all of them.

18. Assisted directly in the **development of Language Programs** in the division including:

19. The development and implementation of the **French Immersion Program**, K-12. b) The establishment of the first **English–Ukrainian Bilingual Program** in the Province of Manitoba grades K-11, offered in both urban and rural areas of the Division.

20. The implementation of the **Basic French** Program for all children of the division, in Grades 4-12.

21. Assisted in the implementation of the **Resource Teacher Program** since its beginning in 1972 and its expansion, with our goal to have at least one full-time resource teacher in each school. Also, the consultative-collaborative model, a first in the Transcona-Springfield School Division, was well-established in the schools of the division.

22. The implementation of **integration**, first in the elementary setting and then in the middle and senior years schools, designed to allow inclusion of all special needs children in all areas of the school, aimed to meet the academic, emotional, social, and physical needs of all students.

23. The establishment of the very successful **Work Education Program** first at Transcona Collegiate and then at the other secondary schools.

24. The initiation and establishment of the **Co-operative Education Program** at the senior years level which was designed to provide skills to students to bridge school with the world of work. This program was a huge success and involved close to 500 employers as partners of the program.

25. The publishing of three school **divisional newsletters** per year.

26. The publishing of **bi-monthly Board Report** was distributed to all union groups and to all media.

Crescendo to Becoming

Graduation Speech That I Delivered as Assistant Superintendent at Springfield Collegiate, Oakbank, June 28, 1989

It is my privilege to have this opportunity to bring greetings on behalf of Superintendent Vera Derenchuk, senior Administration, and Central Office staff, on this happy and important occasion. This is an important occasion not only for the graduates themselves, but also for all stakeholders such as the parents and relatives, teachers, trustees, friends, and the community as a whole, all of whom are well represented here today, to give recognition to the achievements of the S.C.I. graduating class of 1989.

Graduates, your hard work has paid off. You now know that **it's the uphill trip that gets you to the top.** Your diploma is tangible proof of all the hours you spent in the pursuit of this moment. Today you can rejoice in the handshakes and hugs from family and friends, and accept with pride, laughter and tears, the gifts and accolades you will no doubt receive. We also know that these gifts will always be extra special to you because they commemorate a very special moment in your life: **the magic of high school graduation.**

Graduates, you have a great deal to be grateful for. All of you have been given a least **one very special gift,** a gift that was given to you free of charge, with no strings attached...a gift that is probably as unique as you are. You are free to take this gift, nourish it, and allow it to become your greatest /strength, or to neglect it, misuse it—even reject it—until it deteriorates into weakness, fault, and waste.

But what gift do you possess?

You may have the gift of **leadership**. You can use it to motivate and inspire others to develop their own potential; or, you can distort it until you become a manipulator, a user of people to accommodate you, in your private and arrogant ambition.

Perhaps you possess the gift of **determination** and commitment. You are also very lucky, for the force of perseverance can sustain you, when the task before you is difficult or challenging, or you can misuse it and twist it until it is reduced to mere stubbornness, tainted by a total disregard of its effects on others.

Or, perhaps you have been given the gift of **tenderness and compassion,** a sensitivity that instinctively reaches out to soothe someone who is hurting; but if you are afraid to share some of that person's hurt in order to ease it, your gift may be reduced to nothing more than simple pretension. Or, is yours the gift of **superior**

intelligence, *that priceless capacity to absorb knowledge easily and quickly? To you comes the opportunity to hone your fine intellect so that you can contribute limitless benefits to society; but if you choose to let your gift lie dormant, or to misdirect it in a quest for personal power, you can become a burden, or worse, a menace to society.*

Yes, graduates, you can become what you believe you can be.

*In all this one very important reality emerges: each of you possess some extraordinary gifts—gifts that give you the capacity to think, to reason, to make choices, and to feel. **The essence of this message is really this: YOU ARE THE GIFT, the gift of mankind's hope.** Yes, the gift of God's creation itself, and if you should determine to share and to give of yourself you will experience the miracle of the greatest gift of all: **friendship and love.***

I wish to propose a toast to the fact that you, your friends, and your teachers have developed a sense of community, a feeling of belonging. You have become a part of each other now, and by God you are all the better for it.

*Graduates, my wish for you is simple: may you recognize your gifts, and may you nourish them so that you can continue to learn and grow all the days of your life. I wish you that, knowing fully well, that in your lifetime, **"learning a living" will be more important that "earning a living".***

Finally, I wish to extend to you my personal congratulations and continued success....and may God hold you always in the palm of His hands.

Crescendo to Becoming

LETTERS OF RECOMMENDATIONS FOR THE POSITION OF SUPERINTENDENT OF EDUCATION BY MY THREE FORMER SUPERINTENDENTS OF EDUCATION: BOBBY BEND, REEVAN CRAMER, AND VERA DERENCHUK

October 18, 1990

The Superintendent
Selection Committee

Re: Mr. Frank Fiorentino

    I was more than pleased to grant Mr. Fiorentino's request to use my name as a reference in connection with his application for the position of Superintendent of Transcona-Springfield School Division. I would like to take this opportunity to express my reasons for supporting his application.

    As you no doubt already know, we both worked for the Division as administrators from 1965-69. This experience gave me an excellent opportunity to assess his administrative ability.

    One incident in particular comes to mind in this connection. It concerns the recommendation I was required to make to the Board for the position of principal of Murdoch Mackay Collegiate in 1968. It was, without a doubt, one of the most difficult decisions I was required to make during the four years I was Superintendent of the Division.

    Firstly, the administrative position itself was a most responsible one. Secondly, certain major difficulties had developed that were very distressing to the Collegiate itself. I have always been thankful that the appointment of Mr. Fiorentino to the position turned out to be the correct one. This is witnessed by the fact that he held the principalship for seven years (1968-1975) and was then appointed Administrative Assistant to the Superintendent, a position he held for two years. He was then appointed Assistant Superintendent of Education, the position he has held for 13 years, and finally now Acting Superintendent.

. . . 2

BECOMING A TEACHER, A PRINCIPAL, AND A SUPERINTENDENT OF EDUCATION

- 2 -

Another major reason for this reference is the fact that he has served the Division successfully for thirty years, serving as high school teacher, Vice-Principal, Principal, Assistant Superintendent and now Acting Superintendent.

This experience has allowed him to become completely familiar with the problems that a major school division such as Transcona-Springfield has to deal with. In addition, his knowing the complete history of the Division gives him an excellent chance of ascertaining the problems as they develop and deal with them before they become emergencies.

I would like to mention one more of his assets. It is the ability to use "common sense" when it is required.

To sum up, I have no hesitation whatever in recommending Mr. Fiorentino as Superintendent of your Division.

This recommendation is given without reservation, mental or otherwise.

Yours sincerely,

R. W. Bend

Crescendo to Becoming

October 25, 1990

Mr. Reevan Cramer
2101-80 Plaza Drive
Winnipeg, Manitoba
R3T 5S2

To Whom It May Concern:

At the request of Mr. Frank Fiorentino, I am writing this brief comment on our professional association.

Frank was principal of Murdoch McKay Collegiate during my tenure as Superintendent of the Transcona Springfield School Division No. 12. Upon my assumption of that position in 1968, I found him of invaluable assistance.

He provided me with a complete history of the division, its workings and, if I may say, its idiosyncracies. He introduced me to many of its personnel, both senior officers and teachers. He helped me establish contacts with the Transcona local of the Manitoba Teachers Society and also with the general community. His effort was of inestimable assistance to me as a newcomer.

Frank is a man of unquestionable probity. He is also perceptive, sensitive to people and their problems and extremely kind. These qualities with an innate gentleness made for a warm rapport with his students and colleagues.

He was, in my experience, far-sighted and innovative. By way of example, he pioneered the tri-mester system, computer timetabling and was deeply interested in the development of programs in Canadian Studies. He was a sound administrator and an excellent organizer who could maintain "law and order" in what were often difficult circumstances.

I have always counted myself fortunate to have had this professional and collegial relationship with Frank and I commend him to your attention.

Yours sincerely,

REEVAN CRAMER

BECOMING A TEACHER, A PRINCIPAL, AND A SUPERINTENDENT OF EDUCATION

November 8, 1990

Chairperson of the Selection Committee
Transcona-Springfield School Division No. 12

Dear Madam:

Re: Frank Fiorentino

I have worked with **Frank Fiorentino** in his role as principal of Arthur Day School, principal of Murdoch MacKay Collegiate, as Administrative Assistant, and over the past number of years, as Assistant Superintendent. In his role as Assistant Superintendent he was part of the administrative arm of the Superintendent with primary responsibility for the secondary level.

As Assistant Superintendent, Frank was involved in a meaningful way in most of the areas of the Division's functioning, and in this capacity was an excellent support administratively to the work of the Division and to the Superintendent's Department. Particularly in his first thireeen years at Central Office, Frank demonstrated initiative, organization, dedication to the task, and supportive follow-through on those duties assigned to him.

Should you consider it useful to your deliberations, I would be most willing to expand on any of the points in this letter or any other areas of his expertise and suitability for the position not mentioned above.

Sincerely,

Vera Derenchuk

Vera Derenchuk, Superintendent Emeritus and Executive Director
Manitoba Council for Leadership in Education

08/11/90
mr

Crescendo to Becoming

FRANK FIORENTINO, B.A., B.ED., M.ED. SUPERINTENDENT OF EDUCATION
TODD BARANIUK SECRETARY-TREASURER

TRANSCONA-SPRINGFIELD SCHOOL DIVISION NO. 12
SCHOOL BOARD OFFICE PHONE: 224-1271
760 KILDARE AVENUE EAST – WINNIPEG, MANITOBA, R2C 2Z4

FRANK FIORENTINO'S PHILOSOPHY OF EDUCATION AS SUPERINTENDENT OF EDUCATION PUBLISHED IN THE 1990–1991 SCHOOL YEAR

I am very happy to have this opportunity to provide a message for this first edition of our newspaper *CONNECTIONS* for the 1990–1991 school year. It's an opportune time for me to outline briefly some twelve key statements that are quite representative of my thoughts and beliefs about modern day education.

1. *EDUCATION IS A RIGHT OF ALL, NOT A PRIVILEGE OF THE FEW. THE MISSION OF THE SCHOOL SYSTEM IS THE DEVELOPMENT OF HUMAN POTENTIAL.*

2. *THE EDUCATOR'S GOAL IS OPEN MINDS AND HEARTS, NOT THE OPEN CLASSROOM.*

3. *EDUCATION IS A LIFE-LONG JOURNEY, NOT A DESTINATION.*

4. *EDUCATION IS A PARTNERSHIP OF ALL ITS STAKEHOLDERS: STUDENTS, TEACHERS, ADMINISTRATORS, SUPPORT STAFF, PARENTS, VOLUNTEERS, TRUSTEES, BUSINESSMEN, AND COMMUNITY MEMBERS.*

5. *THE PUPIL IS A CHILD OF GOD, NOT A TOOL OF THE STATE—A UNIQUE HUMAN BEING WITH AWARENESS, DIGNITY, WILL, HUMOUR AND LOVE. HE MUST BE THE CHAMPION OF OUR CAUSE.*

6. *THE TEACHER IS A GUIDE NOT A GUARD. AS FACILITATOR OF LEARNING, THE TEACHER MUST BE THE ADVOCATE OF THE STUDENT.*

7. *THE PRINCIPAL IS A MASTER TEACHER, NOT A MASTER OF TEACHERS.*

8. *THE FACULTY IS A COMMUNITY OF SCHOLARS, NOT A UNION OF ROBOTS WORKING WITH INANIMATE, UNFEELING OBJECTS.*

9. *THE CLASSROOM IS THE CRADLE OF THE CHILD, A PLACE OF NURTURING, AND CARING FOR THE CHILD.*

10. *THE SCHOOL IS THE CATHEDRAL OF THE STUDENT. AS SUCH, THE SCHOOL MUST BE THE MOST IMPORTANT, AND THE MOST INVITING PLACE IN TOWN.*

11. *TEACHING IS THE NOBLEST PROFESSION IN THE UNIVERSE.*

AS PEOPLE DEVELOPERS, TEACHERS (AND THOSE THAT SUPPORT AND FACILITATE THEIR TASK) MUST CONSIDER THEMSELVES VERY FORTUNATE THAT THEY HAVE THE OPPORTUNITY AND CHALLENGE TO MAKE A TREMENDOUS DIFFERENCE.

IN THE FINAL ANALYSIS, TEACHERS, EDUCATORS AND OTHERS WHO IMPACT ON THE EDUCATION OF OUR CHILDREN, HAVE THE MISSION NOT ONLY TO RE-INVENT THE FUTURE, BUT TO ACTUALLY CREATE IT.

Frank Fiorentino

Crescendo to Becoming

• •

"You have within you right now the potential to bring more health, more wealth, more power, more success, more freedom into your life than you ever dreamed possible. You don't need to "acquire" this potential, you already possess it. You just need to learn how to use it, direct it, understand it, so you can apply it in all departments of your life. "
—**Michael Monroe Kiefer**

• •

My First Speech as Superintendent of Education to the Total Staff of Transcona –Springfield School Division No.12

Mr. Chairman, Colleagues, Ladies and Gentlemen,

First of all, I wish to extend a very warm welcome and a "Welcome on board" to those that are embarking on the exciting journey that is Education for the very first time, and of course, to all those who are returning to the Division for another leg in the important journey.

This is perhaps the only time of the year when we are likely to be together as a total staff. Following what is now tradition of this meeting to launch the school year, I hope that we greet each other as we have done in past years. So, as I call on each employee group, please stand and take a bow and thus be recognized.

1. *Bus Drivers, and members of the Transportation Department*
2. *Custodians and members of the Maintenance Department*
3. *Clerical and Secretarial Staff in all Departments*
4. *Paraprofessional staff*
5. *Library Clerks and Materials Resource Staff (M.R.C) Staff*
6. *School and other Administrators*
7. *Teachers and Substitute Teachers*
8. *Divisional Support Staff including Child Guidance Clinic Staff, Consultants, Coordinators, Payroll, and Purchasing staff*
9. *And last, but not least, the Senior Administration Team:*

BECOMING A TEACHER, A PRINCIPAL, AND A SUPERINTENDENT OF EDUCATION

- *Gerry Saleski: Deputy Assistant Superintendent*
- *Peggy Hunt: Administrative Assistant to the Superintendent*
- *Todd Baraniuk: Secretary-Treasurer*
- *Bruce Cairns: Assistant Secretary-Treasurer*

The Division is people driven, and the 750 plus people here in this room, are a great force that drive it and make it what it is.

This being the first occasion that I've had to be with the total staff, I think it appropriate that I too introduce myself to you. I will do this by sharing with you three beliefs that I hold very dear:
*I believe that the **classroom is the cradle** of our children in our community. In today's threatened and threatening world, the classroom must remain to be **a caring and nurturing place**. For far too many children unfortunately, the classroom is the only safe and caring place in their community. . . I believe that the **school is the cathedral of our students**. In this day and age the only cathedrals being built are cathedrals called schools, inviting facilities and learning environments that facilitate and enhance the pursuit of excellence in the development of human potential, for that is our true mission, in places called schools.*

*I believe that **the teaching profession is the noblest profession** in the universe. As **people developers**, teachers (and all of us that exist because of the child) have the privilege of working with the best "raw material" in all creation. We should be honored that we have the opportunity, every day, to make a difference, and as we work with children, we have the power to actually recreate the future itself!*

And that is the greatest journey imaginable!
Thank You and Bon Voyage!

> March 12, 1991
>
> Dear Frank;
>
> I am writing this letter to express my sincere appreciation for the support you have given me, both professionally and personally.
>
> Your ability to retain a humanistic outlook, while dealing with figures and dollars is a rare talent. Making the time to share not only the facts, but your thoughts as well, has made me feel like a part of the administrative team of the Division.
>
> You have served as a model for me, and I feel I have benefitted from working with you both as an educator and a person. Thank you.
>
> Sincerely,
>
> Don

A letter from teacher/consultant, Don Reece, typical of several I received upon my leaving the Transcona-School Division No. 12.

AREAS OF MY INVOLVEMENT AND ACHIEVEMENTS AS SUPERINTENDENT OF EDUCATION IN THE TRANSCONA-SPRINGFIELD SCHOOL DIVISION NO. 12

When the previous Superintendent of Education unexpectedly submitted her resignation on June 4, 1990, the School Division was faced with a discontented community including angry parents, staff and students. The discontent arose out of the decision of the School Board to extend the noon lunch break to one and one-half hours as a response to the *Transcona-Springfield Teachers' Association's* request for compensation in return for providing supervision during the noon hour. As well, for the previous two months, the School Board had received delegation after delegation of angry parents who had polarized both "pro" and "con" over the issue of the re-organization of French Immersion facilities. During this transition period, moreover, the Superintendent's Department had undergone great internal changes, with no less than six new members in new, key positions, and all of whom needed ongoing support, direction, and clarification of their roles. Of course, the responsibility all fell on me as Superintendent since the appointment of an Assistant Superintendent did not take place until sometime later in the fall of 1990.

- **The Re-organization of the Superintendent's Department** (Senior Administration) Six new appointments were necessary as the Superintendent's Department underwent a huge transformation caused primarily by the sudden resignation of the former Superintendent and the long-term illness of the Administrative Assistant. This was a high priority transition which I believe I handled systematically, and professionally, and which was accepted by the School Board with a high level of consensus

- **Planning, goal setting, team building and collegial interpersonal relations at the highest level of the decision-making** authority in the Division had never been greater than at this transition point and these needs were addressed calmly and efficiently. The end outcome was an unmistakable sense of cohesiveness, continuity, positive feedback, and personal satisfaction for me to the very day of my early retirement accelerated somewhat because of health reasons.

- **The noon hour issue** with the Transcona-Springfield Teachers' Association (T.S.T.-A.) was resolved to everyone's satisfaction. This was done primarily through my personal initiative and efforts in consultation directly with Henry Wedel, the President of the T.S.T.A. at that time. During my tenure as Superintendent of Education **the morale of the teachers** and other staff in the Division had risen to an unparalleled level that had never been seen before. I believe that this was due mainly to my "open door" policy enhanced through my personal visitations to all the schools of the Division and meetings with all school staffs that were all so well received everywhere I went. This was

Crescendo to Becoming

attested by the many positive letters that I received from teachers and other staff expressing great satisfaction with the process which some described as "a breath of fresh air.

- The **Re-organization of the French Immersion Program** study was objectively considered looking at all factors and included a recommendation to convert *Margaret Underhill School* into a French Immersion School in the east end of Transcona, changing the direction of keeping all French Immersion facilities in the west end of Transcona. This move was relatively quite well received in the community. The very successful, three-day, first of its kind ***Workshop on Wellness*** with input of the Manitoba Teachers' Society was held for members of the administration at Hecla Island on October 1-2, 1990.

- A much needed and long overdue **Reorganization of the Purchasing and Payroll Department** was initiated and recommended by me and ratified by the School Board.

- The **construction of the new College Pierre Elliott Trudeau** was supervised, and the deadline accomplished in time for the re-opening of schools on September fourth, 1990, and the official opening of the school took place on October twelve, 1990 as planned.

- **Budget planning and reformulation** was done and completed on target for December fifteen, 1990. **Staffing allocations** were done effectively and in accordance with, and within all guidelines and budgetary requirements.

14 Winnipeg Free Press, Friday, August 31, 1990

Teachers, trustees resolve dispute over lengthening school day by half hour

By Terry Lulashnyk

A Winnipeg Free Press article on the noon hour dispute with the Transcona-Springfield Teachers' Association

BECOMING A TEACHER, A PRINCIPAL, AND A SUPERINTENDENT OF EDUCATION

November 12, 1991

Mr. Henry Wedel, President
Transcona-Springfield Teachers' Association
23 Capricorn Place
Winnipeg, Manitoba
R2G 2W3

Dear Henry:

I am writing this letter to express my appreciation to you and the Transcona-Springfield Teachers' Association for the wonderful reception held in my honour on Thursday, October 10, 1991 at the Golden Oak Inn. I am well aware of the efforts that go into the organization of such an occasion and I wish to thank you, Darla Sutherland and members of her Social Committee in particular for their hard work in making the arrangements for the evening.

It is said that nothing is so meaningful and personally satisfying as being recognized and honored by one's professional peers. As I found out, that is absolutely true. The event was even more meaningful and unforgetable to me because I know that it was the very first occasion of its kind to be held by the Transcona-Springfield Teachers' Association. For these reasons, I shall always be grateful to all those who were in attendance for they contributed greatly to the special significance of the evening.

You may be interested to know that my "retirement" has in essence evolved into a career change. I have now embarked on a new and exciting second career in consulting and I am presently doing some work in the development of human resources, and communications. As well I am presently doing some work with the Faculty of Education and have some commitments to do other work consulting, still in the field of education. I am very pleased and proud to be able to continue my association in the field of education in general and in the teaching profession in particular.

Again, please convey my appreciation to all the members of the TSTA. I shall always cherish the memory of my association with you and the "magic moment" you provided me on October 10, 1991.

I wish you all continued success and a healthy and satisfying voyage the rest of your journey in education.

Yours sincerely,

Frank Fiorentino

My thank-you letter to the Transcona-Springfield Teachers' Association for the reception held in my honor upon my retirement from the Transcona-Springfield School Division, Nov. 12, 1991

8.
BECOMING A HUSBAND, FATHER, GRANDFATHER, AND A GREAT-GRANDFATHER

Giuseppina (a.k.a. Josephine/Josie) Graziano Comes Into My Life

As far as I am concerned, the best way to become a father is first of all to fall in love with some wonderful young lady, make a commitment to marry, and plan and pursue the formation of a family, complete with the raising of some children. Take it from me, becoming a father, and better yet a grandfather, is the most satisfying occurrence in a man's life. In my view, there is no greater feeling of meaning and fulfillment.

Let me state categorically right here and now, that I wouldn't trade my children and grandchildren for anything in the world, for they are the source and end of everything that is most dear to me. To me, the family unit is the most important foundation of our society, especially today, when the traditional concept of family is being seriously eroded.

Giuseppina Graziano, like me, was born in Amato but she was born in 1939, only three years after my own birth, and we lived only a few houses apart in the same closely-knit neighborhood of our town. She was a member of one of the most respected families in Amato. As destiny would have it, her father left Amato for Winnipeg, on Boxing Day in 1948, only 6 days before our departure on January 1, 1949, and his family including Josephine, followed him to Canda about a year later. She was only thirteen and I was 16 when I let her know that I had "designs" on her, and from 1953 to 1959 I

BECOMING A HUSBAND, FATHER, GRANDFATHER, AND A GREAT-GRANDFATHER

made sure that on occasion, I gave her gentle reminders of that. I knew that her parents were quite traditional and rigid in these matters, meaning that they would not permit her going out on dates under any circumstances, not until there was some substantive "promise" or commitment on my part, and then only with a chaperone if they approved of the young suitor.

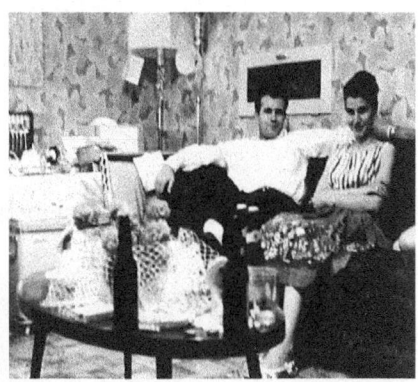

Josie, the love of my life

Although she was quite shy, from time to time I would phone her or go to Transcona to try and see her and try to meet her on the way to and from school. When I was able to reach her by phone, invariably I had brief and very superficial conversations with her. On a couple of occasions, as we got older, I would send her flowers, which she invariably threw in the garbage, probably to show her parents that she was a "mature" and obedient daughter, and not one that would show interest and encourage someone, unless the parents would approve. On one occasion I called her to ask her to listen to radio station CKSB where I was playing with my dance band and dedicated a popular song to her, in the hope that she would listen as I had told her to do. I doubted that she would listen, but in any case I wanted her to know that I was still interested and that my band was becoming a success.

It was in 1959 just before I embarked on my career as a teacher, that I went to formally meet with Josie's father and mother to declare my intentions and ask them, for her hand in marriage. The meeting was more uneasy for Mr. Graziano, her father, than it was for me, for I knew what to expect, for and my father had "coached" me quite well in preparation for this important occasion.

Crescendo to Becoming

The bride is taken to the church on time, and in style: to the left is Josephine as she arrives at the Holy Rosary church accompanied by her father Giacinto Graziano. The decorated beautiful automobile is a 1959 Chevrolet with the fins and all, and belonged to Giacinto (Don) Graziano, Josie's brother.

The Groom's Wedding Party and Support Group

GROOM-IN-WAITING OUTSIDE THE HOLY ROSARY CHURCH, SHERBROOK STREET, (1960) *Left to Right:* Frank Falvo, Franco Masi (best man), Me the happy groom, Ferruccio Moscarda, and Giacinto Graziano (my brother-in-law)

<u>FRANK FALVO</u>, a good friend of mine, had gone to work in a Winnipeg factory as a tailor upon arrival in Canada. He was the only one from my hometown that actually sought me out several times to find out from me

176

BECOMING A HUSBAND, FATHER, GRANDFATHER, AND A GREAT-GRANDFATHER

what was it like to go to school in Canada. He had begun to attend night school but found the process painfully slow and tedious. On his insistence, I had gone to the Administration of the University of Manitoba to request information on the "Mature Student Program" that had just been implemented, whereby an older students could attempt one or two university courses, and if successful, would be allowed to enter university on a regular basis. So, that's exactly what I suggested to him, and that's what he did, as he was accepted to enter first year Arts at the University of Manitoba. On this basis, Frank entered the University of Manitoba to pursue his dream, and after his university studies became a university professor in historic University of Charlottetown in New Brunswick.

FRANCO MASI, my best man, used to live with the Graziano family where his uncle Leopoldo and his wife Concetta, Josie's oldest sister, also lived at 602 Bond Street in Transcona. Although I knew him from Italy when we were children, I really got to know him better when I started courting Josie. He impressed me highly, for he was surprisingly quite well-read, and was a multi-dimensional young man, quite different than other young men from Amato. From the beginning we enjoyed each other's company, and like me, he liked to read, he liked sports, music, and chess. We often got into some very interesting discussions, debates and arguments, especially since he tended to admire the philosophy of Marx and Lenin in those days, and I favored the philosophies of such thinkers of St. Augustine, Rousseau, Descartes, and Kant. After living in Canada for about 12 years, Franco, upon the insistence of his father, decided to return to Italy where his father and family were happy to have him. Even though he lives in Amato, we are still in frequent contact with one another, and to this day, he remains a great, great friend, and because of his compassion and intellect, he remains to be one of my most favorite people.

FERRUCCIO MOSCARDA was the Italian guitar player in my two dance bands. We also had become best of friends, so much so, that when his daughter Liliana was born, his wife Dorotea and him, asked me to be the Godfather and baptize her. We saw a great deal of each other as members of the dance band for about 16 years, but when I gave up music, our interests went much on separate paths. He continued to play for many, many years, and I focused more and more on my career in education and my family. We reconnected somewhat when I was the Vice Consul of Italy, as our paths crossed on several occasions. While we did remain friends, we do not, unfortunately, see much of each other, especially since Dorotea's premature death several years ago.

GIACINTO "DON" GRAZIANO is Josie's brother, and it was only natural that he would be one of the groom's group members. We became "brothers-in-law", by my marriage, but we actually became more like real brothers, and lived more like we were members of the same family for a long, long time. For 41 years, from 1960 to 2001 we were in fact inseparable, and saw each other almost every day or so. Even geographically we gravitated together and have always lived in close proximity to each other, always on the same street, even to this day (2024). Amazingly we shared almost everything, and did everything together, including raising our families in similar fashion.

My bond with all the Grazianos was always very strong, cemented no doubt, by the fact that his mother, (my mother-in-law Maria Graziano) lived with us, in my house, with my family, for approximately thirty-five years pretty well until she passed away in 1997. Regrettably, however, our very strong relationship went totally sour, once he and his sister Josie had a disagreement over their relationship with their uncle Joe. The misunderstanding over this brother-sister squabble lasted awhile, and the two of them, and indeed all of us, were again brought together in forgiveness of each other as a wish and great suggestion by our dear daughter Franca in her dying bed, on December 11, 2011, only four days before she passed.

Specifically, when Don was approached by Tony, my son, to see if he wished to see Franca for the last time, he "jumped" to the opportunity, and both he and his wife Felicia came immediately to the hospital to see Franca. Our family reunion together with our dear Franca in the hospital room was something all of us will never forget, for it was so beautiful a moment of pure joy both for Don and, more importantly, for Franca and all of us as well. Although Franca had been moribund for a while, upon Don's entry into her hospital room, Franca seemed to wake up and together they embraced with affection for a relatively long time, while all of us were crying profusely with joy of the occasion, and during which was the most bitter-sweet moment in

BECOMING A HUSBAND, FATHER, GRANDFATHER, AND A GREAT-GRANDFATHER

the life of all the members of my most immediate family. And, today thanks to Franca's wish, our relationship with Don is and remains stronger than ever.

Our Wedding Day, August 20, 1960

After one year of courtship, Josephine Graziano and I became Mr. and Mrs. Fiorentino on August 20, 1960. We were married at the Italian Holy Rosary Church located then on Sherbrook Street and Bannatyne, with young Father Provost officiating. As Italian weddings go, it was a relatively small, but an elegant wedding, done in good taste, consisting of approximately 225 people in all, and included our respective family members, some relatives, and intimate friends. The dinner and dance reception was held on the fifth floor of the Marlborough Hotel in the beautiful classical hall, unusual for those days when most of the wedding receptions were then held at church basement halls.

Everything about our wedding was wonderful even though it had put us in debt for about $2,000. which was a considerable amount of money for those days. Although Josephine was not too happy about this large monetary expenditure, I still believe to this day that it was well worth every penny!

JUST MARRIED! August 20, 1960, in front of the Holy Rosary Church on Sherbrook Street Winnipeg. Newlyweds Mr. and Mrs. Fiorentino with our respective extended families

Upon returning from our honeymoon at Banff, Lake Louise, and Edmonton, we moved to a suite in a small house on Garfield Street between Ellice and Portage Avenues in Winnipeg that we had already rented beforehand. About a month later, late in the month of September, our brother-in-law Leopoldo Masi, his wife Concetta (Josie's sister) and their two children Marianna and Franca left Canada to be permanent residents in Italy as Leopoldo wanted his two girls to be brought up and educated in Italy. Soon after they left for Italy, Josie's mother and father encouraged us and insisted that we should move in with them and occupy the spaces that Leopoldo and Concetta occupied and lived in at 602 Bond Street, Transcona.

BECOMING A HUSBAND, FATHER, GRANDFATHER, AND A GREAT-GRANDFATHER

The Happy Bride and Groom, Frank and Josie Fiorentino, August 20, 1960

The new bride and groom at the wedding reception

Best man Franco Masi, Newlyweds Frank and Josie and Matron of Honor Caterina Falvo

Our Honeymoon at Lake Louise, Alberta, Canada

Although we would pay our portion of the food and other house expenses such as hydro, water, etc., we would save the money that we would otherwise have to pay for rent elsewhere. As Josie seemed to be comfortable with this idea, and as I was teaching at Transcona Collegiate in Transcona within walking distance from home, I agreed with the move.

I must say that I was treated royally by the Graziano family during my whole stay with them for approximately 7 years. My mother-in-law Maria couldn't do enough for me, and I particularly admired Josie's father, (who incidentally also admired me) my father-in-law Donato Graziano, a wonderful man who was not only strong physically, but also strong in character and a well-respected man in the Italian community of Amato as well as in Winnipeg. He was a man of honor, principle, and integrity. I became very fond of him and often we confided in each other. Bu regrettably, only five

BECOMING A HUSBAND, FATHER, GRANDFATHER, AND A GREAT-GRANDFATHER

years after we were married, the unthinkable happened. We were all devastated by his sudden death in 1965, the result of a massive heart attack. It was a shocker, considering that only two weeks before, we witnessed the greatest snow fall in the history of Manitoba, and I remember my dear father-in-law shoveling snow like a man half his age.

About six months after we were married Josie became pregnant, and three months later she abandoned her job as a teller at the Bank of Toronto in Transcona, for we both decided that it was important for her to stay home and focus on raising the children.

I have always considered myself blessed and fortunate having such a caring and loving family. My wife Josie has been totally and categorically committed to the well-being of all our family members. In many ways she is the "strongest" member of our family, dependable and steadfast. She is the most unselfish person I have ever known. The unconditional love and care she has shown, not only to me and the members of our immediate family, but also to her own mother, has always been remarkable if not unbelievable. It is also interesting to know that my mother-in-law, who always assisted my wife in raising our three children, lived with us as an integral part of our family, and had a great influence on our three children. Before she died at the ripe old age of 91, unfortunately we had to place her at a seniors' residence, for Josie could not take care of her needs at home twenty hours a day, even though she did that for quite a long time, until it became impossible to do so. Just the same, Josie was devastated by this move, and could not do enough for her mother while she was in the seniors' home for about one and half years before her death.

What follows below are some comments on the people that I care most about, and that I believe care most about me. All have contributed immensely to my existence and ***joie de vivre***, and all have given me hope, faith, fulfillment, pleasure and unconditional love. All have been an intrinsic part of who I am and whom I have become, and we now have a bond that I am positive will be forever.

My Family

What I want to attempt to do here and now is to **speak directly to each of those dearest to me,** as I try to put into words what they have meant to me, what I have felt for them, expressing to them the unending and profound eternal love I have for each of them. But before I do that, let me say only that when it comes to my own children and my grandchildren, I have always had high expectations of them, and that is based on the notion that I want to show the highest respect for them, and not treat them as poor and incapable. While I always will accept the fact that whatever they want to be its ultimately their own choice, I tried to influence you all to go for the highest and best heights you are capable of reaching and achieving, knowing that my position has been clear to all of you: **don't just be content to make a living, but aim always at making a difference!**

To My Wife Josie:

A man named Meister Eckhardt once said that *"If the only prayer you ever say in your entire life is "thank you", it will be enough."* I do believe that you are the type that would probably be satisfied with a simple "thank you". Although that may very well be the case, I still wish to say the following to you: **Josie,** you have been my first and only love. As you know I was attracted to you when you were barely thirteen years of age. You became and are still my loving and lovable soul mate. You have been a faithful and a super partner beyond reproach. You absolutely know the meaning of the word *"commitment* reach our sixty–fourth wedding anniversary in August 2024, and most of the credit for this. remarkable achievement has to go to you.

Me and my lovely wife Josie

BECOMING A HUSBAND, FATHER, GRANDFATHER, AND A GREAT-GRANDFATHER

Since our coming together in 1960, I know firsthand that you have been an ideal and devoted mother to our three children and a fantastic grandmother to our twelve delightful grandchildren who love and adore you so much. Not only that, but you were such a caring, supportive, and kind daughter to your dear mother, who lived with us for some thirty–five years. You have actually helped significantly particularly in the raising of six of our grandchildren, i.e. Tony's children, when they were actually "abandoned" by their mother at a very early age of five, eight, and twelve, and Franca's children particularly since Franca was stricken with cancer July 12, 2010 (more on this later). To our daughter Franca, you were an angel of mercy, and as she became more and more dependent on you, you responded by being there at her every "beck and call" and every step of the way. For sure, you are "the salt of the earth" and you have been a marvel to us all. For all that you are, thank you and know that I still love you profoundly with all my heart.

To My Son Tony

My son Tony (left) with me

Tony, as our first child, you were truly the miracle that came into our life. You were and are the solid pillar and cornerstone of our family. I still shiver with delight when I think of the happiness and love you brought to my life when you came into our world. You were a bundle of pure joy, and we can only thank God for the happiness you brought to me and to all of us.

I remember that when you were a student in junior and senior high school I had you convinced for a while to go into law, and you did so for a while. But, it became evidently clear, that you were doing that to satisfy my ego, and that you had our own plans and dreams.

As you may very well know, I have always been a staunch believer that you do not take away the dream of youth, and on that basis, I allowed you to make your own choice on becoming what you wanted to be(come). When I did question you as to why you chose teaching, your answer was "Why not

Dad", you didn't do so bad as a teacher". I recall that on the one hand I was perplexed by your answer, and on the other hand, I was oozing with pride, realizing that I had been such a role model that you too, like me, wanted to become a teacher. And what a teacher you have been! For I know you are respected and loved by most of your students and staff, in a day and age that is laden with heavy pressures all around us. I know very well what a terrific high school principal you have been, and you should be still very proud, for you know that relatively few people today can handle the required interpersonal skills, the heavy responsibility, and the commitment to be a caring and effective high school principal.

Tony, I know so very well through reliable sources that you are still having a tremendous impact on the youth in your care, and you will experience a great deal of personal satisfaction as the years move on. You have had a tremendous positive impact, on your students, which slowly and surely it will reveal itself to you, and then you will know for certain, that teaching is the noblest profession on earth. I am sure of that, because I still meet former students of yours, who give me positive feedback on the great influence you had on them. In fact, you should realize that you have a great "family" out there.

As I write this you are now working as a high-ranking high school administrator in Beijing, China and from all accounts after eight years you have received high praise awards and many accolades for your high–quality work you are producing. I know that you have experienced high satisfaction and respect in Canada, but the high esteem people in China have for you is extraordinary. As well, your super, legendary good impact on Chinese young people in China at the present time will be a beautiful legacy of yours when your career is done. Well done, my boy!

Tony, yes, absolutely, you are a man of high integrity, perseverance, and dependability. You have super attributes, and I hope you know that I am very proud of you. I shall eternally love you unconditionally as "my boy" a phrase I coined at your high school graduation.

To My Daughter Franca

Franca, you have been and are our first wonderful "princess." You are definitely a people person, and a lovely human being. I know that you care, and

BECOMING A HUSBAND, FATHER, GRANDFATHER, AND A GREAT-GRANDFATHER

Franca and her son Evan by her side

love people. The fact that you chose Nursing as a career shows the strong human element of your personality.

I recall that so very early in your nursing career, you were assigned to provide professional nursing care to some patients who had contracted AIDS, and how you assumed that commitment with the greatest of care and compassion, at a time, I might add, when not too many health care workers were ready and willing to do so, for fear of the risks that could result in working with the much-dreaded disease. I recall too, that one young AIDS patient wrote a letter to your immediate supervisor, expressing his great appreciation of the great care that you demonstrated toward him. I bring forth the above information only because the episode really defines in some measure, who you really are, and who you have become.

Franca, I am proud of the kind of job you have been doing in the employment sector and are now doing as a responsible Research Assistant at the St. Boniface Hospital. But I am most proud of you for the type of wonderful family you and Rob are raising. Your commitment and devotion to providing the children with a plethora of great experiences is unbelievable. And the fact that you have even extended many experiences to include Tony's children, is so kind and so much appreciated. The only advice I would leave you is to see to it that Rob doesn't continue to overwork as he has done so often to this point.

Franca, I loved you from the moment I first saw you at your birth. I want you to know that you have played an extremely positive part in my life, and the lives of all the members of our family. With your arrival into our world, you made me feel that we had the perfect family. As a little girl you gave us so much to feel good about, as you really were a veritable, beautiful darling. I cannot do justice to the innumerable happy occasions that you gave us. As daddy's first little girl, you gave us infinite pleasure and fulfillment. Your date of birth marks the time and place when I began to feel complete and wholesome. With your arrival, and the ability for us to build our own home in 1967, I felt I had finally made it in Canada, and I felt contented as a person who had everything.

Franca, I'm so happy that you have been blessed in that you have achieved exactly what you wanted when you fell in love with Rob and when you so desperately wanted to marry him. Yes, recognize that you now have a perfect family consisting of a super mother and father, and three perfect children. I am delighted that Rob spends so much quality time with the children, so much so that your neighbors have noticed it, and have complimented me on it. So please count your blessings for they are many.

As your father who will eternally love you, I have only one request that I want you to focus on, and that is, to take control of your wellness, including eating and exercising properly as many of your friends have done before your eyes. I cannot accept that you cannot do it, for I know better. I do not want you to try and see what happens. I want you to do it. Period. But ultimately, you must do it for yourself. Your health and the quality of your life depend on it. Do it, please! Princess, you always have a wonderful way to make me and those around you feel so good. So be happy always.

NOTE TO READER: THE ABOVE HAD ORIGINALLY BEEN WRITTEN JUST BEFORE JULY 12, 2009, WHEN MY DEAR FRANCA WAS OFFICIALLY DIAGNOSED WITH PHASE FOUR, AGGRESSIVE BREAST CANCER. (SEE PAGE 358)

To My Daughter Elisa

My Daughter Elisa on her Graduation

First of all, let me reassure you, **Elisa,** that although you arrived somewhat late in our married life (14 years after your mother and I were married), you were NOT "an accident". The truth is that your mother and I wanted three children all along, but for reasons unknown to us, things just didn't happen as we had planned. I guess God took his time, and boy you were worth waiting for! My view is that when God got busy and finally put you together for us, He created human perfection!

BECOMING A HUSBAND, FATHER, GRANDFATHER, AND A GREAT-GRANDFATHER

I'll never forget how I placed you in the "late entry" French Immersion Program beginning in grade seven and after you stumbled somewhat during the first month or so, you embraced it totally and mastered it well beyond my expectations. Not only that, you graduated from *College Pierre Elliot Trudeau* with the highest honors possible. As that was my last year as a superintendent in the school division, I'll never forget how proud you made me feel when I came to the graduation ceremonies and delivered a speech for the occasion.

How could I ever forget how you were chosen first from the many applicants in the Province of Manitoba, for entry to the School of Optometry at the University of Waterloo in Ontario. For all of us, it was as if we had won the lottery, for going to a university elsewhere in the USA, would have cost us some prohibited sum of money. I'm sure you will recall that when we went to Calgary so that you could register at the University of Oregon, the cost would have been some $41,000 per year. When I told you to let me worry about the money, and that I was prepared to sell our house if I had to, you burst out crying because you realized that it would mean a very heavy burden on everybody. But you were such a deserving person and student, that I was ready and willing to do just that. Although you forfeited the down payment of $500. to the University of Oregon, you were successful in being chosen from the Province of Manitoba to register and attend the University of Waterloo, we all breathed a sigh of relief, for the whole affair became a much more affordable and manageable proposition.

Your academic achievements and your efforts to live apart from the family for four years at Kitchener-Waterloo were unbelievable. I have never been prouder of anyone as I was of you when you walked across the stage on your graduation and received your Doctor of Optometry degree. That was one of the biggest thrills of my life for it represented a triumph beyond my wildest dreams. Elisa, I will never be able to show my appreciation for that defining moment in my life.

Yes, Eli, you have been and are an ideal person. From every point of view, you have been and are still so complete and wonderful. You possess all the best attributes that a person can have. I have known no one that is the complete person that you are. Truly, you have been and are a gift of God. As a child, I always considered you a perfect child, and as an adult, you are now a complete, caring, loving and lovable adult. In Mark, as well, you have found a seemingly perfectly matching companion. When you add the two "jewels" that you have in Ethan and Adam, you have a perfect family unit that gives me unbelievable satisfaction and joy. Eli, you have given me many beautiful and unforgettable moments in my life, but none bigger that the birthday card that you gave me February 20, 2000 that read as follows:

> *"A dad is someone who gives you*
> *the tools you need to build your life*
> *and the knowledge you need*
> *to use them successfully,*
> *the encouragement to overcome obstacles,*
> *and the confidence*
> *to take pride in a job well-done.*
> *A dad is someone who gives you*
> *a living model of excellence to follow."*

* * *

> *"Dad, it takes a special kind of man*
> *to set a course in life and follow through,*
> *no matter what the obstacles.*
> *It takes a special kind of man*
> *to aim for the best, to be the best,*
> *and to pursue his goals*
> *with passion and enthusiasm.*
> *It takes a special kind of man*
> *whose faith inspires faith,*
> *whose determination leads to admiration,*
> *and whose perseverance*
> *always makes him a winner.*
> *It takes a special dad like you."*

* * *

> *"I want you to know how proud I am*
> *to say that you are my dad*
> *& how much I love you!*

BECOMING A HUSBAND, FATHER, GRANDFATHER, AND A GREAT-GRANDFATHER

Thank you so much for all of your support. Without you I never would have accomplished all that I have. Love, Ellie

....

What is really important in life is not only what a person is able to achieve, but also, what he is able to overcome.
—**Frank Fiorentino**

....

«Every single thing you do matters. You have been created as one of a kind. You have been created in order to make a difference. You have within you the power to change the world. "
—*Andy Andrews*

....

Then on February 20, 2009, you gave me the birthday card that read as follows:

*"DAD. Because of your hard work,
I've had everything I could ever need"
Because of your passion,
I'm inspired to do my very best ...
Because of your sacrifices,
I'm closer to reaching my own dreams ...
DAD, Because of you,
I have a lot to be grateful for.
Thank you for being such a wonderful
role model for us & our children.
We love you very much!
Ellie, Mark, Ethan & Adam*

The above comments I consider the greatest reward a father could receive from his children! I am a lucky man indeed!

Crescendo to Becoming

MY EIGHT "GRAND" CHILDREN, AND FOUR GREAT GRANDCHILDREN: 2019

Front Row, Left to Right: Finlay Asmundson, Ellis-Rae Asmundson, Halldor Asmundson and Adam Charbonneau **Back Row:** Frank Fiorentino (junior), Leith Asmundson, Winnfield Asmundson, Amanda Asmundson, Dylan Fiorentino, Josie Fiorentino, Me Frank Fiorentino, Ethan Charbonneau, Adriana Kiz, Evan Kiz, and Austin Kiz

BECOMING A HUSBAND, FATHER, GRANDFATHER, AND A GREAT-GRANDFATHER

SIX OF MY "GRAND" CHILDREN AT A MUC H YOUNGER AGE
*Top row, **left to right**: Evan, Amanda, Adriana, Dylan **Front row:** Frankie, Austin, and Adriana's friend, Mayia Westwood Missing: Ethan and Adam Charbonneau)*

***Left to Right**: Frankie, Tony, Amanda, Dylan Fiorentino, 2019*

Crescendo to Becoming

AMANDA ASMUNDSON (nee Fiorentino)

Amanda Asmundson

I love all my twelve grandchildren immensely. The fact that I focus on Amanda in much greater detail here, it's only because she is the oldest (22 years old when this was written), and is now an adult, and as our first grandchild she is in essence representative of the love that normally engulfs grandparents toward their grand-children, and Josie and I experienced the advent of this beautiful reality with Amanda's arrival into our lives. I don't really know why it is so, but the love that grandparents have for their grandchildren is something very special. And with us, it all came to the surface and became evident for the first time with Amanda.

Talking directly to Amanda now, I wish to tell you Amanda, that I felt so hurt when your mother walked out on you, for you were barely 12 years of age, at a critical time when you needed so much a mother's support. Amanda, throughout that ordeal you were so very brave and faced the cruel reality with astonishing strength. Thank God too, that Nanna Josie in particular, and everyone in our family gave you a great deal of support. We are so thankful that you have developed into a beautiful young lady, beautiful not only physically, but beautiful also in human spirit, warmth and caring, that has become your trademark.

Amanda, I am still very proud of you now at the age of 35 (in 2024), for you got a lot to show for your life so far. You completed a couple of years of university at the College de St. Boniface, and you are now married to Leith Asmundson, a wonderful young man who is a mason by trade. With your high energy and very hard work, you have achieved much already, coupled with your caring disposition toward people in general and children and special needs in particular, you will achieve a great deal more.

Already you and Leith have built a wonderful family, including four young boys who are guaranteed to keep you busy. You have built a new home in the country not far from the town of Anola, and you have built a business,

BECOMING A HUSBAND, FATHER, GRANDFATHER, AND A GREAT-GRANDFATHER

caring for dogs, that you care for immensely. And you have already received a nomination for **Woman Entrepreneur of the Year in Manitoba**. All are remarkable achievements in themselves and all attest to your ability to work very hard and achieve outcomes that will ultimately give you a sense of personal satisfaction about who you have become.

I will never forget the special, unsolicited card you send to Nanna Josie at her birthday on June 14, 2009, which expressed so beautifully, your feelings toward her: *"Nanna, I know I don't say it enough, but I love you more than you will ever know. I have no idea who or where I would be without you. You mean everything to me and I can only wish to turn out to be half the woman you are. I look up to you in every way. And I am eternally grateful for everything you have done for me and for making me the person I am today. You have not only been a grandma but a mom and a friend to me. I just want to say thank you and I love you. Love always and forever, your "princess Amanda".*

And I shall always personally treasure the following thoughts you expressed to me on November 20, 2017. *"My biggest inspiration. , thank you for always being so supportive, for being my biggest critic in the best way. For loving me unconditionally. I wouldn't be where I am without you. You have instilled the most valued thing in life into me, the importance of family. I have followed my dreams in life because of you. Thank you for everything,*

Nonno. Yes there were times, I'm sure you knew,
When I bit off more than I could chew,
But through it all, when there was doubt,
I ate it up, and spit it out, and I stood tall, ... And did it, my way."

DYLAN FIORENTINO

Dylan Fiorentino

Dylan, your arrival in our midst was a very joyous, happy occasion. Especially your father, of course, who loved you from the first moment he saw you, and I remember that I could not get enough of you either. For nine years you were a happy, "bouncing" boy, and suddenly then and there, I felt devastated when it was revealed the day after boxing day 2001, that your mother had left the family and in fact "abandoned" you all. Every day after that, I have felt the greatest pain, knowing that you had to fend for yourselves without a mother at a time when you and your siblings, were in such a vulnerable age. I know that in this broken-up, dysfunctional scenario you had to "grow up" much too fast than is normal.

Dylan, I am so proud of you, that even against all odds, you have not only survived, but thrived and actually you have accomplished much in your areas of interest such as your ten years spent with Earl's Restaurant in a leadership role, and more recently, that you have shown a good deal of initiative in setting up of your business undertaking in the construction sector. Above all else, you have become a wonderful, caring, mature people person that allows me to see nothing but a promise of a satisfying life ahead for you, given the wonderful and relevant qualities and attributes evident in your life so far.

As I write this now, in January 2024, I know that you will be making a meaningful contribution to yourself, your family, and to society.

Dylan, you are a sensible and sensitive individual and a caring, people person. You are also a mature, responsible young man not unlike your father I might add, and I couldn't be more proud of you. No one will ever be able to take away the great qualities you now possess as part of your makeup. Your great qualities of kindness and genuine caring are indicative of who you really have become and should sustain you very well in your life. Trust me on this, my own life is proof of that.

BECOMING A HUSBAND, FATHER, GRANDFATHER, AND A GREAT-GRANDFATHER

I pray that you will make a determined effort to stay the course and follow your dreams, and I'm sure your life will have meaning and satisfaction. Remember that the more you believe and invest in yourself the more relevant your life will be, as you persevere to reach your dreams and goals with honesty and integrity and without wavering. Trust me, you are now well on the way to become the best that you can be.

FRANKIE FIORENTINO

Frankie Fiorentino

Frankie, I was so happy when you were born and delighted and very proud that you were named after me. You and Dylan have the added responsibility of carrying on the Fiorentino name and I am concerned somewhat that this may add to the pressure that you may already feel. I have also felt the anguish that you, as the youngest of the three children, were the most vulnerable when your mother walked out on you when you were barely five years of age. Frank, you have been a very brave young child, placed by cruel circumstances in the middle of it all, for loving both your mother and father, you were placed in a difficult position to choose, when in fact you could not do so, for clearly you were so young and indeed in need of both your parents.

Frankie, you were a brave tough kid growing up, and I was so proud to see you play high school football with such grit. enthusiasm, and determination. Your true character as a contributing team member and your perseverance was obvious when I saw you play. You fought hard and honestly for every yard you could gain. Again, I am so very proud of you still, and you surely must be too, or you were a credit to yourself and to your team. Trust me, when I say that you too have demonstrated that for sure you have what it takes, i.e. wonderful qualities and characteristics in your make-up, to become every-thing you dream about, and know that you have also, ample drive and intelligence to become something and someone wonderful and worthwhile.

Crescendo to Becoming

I have met many young people in my life as an educator and believe me when I say that at your age you demonstrate more potential than many young people today. What you must do now is to determine your desired path, and don't let anybody dissuade you from reaching your dreams and goals, not even yourself, for we both know that you have abilities and tenacity to do it. The road to achieving what you want is much shorter than the time that you have to enjoy your efforts during your whole long life. For me, the best decision I ever made was to stay in school even though at age thirteen I had to start all over in grade one, for I could not speak a word of English at age thirteen when I arrived in Canada. So, again, stay close to people that care and love you, and set and follow your own dreams and goals whatever they may be, with confidence and all the tenacity that we know you can muster.

You and I know that you are abundantly motivated by hard work, and that is a quality so rare today in young people like you. You have demonstrated this quality without any doubt in your ability to produce and create beautiful work in your tile setting business, and in that I believe you have found your probable path to become truly a success.

Wonderful Austin, Adriana, and Evam Kiz, (Franca's kids) 2019

BECOMING A HUSBAND, FATHER, GRANDFATHER, AND A GREAT-GRANDFATHER

ADRIANA KIZ

Adriana Kiz: a younger version

Adriana, you have been and will always be *"my little Angel"* as I have often called you. You were born in Welland, Ontario due to the fact that at that time your parents were living in nearby St. Catherines, close to nearby beautiful Niagara Falls. Prior to your birth, your grandmother Josie had been with your mother supporting her well over a month, and I had come there on time, awaiting your birth. The day you were born I remember your father driving me to the hospital, and I asked him to stop at a liquor store to buy a bottle of champagne to bring it to the hospital and celebrate the special event of your birth. Your dad was very uneasy and apprehensive about doing something like that and tried to dissuade me from going ahead with my plan. I reassured him that this was not the same as bringing and consuming alcohol at the hospital, but a memento occasion. In any case, we did celebrate your birth in this fashion, (the Head Nurse in charge was quite ok with the my suggestion) and it was then the first time I held you in my arms. Present at this beautiful occasion were your mom holding you lovingly in her arms, and your dad, Nanna, me and of course, you as the center of attraction.

Now, in 2024 you at age twenty-seven and for sure you are "miss sophistication". Already you now express yourself in a mature adult fashion. In many ways you are mature well beyond your chronological years. As well, it's already evident, that you are not only smart, but strikingly beautiful, for you are already a beautiful young lady.

You have always impressed me since early in your life, that you seemed to know what it would take to make it big in your life, and to make a positive difference. The kind of projects you chose to research in *St. Mary's s Academy* for school year 2010-2011 were great, as they were in the *Mennonite Brethren Collegiate Institute* (MBCI) in 2011–2012, and later at Miles MacDonnell taking the challenging *International Baccalaureate Program* and doing well.

Crescendo to Becoming

Adriana, you have demonstrated consistently great potential academically and intellectually, and consequently as a result, I must admit that I have very high expectations of you. With your acceptance into the study of Medicine in Granada last year (2023) you have finally found your path that will lead to your honorable mission in life. You rightfully set bold goals that I know you can attain, if you only will determine to do so. If you stay focused and "on course", you can and will surely have it all in the vast field of Medicine.! **So, Carpe Diem!!**

EVAN KIZ

Evan Kiz

Evan "my boy", from the very first day you were born, you were so perfect and so well-formed and defined in every way. Your physical features were perfect and as a result you were the cutest little boy ever. Of course, now you have become so "cool, calm and collected", and so debonair. The school photographs that you have ought home from school are unbelievably striking. Evan, you are and have always been a wonderful, affectionate human being. Your striking good looks. are a reflection of your mother's and father's good looks. I compliment.you for becoming a loving and lovable individual, particularly in your relations with Nanna Josie. You have developed a wonderful personality which should help you to become whatever you choose to become. I am quite certain that whatever career choice you make, will make all of us proud, and I know you will make a solid contribution to your family, to your community, and to society in general, for you are a very caring individual, caring for people, for animals, for the environment, and overall, for the planet. I feel that you **can** and will make a big, positive difference to those that are close to you. I only wish that I could be there to see it all.

Although you don't seem to be overly athletically inclined, it now seems obvious that you are not the competitive type, a necessary attribute necessary

BECOMING A HUSBAND, FATHER, GRANDFATHER, AND A GREAT-GRANDFATHER

to excel or do well in sports. Therefore, you may need to find some recreational activity that you enjoy doing, or at the very least, set up a program of physical exercise designed to keep you fit (as you are already doing). When you were much younger, you also tried to learn to play the clarinet and the guitar, but you also found out that the world of music is not where your aptitudes and tendencies are.

You had taken a Masonry Program for a couple of years at Red River Community College and almost received your Red Ticket (Apprentice Status) but unfortunately you gave that up close to when you would have completed it. Nevertheless, it still remains an option for you although unlikely. (Nobody can take away what you learn!). You also tried car sales, and you were pretty good at that as well. But it was with door-to-door sales of pesticides that you have proven that you have very good skills in the field of sales. So, your career quest is still on-going, a work-in-progress you might say. Regardless, you are a very caring person, and I have no doubt that you can do very well in a field you choose that relates to your caring and your genuine good feelings for people, animals, and the environment etcetera. In the scheme of things, being such a wonderful people person is much more relevant, than to be good at competitive sports and the like. So, pursue your dreams, and never give up!

AUSTIN KIZ

Austin Kiz

Austin, I was there when you were born in Hamilton, Ontario on May 25, 2000, a new beautiful, millennium baby. From the very beginning you were incredible, for you immediately captured our hearts, and I loved you from the first moment you arrived in this world. Austin, you possess many special qualities, very special personality traits, and you are simply special in any activity you take part in, for you quickly become the center of attraction. I believe that you are gifted in several areas of endeavor, including intellectual, social, and physical areas.

Crescendo to Becoming

You also have an outstanding caring attitude as you have shown toward me and many others. All of these qualities have contributed to you becoming a loving and lovable child and one that has brought us immeasurable joy and delight. Austin, when you were a ittle boy I teased you so much. Many times, I would say: *"I don't .like you"*, and then wait for your reaction, and then say to you *"I love you"*. I also have often said to you: *"you are my hero"*, and in many, many ways you are, for you seem to do everything with a certain "gusto", enthusiasm, and passion. For example, I will never forget the very first time you started to play hockey and how tremendously well you learned to play in the very few years that followed, and what an exciting player you were. I also fondly remember how you made Nanna Carmelina (my mother) so happy when you were still two or three years old. You were so friendly and lovable with every member of our family. And how could I forget the first time you went to *Camp Arnes* in the summer of 2009 for a week. When you came back, you showed us everything you had learned, -- games, songs, arts and crafts. You had picked up and memorized every word and every gesture, and every nuance of everything you had done, including the singing of grace before each meal. Do you remember?

Austin, I have often referred to you as a *"whipper snapper"*, that's because you are such a fast learner and fast thinking on your feet in everything you do. But what I want you to know above all else is that I have loved you profoundly since the day you were born and that you have provided a great deal of joy for me and all the members of my family. You have the ability and character to be both loving and lovable and these are super attributes that should serve you well during your whole life.

I have nothing but the highest expectations for you. And you can have it all. You can be whatever and whoever you want to become, so reach for the highest star, seize whatever opportunity comes your way, (*carpe diem!*) and be the best at what you want to be and do. I am more than certain that your growth and achievements will be remarkable and worthwhile. If you want to make me happy, you will become the best you can be in a relevant field of your choice. I am convinced that you can and will make a worthwhile contribution, and thus make a positive, meaningful difference in everything you "touch" as you have already so well demonstrated!

BECOMING A HUSBAND, FATHER, GRANDFATHER, AND A GREAT-GRANDFATHER

Adorable Ethan and Austin Charbonneau, year 2019

ETHAN CHARBONNEAU

Young Ethan Charbonneau

Ethan, when I originally wrote this part you were five years old, and just entered Kindergarten at Birds Hill Elementary School. By the time you began your formal education, you had demonstrated beyond any doubt that you were a uniquely intelligent child. Already at the very early age of two years, not only were you one of the cutest little boys I have ever seen, but you also demonstrated a certain, promising intellectual capacity. For example, when I asked you *"How come you are so good looking?"* In no uncertain terms, your answer seemed to get not only more mature each time, but also more and more sophisticated. At first you used to say that it was because of your mother and father, but then soon after you would answer that probably God made you the way you are.

Ethan, very early in your life, you demonstrated a clear sense of uniqueness and a propensity for independence. From the earliest days of your life. It was amazing how you responded to the affection of your parents, grandparents and others, including your pre-school teachers. It seemed that you loved and trusted everyone, and so I thought of you as a person with very high people orientation.

It appears obvious to me too, Ethan, that you are quite intelligent, for you demonstrate this fact in many ways. For example, I remember that you knew the alphabet before you had completed two years of age. You have been a well-adjusted young man for some time now, and I am impressed by the fact that you seem to understand what is right and wrong. The fact that you attended "nursery school" when you were two years old has impacted very positively upon you, and you now seem to be well-advanced for your age.

We're now in January 2024, you are seventeen years of age, and in grade 12 at M.B.C.I. It's already four years since you asked me to be your sponsor at your Church's Confirmation into the Roman Catholic Religion, and I was delighted to accept, and I shall always consider it an honor to be your Godfather. You were a member of the R.E. Royals Hockey Team, a member of the MBCI Music Band for two or three years, and active in hockey and many other activities. In short, you have made a great start in all aspects of your life so far, and I could not be more proud of you.

Ethan, you are a wonderful person already, and you demonstrate great promise. You are now ideally positioned to experience inevitably great success and a personally satisfying and fulfilling life in a path of your choice. So, choose well my boy, and let me give you a big thank you for enriching our lives.

ADAM CHARBONNEAU

Adam Charbonneau, on his first fourth of July birthday, 2009.

Adam, on July 4, 2024, you will be exactly sixteen years old, and already you seem to be Ethan II in many ways. I can't get over how cute you were as a little boy, and still are! You have beautiful, penetrating, clear blue eyes, and a character that is distinctly your own, and we would not have it any other way. Adam, you are sure learning fast, partly and simply by observing and watching Ethan no

BECOMING A HUSBAND, FATHER, GRANDFATHER, AND A GREAT-GRANDFATHER

doubt. You are already being quite assertive and, uniquely opinionated. You also know exactly what you want and how to get it. When we come to your house and you come to greet us, you are simply fantastic by the expressive ways you demonstrate that you are so happy to see us. You have already a strong sense of independence and you are quick to show emotion and intimacy. Putting it bluntly Adam, you are affectionate and simply adorable.

Adam, you are intellectually very bright, which should help you go far in your success path whatever that might be. But your best qualities, as far as I'm concerned, are the human qualities and traits that make up your personality. In this area, you have the very best attributes in my opinion, for you are both loving and lovable, the highest of human conditions! So, how far and how high you can go in whatever path you choose in life, is strictly up to you with whatever limitations being those that your yourself might place in your path. I shall follow you with the highest interest, as one of my most favorite people on earth.

MY FOUR GREAT GRAND CHILDREN:

THE AMANDA AND LEITH ASMUNDSON FAMILY,
Including My Four Great Grandchildren, in the year 2019.
Front row, left to right: Ellis-Rae, Halldor, Finlay, and Winnfield.

My four great grandchildren are unbelievably both cute and adorable. I must compliment both their parents, Leith and Amanda, for the great way they are raising these beautiful children, for the children's life is already rich and full of varied positive experiences and excitement.

Still in their very young life, the lucky children have already experienced a meaningful variety of activities/experiences including the following:

- seasonal activities of all kinds;
- formal and informal pre-school engagements;
- trips to the country to experience 'flora and fauna';
- trips to farm and related activities;
- caring for a variety of animals;
- visits to various locations throughout the province;
- camping, picnics, fishing, gardening, and music lessons (piano),

FINLAY ASMUNDSON

The twenty-ninth of May 2013 in Thompson, north Manitoba was when and where you were born, and your Grandfather Tony and Uncle Dylan were there to support Amanda your mother, and to greet you when you were born. Me and Nanna Josie came there to meet you on the second day of your life, and together with your mom and dad, we had a drink of champagne to celebrate your arrival much the same as I have done with most of my other grandchildren.

Yes, every newborn is special in his or her unique way, but you were extra special because you were the first to give me the title of "Great" Grandfather which I will always cherish.

You may not be aware now, that you lived with Nanna and me, in our house, for about a year, while your parents were building your new home just East of Anola Manitoba where you now live, and during that time we enjoyed each other's company wonderfully. You have brought a great deal of joy to me and Nanna Josie as we saw you grow up as a very cute little boy. In a way you were a Godsend, a great gift from heaven that we needed so badly, especially that you came as a living gift to us, only a couple of years after the loss of our dearest daughter, Franca to cancer.

BECOMING A HUSBAND, FATHER, GRANDFATHER, AND A GREAT-GRANDFATHER

Finlay, you should have been named "Pure Energy" for when you were very young, you always seemed to be in perpetual motion, always with unsatiable curiosity, busy exploring the world around you, and always focused on doing "your thing". But this phase has remarkably changed to what you are now, a sensible and sensitive, caring young man, who cares a lot about all living things. One of my hopes for you is that as you get older you find your own path that will give you meaning, relevance, and good fortune. My advice to you is that you stay and pursue music at least as a hobby. After hearing you at the piano recital I know that you have enough talent to appreciate what the world of music can offer you. One day you will know how music enhanced and enriched "Great" Nonno's life.

HALLDOR ASMUNDSON

Halldor, you were born July 25, 2014, at 2:47 a.m. weighing 7 pounds 6 ounces measuring 19.5 inches in length.

Keeping with tradition, Nanna Josie and I came to the St. Boniface Hospital to meet you and to celebrate your arrival into our midst with

a glass of champagne. We were so happy to see you and to thank you for making us "great" grandparents for the second time.

I know that your mother, father, and brother Finlay were very happy to have you join them and no doubt you will make their lives whole and more complete. As for me, I wonder as I write this, for how long I will get to see you grow and develop and provide a measure of happiness that only children like you can provide.

On June 24, 2024 I saw and heard you play at the piano recital, and you were simply wonderful and one of the very best of all the solo performers. I hope that you will stay with it for I can tell you have the innate ability. (maybe you have inherited the musical genes from your great *nonno*). In any case don't ever quit music for it can improve the very quality of your life, as was the case in my life, for you definitely demonstrate that you have a promising talent!

WINNFIELD ASMUNDSON AND ELLIS-RAE ASMUNDSON

Winnfield, you were born October 3, 2017, and Ellis-Rae on June 29, 2019. Both of you are still quite young, but for sure you are nevertheless, a relevant part of our family. You are easily engaged in any activity that is presented or planned by your caring parents, Leith and Amanda. Both of you are quite responsive and already constitute a "dynamic duo". You are a veritable bundle of joy, that bring nothing but happiness to us when you come to visit Nonno and Nanna. Without a doubt, at this young stage of your life, amazingly, you are not only adorable, but also loving and lovable. May God always protect you and hold you both in the palm of his hands.

To My Four Sisters: MUSETTA, MARIA, DELFINA, ELEONORA (NORINA) and One Brother, ONOFRIO:

I have elaborated somewhat earlier in this book, how I had to "grow up" relatively very fast and assume adult roles and responsibilities quite pre-maturely in my life. I wish to underline it here, for it's an irrefutable truth which I want my siblings to know, for it fell upon me to help sustain the family in every way imaginable, primarily whatever financial support I could provide to help meet the many family needs.

In this scenario I was very close to my brother and sisters, including my older sister **Eleonora**, who chose to get married as quickly as possible, and thus "escape" from the needy and frustrating conditions that our family was in when she was close to only twenty years of age.

I did everything I could in a supportive role for a good eleven years from the moment we arrived in Canada until August 20, 1960, the date of my marriage. I had given so much of myself, that even when I got married, I had to borrow the money to do it. But I did it willingly, with no strings attached, for I knew that with the professional qualifications that I had earned through education, I would, in time, be able to realize my own dreams

From the moment I got married, my focus turned more inwardly in a more selfish way, for I had a lot of catching up to do. Except for Musetta, all the children younger than me were all by now (1960) in their teens, and in a much better position to survive and to take care of themselves if need be.

BECOMING A HUSBAND, FATHER, GRANDFATHER, AND A GREAT-GRANDFATHER

In any case, at this point in my life, all my energies were redirected to my newly acquired wife, to launching my new career in education, to advancing my university studies for a further five years (evenings and Saturdays) in pursuit of my master's degree and the Professional Certificate in Education, together with the growing and nurturing of my own family. Sadly, this restructuring in my life caused my brother and sisters to grow somewhat distant than ever before, and more and more so, as the years went by. While we saw each other at most key points and occasions in our lives, and as they too focused on pursuing their own interests, we lost the closeness that we had enjoyed theretofore.

As stated above, Eleonora got married relatively young to a son of an Italian family from our town of Amato in Italy who were living in Transcona, but unfortunately the marriage ended in divorce probably due to the fact that as a couple, they could not have any children, and I think that having children was something that my sister had to have

Delfina responded to "an inner calling" and entered a convent in Sherbrooke, Quebec, and became a nun in spite of my repeated attempts to keep her from making such a drastic move. After approximately five years in the convent working in the kitchen, she left the order just before she had to take the final vows for working in the kitchen day in and day out was not the vision and the kind of life mission that she had anticipated, for she clearly wanted to donate her life in helping those in great need, more or less to follow the example of Mother Teresa. ... . Once out of the convent, Delfina met and married Kauser Jaffri, a gentle and kind person, a mechanical engineer from Pakistan and both moved first to Nanaimo B.C. and then to Detroit, Michigan where he could find available work in his line of his expertise.

Delfina, perhaps because of her age proximity to mine, has always occupied a special place in my heart. I remember how dearly and how much I loved her in Italy when I was a child, and how much I cried and missed her when I was in Monte Cassino with my father right after World War II.

Maria married Walter Volberg, a television technician of German descent and eventually moved to Vancouver, B.C. They had three children, Ryan, David, and Randall, and to my knowledge, they all presently live in Vancouver and all are doing quite well.

Crescendo to Becoming

My brother **Onofrio** (Norf) became a teacher and later a principal of a challenging upgrading school named *Park Circle* consisting basically of approximately 150 children with special needs. He married Cheryl Chudley his high school sweetheart and a bright former French student of mine, and they had two intelligent and creative children: Jamie a musician, and Jon now a promising professional writer.

Later in his career, Norf, (Onofrio) also became a principal, but of an elementary school, and also in the same school division where I worked, and as a result, I interacted more with him than all my other siblings. Norf and Cheryl are now living in Montreal originally moved there from Winnipeg to be close to son Jon who was then a professor of Creative Literature at Concordia University.

Of the six children in our family, **Musetta** was the only sibling that was not born in Italy. She was born in Winnipeg, in October 1951 not quite two years after our arrival to Canada, and many times we used to tease her that she was *l'americana*", i.e. "the American" and not Italian-born like the rest of us. She married, a successful businessman in Winnipeg, and together they have five children.

After I retired from the Transcona-Springfield School Division in 1992, I worked with a Winnipeg business company (half days), as a consultant on two separate occasions: the first term in 1992 for about eight months, and the second since 2007 to November 2014. This I did with some degree of enjoyment, in addition to running my own business, **People Developers,** to make sure I always had something to do, rather than stay home and do nothing, which was not much to my liking *per se*.

• •

*"I honestly think it is better to be a failure at something you love,
than to be a success in something you hate"*
—**George Burns**

• •

9.
BECOMING "FREE" AT "FREEDOM 55"

BECOMING "FREE" AT AGE 55 was a dream of mine at the back of my mind for many years. The dream aimed at being able to officially retire from work at age 55. The dream/goal was realized and represented a big achievement financially and otherwise in terms of the quality lifestyle that it can bring with it. In order to achieve it, one must develop and follow a sensible plan, live a reasonable, balanced life financially, and not expect instant gratification with every economic move that is made.

For me, "freedom 55" does not mean that you retire and do nothing, rather it means that you can pursue work that you really enjoy doing, work that you like to do, rather than *work that you have to do*. When I did achieve this goal, I began to do everything in my terms, and the idea of work was no longer viewed as a "job". There is so much to life and so much scope at this stage of one's life!

Retirement at 55 is generally a great achievement that I recommend to anyone that has a possibility to do it. It is an exciting stage in our life that offers us an opportunity to become something and someone that we dream about all our life. This third stage in our life is often referred to as the "Golden Age" period, a period from age 55 to 80, for it can be, and even should be, a period in our lives when everything comes together as it were, and a time when some of our dreams should be realized. It's the period before old age really sets in at age 80. In theory that is so, but in actuality all kinds of scenarios are possible during retirement as well. For sure though, it is the third big period in our lives when we can finally, still, become what we wanted to be all along.

Retirement can be a beautiful period when most of us have some disposable income to do some of the things we always wanted to do, but couldn't, because we lacked money, or lacked the time, or for some other more pressing reason. But retirement can also be a trying time, a time when many of us seniors experience health issues that threaten our very existence on this earth. It is in retirement that we advance into an older age when we witness many situations that give us a great deal of grief as we experience a real sense of loss of many people we have known and or worse still, people we have loved.

What "Freedom 55"?

I am happy to say without reservation, that I had a great, satisfying career in my chosen field of education. Throughout my career I hardly ever thought about retirement, but as the years passed and I reached age 50, I began to think about it now and then, and then a lot more after age fifty-two, probably because at that point I had some emerging health challenges that impacted pretty well everything I was doing. So, I began to think seriously about alternatives that I would really enjoy doing. What I really wanted was an opportunity to reinvent myself and do some things that so far in my life had eluded me.

So, in 1988, with the hope that in my "retirement", which I anticipated would begin in about 3 years' time, I would have something interesting to do, I bought a travel agency, a franchise out of Ontario. The travel agency was located right in downtown Winnipeg, in the newly constructed Portage Place Mall and faced Portage Avenue across the street from the historic Hudson's Bay Company department store. Soon after I got involved in the travel business, things generally in the whole industry went from bad to worse. There was such competition to say the least and big travel companies made it impossible for the competition to survive. For example, they would reduce a return fare Winnipeg to Toronto to a meager $99.00 and at 8% commission (i.e., $8.00) for the agency, which was totally insufficient to meet the cost of the Saber computerized reservation booking system, which cost close to $12.00 for each basic domestic booking. In this scenario, even though I was able to increase annual gross sales from $1,200,000 to over $2,000,000., at best we still barely ever broke even.

To my disappointment, we also found out that as the owner I had very little control over decision-making. In short, for me it was a hard lesson learned, and in 1991 we sold the business at a considerable loss and chalked the whole thing up to experience. They say that generally speaking, leaders are risk takers. Well, I think that I have been somewhat of a risk taker alright.

In the early 1970's I had ventured on to what I thought to be low risk business and went into an investment in the state of Florida that consisted of purchasing five (5) condos in a most beautiful area of the ocean front in Miami Beach. As I was paying some 55% of my salary as income taxes, the idea of the venture was to legally shelter some of the tax money I was paying. For several years the thing went well as planned, but then something happened that has never happened before in the history of Canada: the interest rates skyrocketed to levels never seen before (or since). Believe it or not, interest rates rose to close to 20% and maintaining such exorbitant added costs was well beyond my ability to do so and beyond my comfort level. As a result, I did everything possible to divest myself of such a commitment. I had to regrettably abandon the investment initiative, and consequently allowed the sellers of the units to repossess them, which they were glad to do. Thus, I was able to divest myself of the onerous financial burden. and I could consider myself lucky that I was able to get out of the deal.

A PRAYER FOR YOU ON YOUR RETIREMENT

I chose to retire at age fifty-five and six months to be exact after thirty-three years in the teaching profession. Three years before retirement I had gone to a financial advisor and he researched my specific situation and concluded that if I kept on working after age 55, I would earn exactly $37.00 per day more than if I retired. Since I was working about sixteen hours a day Monday through Thursday inclusive, it was obvious that in essence I would be working for about $2.50 per hour to earn that $37.00. Because I had always worked and earned the highest rates for my category all my career, I had a wonderful pension awaiting me and I knew it would be sufficient to maintain our lifestyle that we were accustomed to, and so I decided to "retire". Besides, I wanted to do something else with my life, something where I could put into practice what I had learned through the many professional development activities and courses I had taken over the last 30 or so years, particularly in the area of human resources and organizational development. So, in November of 1991 I officially and irrevocably retired, a decision I have never regretted for since then, I have been my own boss.

What Retirement?

Prior to retiring, I had discussed the whole idea with Josie and we had both agreed that after retirement I would be alright for me not to do anything for six months, for I had earned the right to do nothing but "vegetate". Well, after six weeks of doing absolutely nothing, I had to sit down and reevaluate who and what I was all about all over again. Being ruthlessly honest with myself, I had to decide and plan what I really liked to do. After due diligence and careful assessment, I came up with an area of endeavor that I felt quite comfortable with. I would become **a** workshop/seminar facilitator/trainer for teachers and other groups of people. I would be **a** *"people developer"*, a phrase which, in 1975 I had coined to apply to teachers and parents, and something which described what I had been all my adult life.

People Developers

After I left the Superintendency of the School Division, I had to re-invent myself and so I did some very serious planning. During the process, I concluded that I wanted to do was work with people, lots of people, as I had done in the previous forty years plus. So, by eliminating those activities that I was sure I did not want to pursue, I set my sights in establishing a small consulting company called *"People Developers"*, a name I had "coined" as Assistant Superintendent of Education, in which defined teachers as "people developers" as opposed to teachers of subjects such as Geography, Mathematics and so on, so that teachers would focus more on the development of the total person, and give less importance on subject matter *per se*.

My son Tony has always been part of this undertaking in a minor way and assisted me in most major school evaluations projects, which, until I really retired, did them at the rate of about one per year. As well, I hired some specialists on a *per diem* basis, educators such as Early Childhood Education and Special Education Specialists, to get a thorough and more comprehensive opinion in these "special" areas. But all Education System Evaluation Reports were always collated, written, and presented by me personally.

Crescendo to Becoming

PEOPLE DEVELOPERS:

WHO AND WHAT WE ARE

PROGRAMS AND SERVICES

PEOPLE DEVELOPERS
FRANK FIORENTINO, B.A., B.ED., M.ED.
1294 Ravelston Avenue West
Winnipeg, Manitoba R3W 1R3
(204) 661-8755   Fax: (204) 661-3834

"The development of human potential is an investment in people excellence."

TABLE OF CONTENTS

1. MISSION
2. PEOPLE DEVELOPERS: WHO AND WHAT WE ARE
   a. AN EDUCATION, TRAINING AND CONSULTING FIRM
   b. THE MANAGEMENT CONTROL TEAM
3. PEOPLE DEVELOPERS: WHAT WE DO
   a. MISSION STATEMENT
   b. PROFESSIONAL AND PERSONAL DEVELOPMENT PROGRAMS, WORKSHOPS AND SEMINARS.
   c. CONSULTING AND MANAGEMENT SERVICES
   d. INTERACTIVE PLANNERS, WORKBOOKS, AND OTHER LEARNING BOOKS AND MATERIALS
   e. PRE-EMPLOYMENT AND RECAREERING PREPARATION AND TRAINING
   f. LEARNING RESOURCES CENTRE
4. REFERENCES
5. "INVESTMENT"

1. MISSION

"People Developers exists for the purpose of developing human potential by providing personal and professional growth experiences, the end-outcome of which is continuous improvement and high quality of life."

The motto of **People Developers** is: *"The development of human potential is an investment in people excellence".* We believe that professional and personal development and training is the essence and lifeblood of improvement and growth. Any professional development program, course or training must begin with the end first, that is, the dream or vision. We must have a clear vision of where we want to end up, and our visualization of the end-outcome must be as clear and precise as possible. When the visualization is most clear, what remains to be developed is the establishment of a path that leads us to our vision and dream. It is at this point that we either really believe that *we can do it,* **or** that *we can't or won't do it.* When we believe that we can, in fact do it, and a commitment to action is achieved, the attainment of the identified targets is almost certain to occur. In short, Napoleon Hill stated it best: **"What the mind of man can perceive and believe, it can achieve."**

The purpose of professional and personal development is growth and improvement. Improvement is desirable because it increases our performance in all our endeavors and with it comes improvement of productivity and profitability. In fact, professional and personal development causes improvement in everything in our life.

2. PEOPLE DEVELOPERS: WHO AND WHAT WE ARE

A) AN EDUCATION, TRAINING AND CONSULTING FIRM

People Developers is a private education and training consulting organization founded in 1991. It consists of experienced, professional, and caring people committed to excellence. The Project Management and Control Team consists of associates from various backgrounds and jurisdictions including associates / consultants from the Aboriginal community. Members of the Team have abundant and demonstrated leadership skills for both the actual delivery and the implementation of the proven programs we provide. And what's more remarkable, is that *People Developers'* programs are leading edge training that is cost-effective and affordable.

The integrity of our work is guaranteed, and our commitment is to deliver and complete the work as promised. Also, there will be on-going monitoring and feedback by the team leader to ensure the attainment of agreed-upon goals and objectives of the project undertaken.

You have our commitment to excellence and our commitment to work closely and harmoniously with you, and those you select to work with us, to ensure the attainment of your aspirations and your goals.

B) THE PROJECT MANAGEMENT TEAM

All assignments undertaken by *People Developers* are carried out on a team management basis. The project management control team is usually made up from the list of highly qualified associates as listed below as an example and other resource people who will be engaged if and when required.

Frank Fiorentino
(B.A., B.Ed., M.Ed.)

* Director, Team Leader
* Education Consultant
* Former Superintendent of Education

Bob Scarth
(B.A., M.Ed.)

* Psychologist, Consultant
* Former Child Guidance Clinic
* Former Assistant Superintendent

Wenda Dickens
(Ph.D.)

* Research Consultant
* Former Director of Research
* Winnipeg School Division No. 1

Katie Dawson
(B.A., M.Ed.)

* Early Years Consultant,
* Early Childhood Programming Specialist

Anthony Fiorentino
B.A., B.Sc., B.Ed.)

* Principal, Sainte Anne School
* Middle and Senior Years
* Administration and Supervision

3. PEOPLE DEVELOPERS: WHAT WE DO

People Developers provide consulting, educational, and training services to a fairly wide variety of clients including school divisions, schools, first nations, government departments and agencies, industries, big and small business, non-profit organizations and others. To date our clients have included teachers, high school and university students, principals, secretaries, paraprofessionals or teacher assistants, custodians, bus drivers, volunteers, salespeople, counselors, employment insurance recipients, seniors, senior management members, chief and councils, managers, and others.

People Developers recognizes that each individual is different and perhaps even unique in terms of "where he's at" relative to his needs for development and growth. For this reason, we believe that the first step in the development of a growth plan is an accurate assessment to ensure the identification of the individual's or organization's needs and style.

A) PROFESSIONAL AND PERSONAL DEVELOPMENT PROGRAMS, WORKSHOPS AND SEMINARS.

People Developers offers over fifty (50) relevant and current topics that are presented with the participants in mind. The focus is always on personal and professional growth and development. All workshops are in fact designed to meet your goals and your own unique, special needs.

People Developers design high energy, skill-oriented seminars and workshops which provide in-depth active presentation of ideas and knowledge to the participant.

Our seminars and workshops are designed to meet the specific needs and expectations of your group, school, organization, business, or corporation. We have the knowledge and skills to design for you a "Blueprint for Excellence" in any area you identify for improvement and growth. We will assist you in the development of a Plan of Action and will profile and target specific strategies that bring professional and personal growth for your staff, whether small or large.

B) OTHER SERVICES BY PEOPLE DEVELOPERS:
...AVAILABLE "ON-LOCATION" OR "IN-HOUSE"

- Facilitator Services
- Consulting Services
- Counselling Services
- Policy and Procedures Manual Development and Writing
- Job Descriptions Manual Academic Upgrading Tutoring Programs
- Train-the-Trainer Programs Heavy Equipment Operators' Program
- Implementation of Parental Involvement in Education
- Accurate and Enrolment Projections
- Surveys on Educational Services and Programs
- Professional Leadership Services
- Professional Development Workshops
- On-Going Consultation with Education Leaders and Staff
- Mentorship Services
- Development of Mission Statements
- How to Run Effective Meetings
- Implementation of School Programs
- Resource Service to the Education Authorities
- Support Services to the Director of Education and School Authorities
- Development of Sound Policies for Discipline, Violence, and Safety
- Peer-Leadership Program Development and Implementation
- Proposal and Report Writing
- Other Services Specifically Designed for Your Specific Needs

C) Seminars ...available to meet all your needs:

- The Personal Excellence Seminar (see below)
- Planning and Programming for Success
- Re-careering as an Opportunity
- Planning: Goal Setting / Goal Getting
- The New Learning Revolution
- How to Take Control of Our Future
- The Power of Expectations
- Career Development
- Peacemaking and Mediation Skills

- Pre-Employment Training and Preparation
- Urban Orientation Program
- How to Find Work
- Indicators of Excellence and Growth
- Are you Ready for Change? How Ready?
- The Power of Communication
- Developing an Education Continuum
- Motivation or Inspiration
- The Power Within You
- Vision And Mission
- Developing People Skills
- Progressive Discipline Strategies
- Self-esteem Enhancement Strategies
- How to Develop an Education Master Plan
- Empowerment Strategies
- Special Needs Students
- Proven Decision-Making Strategies
- Survival Strategies for Seasoned Teachers
- Leadership Styles and Power
- Team Building/Team Functioning
- Accelerated Learning
- Wellness: A Holistic Approach
- Effective Teaching Strategies for Special Needs Students
- Business Planning
- Schools Without Violence: Developing Effective Strategies
- Effective Management
- Planning For Success
- Retirement Planning
- Curriculum Development
- Parental Involvement: A True Partnership
- Schools Without Violence
- How to Develop an *Education Master Plan* for First Nations
- School Growth Plan: Development and Implementation
- The Paradigm Shifts
- Breakthrough Thinking

BECOMING "FREE" AT "FREEDOM 55"

- Creating Effective Schools: What Are the Indicators
- Total Quality Organizations
- Survival Skills for Beginning Teachers
- Strategic Planning
- School Program Evaluations
- Indicators of Effective Schools
- Mentorship Programs
- Time Management
- How to do Enrollment Projections
- Proposal Planning and Writing
- Success Oriented Schools (failure-free)
- How to Conduct Effective Meetings
- Budget Formulation / Administration
- Train-the-Trainer Programs
- Heavy Equipment Operators' Program
- Performance Appraisal Systems
- Urban Orientation Program for Aboriginal
- Attaining Emotional Control
- Listening, Hearing and Understanding
- Effective Public Speaking
- Turning Dreams into Reality
- The Complete Personal Growth Model
- How to Attain Safe Schools
- *People Developers* will design Workshops, Seminars, and Other Projects specifically to your needs and expectations based on the end-outcomes you want to attain!

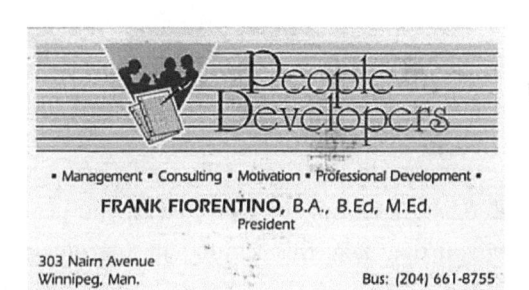

People Developers

• Management • Consulting • Motivation • Professional Development •

FRANK FIORENTINO, B.A., B.Ed, M.Ed.
President

303 Nairn Avenue
Winnipeg, Man.
R2L 0W8

Bus: (204) 661-8755
Fax: (204) 661-3834

- Management Consulting Services
Professional Development Seminars/Workshops
- School Evaluations
- Academic Upgrading Tutoring Program
- Policy Development
- Pre-Employment Training
- Motivation
- Strategic Planning

" *an investment in people excellence* "

My People Developers business card (above) says it all

Crescendo to Becoming

"Quality is the Art of Life!"

THE PERSONAL EXCELLENCE SEMINAR

RESULTS IN:
GROWTH
QUALITY
EXCELLENCE
CONFIDENCE
EMPOWERMENT

The *PERSONAL EXCELLENCE SEMINAR* is a rock solid "foundation workshop that everyone should experience, TO CREATE the kind of person you want TO BE, or to RECREATE OR RE-INVENT yourself into the kind of person you want TO BECOME.

The *PERSONAL EXCELLENCE SEMINAR* is a holistic presentation designed specifically to empower yourself so that you achieve optimum balance in your life and in everything you do.

The *PERSONAL EXCELLENCE SEMINAR* focuses on research-based key indicators, ingredients and skills that must be mastered in order to achieve a measure of greatness in your life.

The *PERSONAL EXCELLENCE SEMINAR* is designed for those who want to enhance their opportunities to achieve peak performance, personal fulfillment, and growth.

The *PERSONAL EXCELLENCE SEMINAR* **focuses** on people and their performance and is designed to ensure the advancement of your personal and professional skills for the attainment of worthwhile goals.

The *PERSONAL EXCELLENCE SEMINAR* may be delivered to you personally on an individual basis, or you may take this seminar in a small or large group setting.

The Mentorship Program
...a personal growth coach for you

WHAT IS A MENTORSHIP PROGRAM?

A Mentorship Program is a special relationship between an experienced professional and an interested newcomer.

WHAT IS A MENTOR?

A Mentor is a "People Developer", a professional "Coach", who facili-tates your "getting a life" by enhancing your improvement and growth. A Mentor helps a person develop his potential to his optimum level. He does this by providing motivation, and inspiration, and by nurturing a person's talents, interests, abilities, and interests.

WHO AND WHAT IS YOUR MENTOR?

* *Your Own "Confidante"*
* *Ultimate Caring Friend and Coach*
* *Guide*
* *Resource*
* *Listener*
* *Advocate*

* *Supporter*
* *Expert*
* *Consultant*
* *Counselor*
* *Leader*
* *Monitor*

WHAT DOES THIS MENTORSHIP PROGRAM PROVIDE?:

* *Vision*
* *Coaching*
* *Guidance*
* *Support*
* *Empowerment*
* *Motivation*
* *Inspiration*
* *Challenge*
* *Purpose*

* *Modeling*
* *Choices/Options*
* *Advice*
* *Training*
* *Expertise-on-Demand*
* *Information*
* *Knowledge*
* *Counseling*
* *Direction*

Crescendo to Becoming

* *Objectivity*
* *Leadership*

* *Development*
* On-going Monitoring

WHAT BENEFITS DO YOU RECEIVE?

- *A clear vision of your desired end-outcomes*
- *A strong, caring support base*
- *Development of a Plan for Success designed specifically for you*
- *A commitment of your Personal Growth and Wellness*
- *An holistic process of discreet and effective services*
- *A performance-based support system through direct coaching*
- *A detailed, consistent, practical approach to decision-making*
- *Great peace of mind in your transition period as; you solidify and build your foundation or renewal of your life*
- *Explore your career path and/or influence and promote your career advancement.*

Note: *By arrangement, your Mentor can be available 24 hours a day.*

TESTIMONIALS
...what people say about us!

◆ "The presentation was very well organized in terms of facility arrangements and material distributed to attendees. You are an excellent dynamic and knowledgeable speaker. The feedback received from our staff has been excellent. The presentation not only contributed to motivate our staff, but also helped them to understand the importance of working as part of a team, and the critical role each of them play at the University of Manitoba."

—Director of Physical Pant,
Assistant Director of Physical Plant
University of Manitoba

BECOMING "FREE" AT "FREEDOM 55"

◆ *"The workshop feedback evaluations are all very positive about the training; in fact, 85% of the participants assessed it as excellent and the remaining 15% as very good".*

—Engineer Peel Regional Authority, Nemaska, (James Bay), Quebec

◆ *"The Workshop feedback forms mirror the positive reaction of the participants to your teaching style with comments such as 'energetic presentation', 'speaker held interest throughout', and 'I loved everything presented'. The presentations on time management, leadership, communication, self-esteem and goal setting were particularly well-received".*

—Research/Analyst Environment Unit National Indian Brotherhood, Ottawa, Canada

◆ *"The positive approach on the issues discussed motivated our staff to look differently at themselves as leaders in their field".*

Winnipeg School Division No. 1

◆ *"I would like to thank you for speaking to our Custodian and Maintenance staff. Indicators of Excellence is ideal for food for thought. The staff enjoyed your message and the evaluations state the same".*

—Assistant to the Maintenance Supervisor,
St. Boniface School division No. 4

◆ *"We received a lot of positive feedback from staff on your presentation".*

—S.O., Chair, L.P.D. Committee

◆ *"Comments from the delegates were very positive and your involvement helped ensure a positive outcome".*

—Program Chair Recreation Conference for Community Volunteers

◆ *"Excellent Presentations! The speaker is not only informative but also dynamic and enthusiastic. Great Workshop!"*

REFERENCES: ...*our credibility* Organizations and Schools that have utilized our services:

- AAA Security Systems
- Antler River School Division No. 43
- Assembly of First Nations, National Indian Brotherhood (Ottawa)
- Assiniboine South School Division No. 3
- Berens River First Nation
- Bloodvein First Nation
- Brandon School Division No. 40
- Brokenhead Ojibway Nation
- Cree Nations of James Bay, Quebec
- Cross Lake First Nation
- Employment and Immigration Canada
- Frontier School Division No. 48
- Garden Hill School
- Grand Council of the Crees of Quebec
- Hollow Water First Nation
- John W. Gunn School
- Little Grand Rapids First Nation
- Lord Selkirk School Division No. 11
- Fairford First Nation
- Pinaymootang School
- Fisher River School
- Manitoba Government
- Canadian Government
- Mikisew School
- Morris-McDonald School Division No. 19
- Mountain School Division No. 28
- Mystery Lake School District No.2355National Indian Brotherhood .
- Otter Nelson River School
- Recreation Association of Manitoba
- River East School Division No. 9
- Sandy Lake First Nation (Ontario)
- Sergeant Tommy Prince School

BECOMING "FREE" AT "FREEDOM 55"

- Seine River School Division No. 14
- Sioux Valley Dakota Tipi
- Somerset School
- Southeast Resource Development Council Corporation
- St. Boniface School Division No. 4
- St. James-Assiniboia School Division No. 2
- St. Theresa Point First Nation
- Sun West Screen and Graphics
- Transcona-Springfield School Division No. 12
- Turtle Mountain School Division No. 44
- University of Manitoba
- Wanipigow School
- Winnipeg School Division No. 1

10.
BECOMING A TRAVELLER

I THINK THAT IT'S TRUE, that *"nothing broadens the mind like travel"*. But the motivation for my travel has been, and is still more than that, much more. Travel to any destination where one has never been before is always a new learning experience that usually enhances understanding, not only of the region explored, but also of its inhabitants, and of its flora and fauna. Personally, I have always found travel not just interesting but exhilarating, but also always a learning experience, contributing something to my knowledge base.

My travels to my native country of Italy though, is something else. It is always a huge emotional occasion. Particularly returning to my little town of Amato where I was born, is always an indescribable event that awakens in me, unforgettable, beautiful memories of my childhood, that is, of my first thirteen years on earth.

Once there in Amato, I cannot get enough of it. Day after day, in early morning, as I usually go for my walk around the whole town, I visit and revisit all the doorsteps of town, fronting invariably empty and abandoned homes, mostly belonging to those that had to emigrate from Amato mainly to far away countries such as Canada, Australia, Argentina, and the U.S.A. I remember well, those dear people that used to live there, and those that have long gone on their eternal rest. The memories of my early days on earth are still so lucid and vivid, for they were so lovingly engraved in my young mind and now cannot be easily erased. Nor do I want them erased. Actually, the great details that I can still recall are simply outstanding and evoke in me strong and poignant feelings that simply amaze me to no end. With this recall ability, I am able to relive tender (and not so tender) early days of my life in my "beloved place", Amato.

BECOMING A TRAVELLER

On several occasions I have gone to the well-kept local cemetery of Amato, with its beautiful family chapels and burial tombs on the many upright walls, for nobody today is buried in the ground anymore, as was the case when I lived there. But to remember those that lived in Amato back to some 75 years ago, it is necessary to visit not only the cemetery of Amato, but as well the mausoleum on Waverly Street and several others in Winnipeg, and many others throughout the world, such as in Buenos Aires in Argentina, in Montreal, and still others in many other cemeteries in other countries world-wide. But no doubt, the vast majority of Amatesi are buried in Amato and in Winnipeg.

Every year since World War II, Amato has fewer people than the year before because it has a constantly diminishing population due to many factors. After the great immigration period that followed the Second World War, Amato has never recuperated the rather dramatic impact. In 1949 when I and my family left for Canada, it had a population well over 2300, and now some seventy–five years later, it has barely 625, if that. I am very saddened that at this point in time, I can't help but think that my beloved town of Amato is slowly, but surely dying. Maybe the great influx of refugees going on in the western world at the present time will give it renewed rebirth and life.

We have travelled to many places with many people, friends, and relatives and in the process have found out how critical it is that those you travel with are totally compatible with each other. Theren is nothing worse than to be in a new land far away from home, and finding out that the persons you are with, don't want to experience any of the things you like to do. It can virtually ruin your vacation or travel package. Sad to say, we did experience some of that (but not too much) and had to put a stop to it and find new travel partners.

• •

"That which constitutes the supreme worth of life is not wealth, not ease, nor fame, not even happiness, but service".
—**Alfred Martin**

• •

Crescendo to Becoming

PLACES I'VE BEEN AND SEEN

I Italy: 1972: 9 weeks (tour etc.)
    2005: 4 weeks (tour etc.)
    2012: 9 weeks
Florida: Miami Beach
          Fort Lauderdale
          Hialeah Park
          Orlando
          Disney World
          Bush Gardens
          Clearwater, Florida
California: San Francisco
          Oakland
          Alameda
          Monterey
          San Jose
          Los Angeles
Anaheim   Disney Land
          San Diego
California: With Franca
          San Francisco
          Alcatraz
          Sausalito
Minneapolis: Several times for prof., reasons: Visit Franca/Rob when they lived there
New York: Visit uncle Onofrio's sons
          Tour of New York
          Ellis Island
          "Cats" in Broadway
Dallas
Chicago
New Orleans

Detroit
Las Vegas
Anaheim
Minneapolis
Baltimore
Chattanooga
North Dakota: Black Hills
          Mount Rushmore
          Chief Crazy Horse
Arizona: Tucson
          Phoenix
Texas: Dallas
Minnesota: Minneapolis etc.
Mexico: Tijuana
          Mazatlán
          Puerto Vallarta
          (many times)
Cuba: Varadero De .. . . Portillo
Hawaii: Honolulu, Waikiki
          (a few times)
Canada: Montreal: (many .. times with family
          Expo World Fair,
          to the Pacific (2x)
          To the Atlantic
          (twice)
          Banff: Three times
          Lake Louise: three times
          Kelowna
          Pier 21 Halifax
          Prince Edward Island
          Victoria, B.C.
          Edmonton: twice

Calgary
Okanagan Valley
Toronto: several times
Niagara
Peninsula
Niagara on the Lakes
St. Catherines, Ontario
Vancouver: twice
Vancouver World Fair
Brandon, MB.
Quebec City
Val D'Or, Quebec
Hollow Water
Reserve Brokenhead
Little Grand Rapids

Black River
Berens River
Fairford
Island Lakes
St. Theresa Point
Cross Lake
The Pas
Bloodvein
Little Grand Rapids
Fisher River
Cree Regions of
James Bay
Sandy Lake, Ontario
Sioux Valley Dakota Tipi

The American Pavilion, Expo 1967, Montreal

Crescendo to Becoming

The modernistic American Pavilion in the shape of a perfect sphere (above) with the monorail going through it was probably the most impressive of all pavilions. The Russian Pavilion was one of the largest but not as imaginative as some of the others.

In any case Expo .67 was a fantastic and an unforgettable experience for all of us.

Then, in 1986 we visited the World Fair in Vancou-ver, but for us it did not at all compare to Montreal Expo '67.

In beautiful Tucson Arizona (1992)
Left to Right: Brother Onofrio Fiorentino, Sister Delfina Jaffri, Me, Rubina Jaffri (Delfina's daughter) and Cheryl Fiorentino (Onofrio's wife)

BECOMING A TRAVELLER

Hawaiian Holiday, January 2000: Waikiki.

*Hawaiian Holiday, January 2000.
"Once a musician, always a musician".*

ITALY REVISITED FIRST TIME IN 1972 AFTER 23 YEARS IN CANADA

"Roma in carozzella", 1972

"Roma in carozzella", i.e. Rome as seen from on a horse and buggy. We rented the horse-drawn carriage all day and went sightseeing in ancient Rome. It was an amazing experience not only for the incredible "view", but for the feeling of being so close to everything in the middle of the action. But even with this most interesting method of transportation it was just too tiring for the children, particularly Franca who was only six years old. So, the next day Josie and the two kids returned to the town of Amato, and it was decided that at least I should carry on with the pre-paid 30-day tour of Italy. Accordingly, I continued on the tour and visited all of Italy from top to bottom, including Venice, Florence, Siena, Pisa, Verona, Rome, Naples, Pompeii, Amalfi, Sorrento, Salerno, and of course, Calabria. It was truly the experience of a lifetime.

BECOMING A TRAVELLER

Procession of San Francesco di Paola, Amato, 1972

With Charlie Mazzone in Taormina, Sicily, 1972, former owner of the famous Rancho Don Carlos nightclub in Winnipeg

Monumento ai Caduti (Monument to the fallen), Rome

City of Paola with Leopoldo, Maria, Tony etc. 1972

Crescendo to Becoming

Famous Trevi Fountain in Rome, 2012

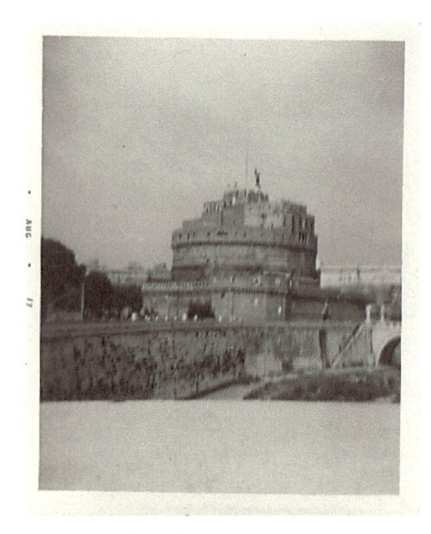

Castel Sant'Angelo, Roma    *Amato Church, Piazza & Palazzo*

BECOMING A TRAVELLER

ITALY REVISITED AGAIN IN 2005, AND IN 2012

Together with my brother-in-law Leopold Masi, a tailor par excellence in our hometown of Amato, in 2005. Leopoldo died in 2007

Part Of Our Italian Family, 2005 **Front Row:** *Luigino Fiorentino and Gian Luca Torchia* **Back Row:** *Elisa Charbonneau, Lorenzo Torchia, Franca Romano, Domenico Romano, Angela Romano, Marianna Marsico, Peppino Romano, Paola Fiorentino, Daniela Fiorentino*

Crescendo to Becoming

Josie and Me, in front of the famous Trevi Fountain, Rome, 2005.

Josephine Enjoying the pigeons at Piazza San Marco, Venice, 2005

The Leaning Tower of Pisa, 2005

BECOMING A TRAVELLER

"Gone to the Birds" in Piazza San Marco, Venice, 2005

Elisa and mom Josephine on the Bridge of Angels in front of the famous Castel Sant'Angelo leading to the St. Peter's Square to the left (2005)

Crescendo to Becoming

Palazzo Galati of Don Bruno Chimirri, Amato, Italy, 2005

Saint Pio Church at San Giovanni Rotondo    *Beautiful Vatican Museum Ceiling, 2012*

BECOMING A TRAVELLER

Italian Canadian Family and Friends, Marcellinara, 2012

Special Dinner Hosted by me with all our Italian Relatives in Italy, August, 2012

Family and Friends awaiting Antonio's Wedding, September 9, 2012,
Left to Right: *Franco Masi, Me, Franca, Antonio, Josie, Eleonora Masi, Peppe Romano, Laura and Isidoro*

Beautiful Positano in the Amalfi Coast, July, 2012

BECOMING A TRAVELLER

Adriana Kiz, Dylan and Tony Fiorentino at St. Peter Square, July, 2012

View of Amato from window of Maria's (Josie's sister) house where we stayed in 2005 and 2012

Crescendo to Becoming

Me, Laura Masi, and Josie, at Antonio's Wedding Day

Street Lights at Amato during Festa di San Francesco di Paola, August, 2012

The Unique" Trulli" Housing Structures of Alberobello

BECOMING A TRAVELLER

The Beautiful Wedding of Antonio and Antonella Torchia, Sept. 9, 2012

Josephine with our friends Vincenzina and Giannino Calista in Puerto Vallarta, Mexico

• •

"Time is not measured by the passing of the years, but by what one does, what one feels and what one achieves."
—**Jawaharla Nehru**

• •

11.
BECOMING A VOLUNTEER COMMUNITY BUILDER

1. Founding Member of the Italian Canadian Club of Winnipeg
2. Leader of the Italian Community of Winnipeg
3. Member Board of Directors, Creative Retirement Manitoba
4. President, Italian Canadian League of Manitoba (1992-1994)
5. Honorary Vice Consul for Italy from 1998 to 2007
6. Member Board of Directors, Centro Caboto Centre (1 year)
7. Board Member, Villa Cabrini (3 Years)
8. Adult Ambassador for the 2009 Winnipeg Folklorama Festival (Italian Pavilion)/
9. Member Board of Directors, Heart and Stroke Foundation of Manitoba, 2010 to 2016
10. Member River East-Transcona Community Health Advisory Council of the WHRA (2012 - 2015)
11. Committee Member for the Transcona Centennial Celebrations (2012)
12. Member of the Transcona Centennial Celebration Steering Committee
13. Member of The Transcona Historical Museum
14. Member of the Retired Teachers Association of Manitoba (RTAM) including Member Board Director one year.

Founding Member of the Italian Canadian Club of Winnipeg

After graduating from high school, I continued to be active in both soccer and softball at the community level. As part of this involvement in soccer, I became a founding member of the *Italian Canadian Club,* the organization that sponsored the *Italia Soccer Club,* and I became an active soccer player as its first goalie for some nine years, culminating with winning the first provincial senior soccer championship in 1959.

The Founding Members of the Italian Canadian Club, 1953
First Row, left to right: Maria Buccini, Dominic Caligiuri, Ralph Cantafio, Father Fiore, Peter Bogdanich, Frank Mignacca, Ugolino Frognolato, and Bernardo Tucci
I am in the Middle Row, second from the right.

Becoming active again in the Italian community was relatively an easy transition for me in the early 1990's. It had been a long time since I was very

Crescendo to Becoming

actively involved in the development of the Italian community, even though I made sure that I kept myself informed about its key happenings and activities.

After forty-three years in Canada, soon after I retired from my chosen professional career in Education, I ventured into the consulting field in education and training. At this juncture, I was approached by respected members of the Italian community to consider getting actively involved once again in the affairs of that community.

In 1991, it was Mario Audino especially, that approached me and asked me to consider letting my name stand for the election for the position of President of the *Italian Canadian League of Manitoba*, and I must admit that I had mixed feelings to let my name stand. I knew that this was a difficult and onerous task, but I also knew that this was perhaps the opening I needed to get into the heart of the matter, help out and make some kind of contribution to the Italian Community of Winnipeg, which at this time was in a complete state of disarray, and close to collapse. There was a great deal of mistrust in several areas of the community and the *"Lega Italiana"* had fallen into disrepute and had reached the lowest level of its relatively short life. Just before I took over, the president was a lawyer whom I had never met, except through the press, who was himself involved personally, apparently in some legal matter, and might have to serve some time. There was nothing but mistrust everywhere, and I knew that especially in this scenario, I could cause positive change that would be beneficial and appreciated by the many good people in our community.

The Italian Canadian League of Manitoba (ICLM) was founded in 1964 and in 2014 it celebrated its fiftieth Anniversary. The unifying concept of the "Lega Italiana" or "Italian League" as the umbrella organization representing all the Italian associations and clubs in Winnipeg, was envisioned initially by the Italian Vice Consul of the day, John Mottola, incidentally my *paesano* also from *Amato*, who saw great advantages in having the Italian community of Winnipeg speak with one strong voice as the advocate for its collective goals, objectives, and needs. As supportive consensus for the concept grew, the union of the various clubs was achieved and the ICLM became a reality. From the time that this union was achieved, there is little doubt that the Italian community has contributed significantly to the growth, enrichment,

BECOMING A VOLUNTEER COMMUNITY BUILDER

and the actual community-building process, of what is now a vibrant and growing City of Winnipeg.

The thirteen member clubs that were active members of the *Italian Canadian League of Manitoba* in 1998 were:

- *Amici Abbruzzesi*
- *Associazione Basilicania di Winnipeg*
- *Centro Caboto Centre*
- *Fratellanza Amatese*
- *Giovanni Caboto Society*
- *Gruppo Alpini*
- *Gruppo Sportivo Italiano*
- *Italian Canadian Foundation of Manitoba Inc.*
- *Italian Youth Association*
- *Lupa di Roma Lodge*
- *Dante Alighieri Cultural Society*
- *Roma Society*, and
- *San Mango d'Aquino Society*

In 1991 as in the past, each member club was represented on the Board of Directors of the League by a Director designated annually by each member club, who has an active voice in formulating and articulating the League's vision, and its commitment of delivering on its mission. This primarily consists of actively promoting the great Italian heritage and culture, including its beautiful "romantic" language, history, traditions, food, art and music. This is accomplished through the implementation of various undertakings and endeavors in such fields as education, dissemination of information, and through social, athletic, recreational, culinary and many other activities.

During the first 60 years of its existence, the ICLM has seen remarkable changes and growth. During its existence, it has operated to date, out of three locations in Winnipeg: the first being the basement of the *Holy Rosary Church* when it was located on Sherbrooke and Bannatyne (everything Italian in Winnipeg started there), the second, in the *Casa d'Italia* on Notre Dame Avenue between Sherbrooke and Isabel Street, and the third, in the present location at the *Centro Caboto Centre* on Wilkes Avenue. The last two locations were initiatives of the ICLM, the *Casa d'Italia* which was bought outright from funds

Crescendo to Becoming

raised in the Italian community in 1982 and the $4.5 million Italian Cultural Centre at the *Centro Caboto Centre* which was constructed in 1997–98 with financial support from the three levels of the Canadian Government: federal, provincial and with some assistance from the City of Winnipeg, and over $1.3 million raised from donations of the Italian community itself.

The collective success of the *Italian Canadian League of Manitoba* is representative of the individual success of every Italian in Winnipeg for it is symbolic of the efforts and perseverance of its people, and as such, it helps to define who we are.

As President of the League, I was, *de facto*, the chairman of the Board of Directors. In this role I found that emotions ran high among the people representing the clubs and they had developed some very poor habits of debating to say the least. I quickly adopted the <u>Roberts Rules of Order</u> and had to insist on many occasions, that everyone had to speak only after the board member had been recognized by the chair of the board. At another occasion, I had to give the Board a lecture insisting that members talk and focus on the issue being discussed, and **not** on criticizing people at a personal level. This took a while to achieve, but after being firm for several months, the Board was beginning to adapt and adopt the methods I introduced and insisted upon.

The "headquarters" of the Italian community was the ***Casa d'Italia*** building on the south side of Notre Dave Avenue between Sherbrook and Isabel Streets. Shortly after I took office, I found out that the taxes on our building had not been paid for two years, and upon my election in the spring, I received further notice of taxes due for the third year. We now owned the City of Winnipeg some $54,000. for unpaid taxes, and as we would be in arrears for three years, the city had the power to sell the building if they so choose, to recoup the taxes owed them. As we had no money to pay the taxes, I initiated a gutsy strategy to make a presentation to the City of Winnipeg Board of Revision, and presented to them a position that our building was assessed wrongly for years, that their "Commercial 2" designation for our building was the wrong one, for we were not a business, but a cultural center, catering mainly to the needs of our ever-growing seniors that frequented the center.

Supported by pictures and slides, our delegation argued that we were in fact, a charitable organization that accommodated seniors from morning to night, for seniors would come to play cards there day after day, would go home for lunch and supper, and come back to play some more, usually until ten or eleven at night. As well, we had a library mainly consisting of Italian Literature, books, posters, and other authentic Italian materials, which were in demand by the Winnipeg and urban public schools, and we loaned many without charge. We argued vociferously that we were truly a cultural learning center, and we should be taxed as such, and not as a commercial business.

After three presentations to the city, we held to the position that there was another classification that we could qualify under, a clause that had come into effect three years earlier. When we learned of this, we quickly turned the matter over to our lawyer, and consequently the City agreed to reclassify the property and did so retroactively to several years earlier. The result of this decision was that instead of having to pay $18,000. per year in taxes, we were now required to pay only about $8,000. per year and the conclusion at the end of the day was that we had in fact been able to wipe off the total debt with the City of Winnipeg with one bold move, and the *Casa d'Italia* was now hopefully, a sustainable undertaking.

In order to take control of the financial mess that we were in, I recommended and/or implemented several other changes. We hired a part time person for Sundays and stopped the financial drain that usually occurred on Sundays when people would gather to watch "live" on our big screen, the soccer games taking place in Europe that we were able to pick up with the twelve-foot reception large dish that was placed on the roof of the premises. It seemed that on Sundays people were accustomed to enjoy *panini*, (homemade bread buns with *prosciutto*,) sandwiches including a cold beer and other beverages, without paying for them, for most of the time there was no one left in charge.

In order to realize some needed income, we instituted a daily luncheon program and attracted many people from downtown Winnipeg for a full lunch at a very reasonable price. I reviewed every contract that the *Casa d'Italia* had with various providers of goods and services and did not renew any without first searching out other alternatives. One of the biggest saving using this approach was realized with the weekly garbage pickup. We dropped the company we were using, paying over $7,000. per year, and contracted with their competitor, for well less than $5,000. per year which saved us almost $3,000. I even discovered that the *Casa d'Italia* was paying some company for two printers instead of one. We returned one and paid reasonable rent on the one we did keep. The final strategy was to apply for grants under any and all areas of government that provided support of multi-cultural activities and programs. This provided us with close to a $30,000. grant income at the beginning, but unfortunately such grants diminished considerably or disappeared altogether soon after as time went on.

But all of the above was short term. The *Casa d'Italia* was in great disrepair and it was not meeting the needs of the Italian community of Winnipeg. The facilities themselves were inadequate and needed a lot of space additions and renovations. I formed a Building Project Committee at the Board level to investigate what we needed and wanted and what would be the best ways or ways to meet our needs and achieve our mission. After eight months of review I remember that I reported to the board our committee's conclusions, namely that the *Casa d'Italia* on Notre Dame had outlived its purpose, and even more immediate was the reality that instead of some minor change, "major surgery was needed". After several options and alternatives were looked at, **it was decided by the Board that we would recommend to the community that new facilities were needed** and proceeded by sending out a survey to every Italian home in Winnipeg to ascertain if there was agreement with this conclusion. Along with this, we also asked Italians to have input on what specific facilities they preferred being included in the new building.

While this was going on, my uncle Gus Cosentino and I met several times in private and were involved in dreaming and thinking of creating an "Italian Village", consisting of a Cultural Centre that included new school facilities to house our *Dante Alighieri School* including a Library, a Soccer Field, a Church, an authentic Italian Restaurant, and space for publishing a monthly Italian newspaper. Preliminary exploratory talks were initiated with the three levels of government, specifically with Member of Parliament Lloyd Axworthy (Federal) Premier Gary Filmon (Provincial), and the then City of Winnipeg Mayor Bill Norrie, to explore the possibility and feasibility to obtain funds to build a new cultural center that would include a home residence for seniors. We found out that in principle it was indeed possible to get some (substantial) support from the three levels of government in a variety of ways including financial support, with the proviso that our Italian community would mobilize its forces and make a commitment to contribute its fair share of the costs, that is, at least twenty-five to thirty percent of the projected capital costs.

BECOMING A VOLUNTEER COMMUNITY BUILDER

The following ages contain copies of documents that show clearly the events of the *Italian League of Manitoba* in 1992 during the period that I was president. They show the plans and actions that were planted and taken during that period, as we moved slowly but assuredly toward the construction of a new Italian Cultural Centre. **It was this, in fact, the beginning of what later became the *Centro Caboto Centre*.**

Italian Canadian League of Manitoba
556 Notre Dame Avenue
Winnipeg, Manitoba
R3B 1S5

Maggio 1992

Notiziario Informativo

CHI E' IL NEOELETTO PRESIDENTE DELLA LEGA ITALO-CANADESE ?

Nato ad Amato in Italia, il professore Frank Fiorentino, si e' distinto nel campo dell'insegnamento e dell'amministrazione scolastica.

Ecco i suoi titoli di studio e le sue qualifiche professionali:

Permanent Professional Certificate, University of Manitoba 1962.
Bachelor of Arts Degree, University of Manitoba 1961.
Bachelor of Education Degree, University of Manitoba 1963.
Master of Education Degree, University of Manitoba 1965.
Principal's Certificate 1968
1959-1966 Teacher Grades 7 to 12
1966-1967 Vice Principal, Arthur Day Junior High.
1968-1975 Principal, Murdoch MacKay Collegiate
1975-1990 Assistant Superintendent
1990-1991 Superintendent of Education.

Frank Fiorentino

AUGURISSIMI...
PER UN BUON LAVORO.

GLI EDITORI DEL NOTIZIARIO:
- Gildetta Esposito
- Beatrice Cardillo e
- D. Romano,

In this issue...

p . Chi e' il nuovo Presidente ?	p 8-9 Lo Sport
p 2- Il nuovo direttivo della Lega	p 10- Rapporto L.Vacca
p 3- Discosso del Presidente	p 11- Rapporto di P.Cespe
p 4- Cont.	p 12- In Cucina
p 5- Cont.gli allievi della scuola Dante Alighieri il "Culturama"	p 13- Folklorama
	p 14- Cosa troviamo alla Casa D.
p 6-Lettera di T.Campanelli	p 15- Messaggi della Lega
p 7- La Puglia	p 16- Upcoming Events.

The above is a copy of the front page of the Italian newsletter in Winnipeg called "Notiziario Informativo" dated May, 1992. It announces my election as President of the Italian Canadian League of Manitoba which for me represented a movement to return to my roots and thereby give me a forum to make a positive contribution to the Italian community of Winnipeg.

Dear   ;

As you probably know, the Italian Canadian League of Manitoba is in the process of reviewing and re-launching its plans for a new community centre.

The League is determined and committed to work with any individual, group, organization and club who are willing to play a constructive role in expediting the process.

A special Committee has been set up to coordinate this effort and to ensure that the proposed plans will reflect and meet the needs of as many people as possible.

Attached is a copy of the questionnaire that is being used to gather relevant information.

Committee members will contact you to set up a meeting with you and all members of your organization to discuss the project and seek your input and advice on its various components.

Thank you for your cooperation,

Frank Fiorentino,
President

BECOMING A VOLUNTEER COMMUNITY BUILDER

Italian-Canadian League of Manitoba
556 NOTRE DAME AVENUE, WINNIPEG, MANITOBA R3B 1S4
PHONE (204) 772-3090

Dear Friend:

Four years ago, the Italian Canadian League of Manitoba conducted a survey on the interests, needs and aspirations of our community. A major component of the study focused on the concept of a centre where social, cultural, educational and recreational activities, programs and services could be provided to benefit the entire community.

Determined to pursue this goal, the League now intends to review and update its bank of information on the changing needs of the community in order to develop the most comprehensive, realistic and suitable plan for such a facility.

To this aim, please complete the attached questionnaire and forward it in the enclosed pre-stamped envelope by _____.

Thank you for your cooperation.

Yours truly,

Frank Fiorentino
President

NATIONAL CONGRESS OF ITALIAN-CANADIANS, MANITOBA DISTRICT

Crescendo to Becoming

of Manitoba

556 NOTRE DAME AVENUE, WINNIPEG, MANITOBA R3B 1S4
PHONE (204) 772-3090

Carissimo(a) amico(a),

Quattro anni fa, la Lega Italo Canadese del Manitoba ha condotto un sondaggio sui bisogni e le aspirazioni della nostra comunità. Buona parte dello studio era basata sul concetto di un centro in cui si potessero svolgere attività e programmi di carattere sociale, culturale, educativo e ricreativo a beneficio dell'intera comunità.

Volendo procedere con questa iniziativa, la Lega ritiene necessario aggiornarsi sulle esigenze presenti e future della comunità ed incorporarle in un progetto integrativo per l'eventuale costruzione di un nuovo centro.

A tale pro, pregasi voler compilare il questionario allegato e spedirlo nell'apposita busta entro il _____.

Grazie per la Sua gentile cooperazione.

Il presidente
Franco Fiorentino

NATIONAL CONGRESS OF ITALIAN-CANADIANS, MANITOBA DISTRICT

BECOMING A VOLUNTEER COMMUNITY BUILDER

QUESTIONNAIRE ON THE NEED FOR AN ITALIAN COMMUNITY CENTRE

First and last name: _____

Age Category: 0-20 ___ 21-30 ___ 31-40 ___ 41-55 ___ over 55 ___

Sex: Male ___ Female ___

Marital status: Single ___   Married ___   Number of children
                 Divorced/Separated ___   Widowed ___   at home under 18 ___

In your opinion, how important would it be for the Italian Canadian community to have a centre with the following features? (Please place a check mark under the numbers from 1 to 5 to indicate the degree of importance.)

	1 Not Important	2 Somewhat Important	3 Important	4 Very Important	5 Extremely Important
Auditorium (with stage/music/dance/theatre)					
Banquet hall					
Classrooms					
Cocktail lounge					
Commercial/retail space					
Day care centre					
Exhibit/exposition space					
Fitness centre/gym					
Green space					
Library/educational resource centre					
Meeting rooms					
Multi-purpose room					
Office space for clubs/organizations					
Recreation/games room					
Restaurant					
Sports bar/café					

Other (please specify): _____
_____
_____

PROGRESS REPORT

Submitted to:

BOARD OF DIRECTORS

ITALIAN CANADIAN LEAGUE OF MANITOBA

Prepared by:

EXPANSION/BUILDING COMMITTEE

February, 1993

BECOMING A VOLUNTEER COMMUNITY BUILDER

INTRODUCTION

In keeping with tradition and in order to meet constitutional and operational requirements, the newly-elected executive and the entire Board of the Italian Canadian League of Manitoba recognized the need for a **Building/Expansion Committee**.

At the June 15, 1992 Board meeting, the Committee was officially mandated to:

"study feasibility and provide suggestions and recommendations to the Board regarding:

    a) centro culturale
    b) seniors' home
    c) new Casa d'Italia."

As the seniors' residence project was being pursued by another group, namely the Italian Canadian Community Development Corporation (ICCDC), the Committee basically targeted three objectives:

a) determine the feasibility of expanding the existing Casa d'Italia at 556 Notre Dame

b) determine the feasibility of relocating by purchasing an existing building and renovating it to suit the needs of the Italian community

c) determine the feasibility of relocating by identifying a suitable site and building a new community centre.

The **Building/Expansion Committee** consists of:

    Domenico Romano (chair)   Domenico Sacco
    Greg C. Fiorentino   Salvatore Rapisarda
    John D'Ignazio   Nino Tesser
    Franco Grande   Mario Audino (ex-officio)
    Gerry Scerbo

Crescendo to Becoming

- 5 -

Option 1 - **Nocita's Proposal / River Avenue Property**

The Nocita family owns 2 (100 ft. x 165 ft.) lots separated by a 16 ft. lane fronting on River Avenue between Scott and Bryce Streets. The entire site is ± .8 acres. A presentation was made to the Committee in March, 1992. The Nocitas would make the land available for development; their proposal envisages a cultural centre, a seniors' housing complex, commercial/retail space, and underground parking. Details as to what is meant by "making the land available" and lease-back conditions on the commercial/retail space have not been provided.

Because of the central location, the proposal should not be abandoned and the Nocitas could be approached to spell out terms and conditions in writing.

However, there are certain drawbacks about this site: the size, the high cost of building and maintaining an underground parking, the frontage on a one-way street limiting access to and exit from the site.

Option 2 - **Working with the Italian Canadian Community Development Corporation**

The original intent of the Italian Canadian Community Development Corporation (ICCDC) was to pursue a site large enough to accommodate several components: a senior citizens residence, a personal care home, a cultural centre, a piazza and, eventually, a church. This would ultimately result in the creation of an "Italian Village" which would prominently place the Italian Community on the demographic, cultural, economic and political map of Winnipeg.

The ICCDC has recently succeeded in assembling approximately 12 acres of land on the north side of Wilkes Avenue almost at midpoint between Waverley Street and Kenaston Boulevard.

262

BECOMING A VOLUNTEER COMMUNITY BUILDER

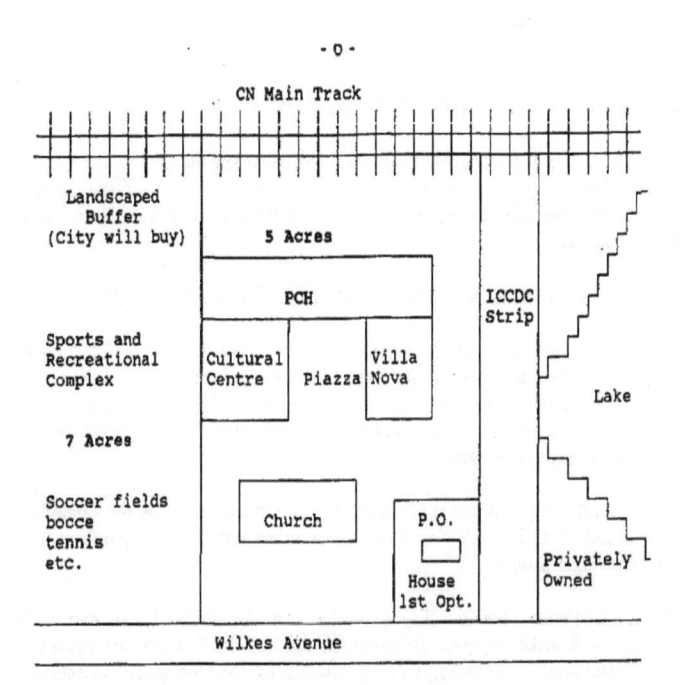

```
                        - o -
                    CN Main Track
|||||||||||||||||||||||||||||||||||||||||||
-------------------------------------------
|||||||||||||||||||||||||||||||||||||||||||

Landscaped
Buffer
(City will buy)    5 Acres
                 ┌─────────────────────┐
                 │        PCH          │ ICCDC
Sports and       │                     │ Strip
Recreational     │ Cultural  │  Villa  │
Complex          │ Centre    │  Nova   │
                 │      Piazza         │         Lake
                 └─────────────────────┘
7 Acres

Soccer fields
bocce             ┌─────────┐   P.O.
tennis            │ Church  │   ┌───┐
etc.              │         │   │   │       Privately
                  └─────────┘   House        Owned
                                1st Opt.
─────────────────────────────────────────
                  Wilkes Avenue
```

This land, adjacent to the man-made lake which separates it from the new Emmanuel Pentecostal Church, is now fully serviced. Plans are well underway to build a 60-apartment senior citizens housing project known as "Villa Nova". The contract has already been tendered; construction is scheduled to start in February and it should be completed by the end of October, 1993. This building may very well be the catalyst for the implementation of the other phases of the master plan. The ICCDC will cooperate with any individual, organization or group of organizations who are willing to play a leading and constructive role in expediting the process. The Cultural Centre should benefit the entire Italian community; therefore, it should reflect and meet the needs of as many people as possible.

The League is perceived to be the logical coordinating force to spearhead the development of a Cultural Centre. To this aim it must demonstrate stability, consistency, direction and continuity.

CONCLUSIONS AND RECOMMENDATIONS

EXPANSION OF THE EXISTING CASA D'ITALIA

Based on the limited space, the functional restrictions and the general apathy of the Italian Community towards the existing cultural centre on Notre Dame Avenue, it is the recommendation of the Committee that the existing Casa D'Italia should not be expanded.

PURCHASE AND RENOVATION OF AN EXISTING BUILDING

It is difficult to find a building large enough, in a good location and at the right price to make this option feasible. It is the recommendation of the **Expansion/Building Committee** not to purchase an existing building and renovate it, unless, of course, the right property with the right features would become available at favourable conditions.

With respect to the building at **Main Street and Church Avenue**, the Committee recommends that the Italian Canadian League of Manitoba does not purchase it for the following reasons:

a) the Committee does not dispute the fact that a bingo hall in this part of the city will make money. However, in light of the fact that the provincial Government is expanding its bingo operations, the Committee is concerned that this would impact negatively on the projected revenues;

b) the building is not conducive to the establishment of a cultural centre and its location does not reflect the demographics of the Italian community;

c) the Committee feels that it is not the League's mandate to be in the bingo business.

BUILDING OF A NEW CULTURAL CENTRE

It is the recommendation of the **Expansion/Building Committee** that its energy and focus be directed towards the identification of a suitable site and the construction of a new community centre.

It is the opinion of this Committee that a new community centre would convey a message of renewal, ongoing development and unity.

BECOMING A VOLUNTEER COMMUNITY BUILDER

At its November 26, 1992 meeting, the Committee decided to form a sub-committee to review the current and future needs of the community, formulate a comprehensive proposal based on clear priorities and develop a conceptual plan.

Presently, the sub-committee consists of the following members:

Greg Fiorentino (co-chair) John D'Ignazio (co-chair)
Gerry Scerbo Jack Abiusi
Maria Lonardelli (ex-officio) Stan Carbone
Mario Audino (ex-officio).

As the tasks become increasingly complex and demanding, additional members will have to be identified and enlisted.

The purpose of this report is to inform the Italian Canadian League of the Committee's progress to date and to offer suggestions/recommendations for appropriate action.

My Friend Mario Audino (left) who Insisted that I run for President of the Italian Canadian League of Manitoba.

Crescendo to Becoming

THE ITALIAN CANADIAN COMMUNITY DEVELOPMENT CORPORATION
C/O 433 RIVER AVE.
WINNIPEG MANITOBA R3L 0C3

PH: (204) 284-2900

Ms. Roberta Novel					September 9, 1992
Adm. Director
Italian Canadian League of Manitoba
556 Notre Dame Avenue
Winnipeg, Manitoba, Canada R3B 1B4

Dear Ms. Novel:

Please refer to your letter of August 26th concerning the development of various programs in the Italian Canadian community.

We shall be pleased to have you and your President Frank Fiorentino join us at our next Board of Directors meeting Thursday at 7:30 pm, October 8th, 1992, 4th floor, Villa Cabrini, 433 River Avenue.

Ms. Kelly Scarpino and Mr. Nello Longobardi will be our representatives at your next regular Board of Directors meeting scheduled for September 21, 1992. Will you please contact Ms. Scarpino and Mr. Longobardi directly, telephone 284-7660 and 261-9862 respectively as to time and place of the meeting.

Yours truly,

A. A. Cosentino, President

cc: Kelly Scarpino
    Nello Longobardi

BECOMING A VOLUNTEER COMMUNITY BUILDER

VILLA NOVA
BY THE LAKE

Villa Nova... the "new house"... carefree retirement living in an all new Non-Profit apartment community designed especially for Seniors 55 or better!

Smith Carter

ITALIAN CANADIAN LEAGUE OF MANITOBA

EXPANSION/BUILDING COMMITTEE MEETING

December 9, 1992 - Casa d'Italia

PRESENT:	Domenico Romano	Franco Grande
	Nino Tesser	Mario Audino
	Greg Fiorentino	Domenico Sacco
	John D'Ignazio

ABSENT:	Salvatore Rapisarda

GUESTS:	- Joe Bova, Vice-President
	Italian Canadian Community Development Corporation
	(ICCDC)
	- Franco Fiorentino, President
	Italian Canadian League of Manitoba

1. Having specified that he was not speaking on behalf of the ICCDC, but rather on his own behalf, Joe Bova gave an overview of the history and background which led to the formation of the ICCDC, the short-lived partnership with the League and the subsequent souring of the relationship between the two organizations.

   The original intent of the ICCDC was to pursue a site large enough to accommodate several components: a senior citizens residence, a personal care home, a cultural centre, a piazza and, eventually, a church. This would ultimately result in the creation of an "Italian Village" which would prominently place the Italian Community in the demographic, cultural, economic and political map of Manitoba and Canada.

   The ICCDC has recently succeeded in assembling approximately 12 acres of land on the north side of Wilkes Avenue almost at midpoint between Waverley Street and Kenaston Blvd. This land, adjacent to the man-made lake which separates it from the new Emmanuel Pentecostal Church, is now fully serviced. Plans are well underway to build a 60-apartment senior citizens housing project known as "Villa Nova". The contract has already been tendered; construction is scheduled to start in February and it should be completed by the end of October, 1993. This building may very well be the catalyst for the implementation of the other phases of the master plan. "The land is there; some kind of Cultural Centre will be built on that site with or without the League's involvement and support". Ideally, the planning and building of the Cultural Centre should be spearheaded by the League but with the direct cooperation of all Italian organizations. Since the Cultural Centre would benefit the entire Italian community, it should reflect and meet the needs of as many people as possible. The ICCDC will cooperate with any individual, organization or group of organizations who are willing to play a leading and constructive role in expediting the process.

2. Franco Fiorentino expressed empathy and support, in principle, for the main thrust and concept of the project on Wilkes. "The League too has a dream" and this dream should be realized for the benefit of the entire community. Franco also mentioned that he had spoken with Gus Cosentino about the project just a few hours before his death. In Gus's words: "The train is at the station and it's ready to leave; you can get on board if you wish".

BECOMING A VOLUNTEER COMMUNITY BUILDER

- 2 -

3. Joe Bova reiterated that the ICCDC wishes to work with groups such as the League, Villa Cabrini, Knights of Columbus, The Church, and others. The overall project is big; the initiative is for the entire community; we must think big to succeed. There is good will within the ICCDC and there is also a standing invitation for the League's president to attend their next meeting and study the master plan. Joe also sketched on the board the site in question and the potential relationship of the various components.

   Presently neither White Ridge nor Lindenwoods have a community centre. ICCDC could perhaps build one on this site and lease back to the city some major components.

4. The committee agreed that the League's president and first vice-president, along with Don Romano, should attend ICCDC's next meeting.

5. The sub-committee, consisting of Greg Fiorentino, John d'Ignazio and Jerry Scerbo, will be expanded to include: Jack Abiusi, Maria Lonardelli, Stan Carbone and others. It is desirable to recruit additional women members, both for the sub-committee and the committee as a whole. John and Greg will co-chair the sub-committee.

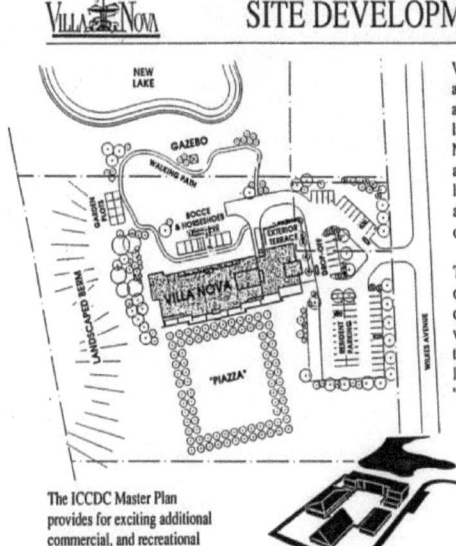

VILLA NOVA — SITE DEVELOPMENT PLAN

Villa Nova residents will enjoy a quite parklike character and atmosphere with a dramatic lakefront focus. The Villa Nova site takes up over 5 acres and will include professionally landscaped grounds with social and recreational opportunities overlooking the lake.

The building features an optimal north - south orientation, allowing sunrise views overlooking the lake to the east and sunset views looking over a landscaped "Piazza" or square, to the west.

Site Development Features include:
- Formal entrance drive and drop off area
- Ample resident and visitor parking
- Large exterior terrace overlooking the lake
- Exterior, resident exercise/ walking path with night lighting
- Screened gazebo at the waters edge with decorative lighting
- Vegetable and flower gardening plots for resident use
- Bocce courts
- Horseshoe pits
- Landscaped "Piazza" or square to the west

The ICCDC Master Plan provides for exciting additional commercial, and recreational developments to enclose the "Piazza" in the future.

Smith Carter

269

Crescendo to Becoming

L'Incontro

italian canadian league of manitoba

Volume 1 - Issue 2   DIREZIONE / REDAZIONE CENTRO ITALIANO   Giugno, 1998
1055 Wilkes Ave. Winnipeg, Manitoba Tel 487•4597 Fax 487•4608

Centro Italiano Caboto

Grand Opening in June!

Tutta la comunità Italiana è invitata a partecipare all'apertura ufficiale del nuovo Centro Italiano "Caboto" Domenica 14 giugno ore 7:30 di sera.

Mark your calendars! On June 14, 1998 it's the long-awaited Grand Opening Celebration of the Caboto Centre, 1055 Wilkes Avenue. It's sure to be a wonderful event.

The Opening Ceremonies Committee has been carefully planning the day's events which will begin 7:30 p.m. They will take full advantage of all the 27,000 square foot complex that its 7 acres has to offer. The day will include the official ribbon cutting ceremony, speeches, and entertainment.

Drop By Now!

But, you don't have to wait until June 14th to visit the Centre. Drop by now, and soak in the wonderful look and feel of this spectacular building.

Italian Community Creates Centre for Next Millenium

The Italian Canadian commnnity has just completed a joumey that has created a $4 million, 27,000 square foot Caboto Centre on Wilkes Avenue in south Winnipeg. Proudly situated on 7.2 acres, the Centre will be a centrerpiece for the community.

In recent years, the Italian community in Winnipeg has carved a strong and vital presence in our city's social, cultural and economic landscape. The new Centre will enhance this presence, and likely formulate new ones for generations to come.

An early and generous supporter of the Centre, Arthur V. Mauro, sees the Centre as offering facilities and activities that will enhance the quality of life for the entire community

"It will do more than honour the contribution that members of the Italian community have made to Manitoba and Canada. It will stand as a symbol of our gratitude to this great country," he said.

Vivian Albo, who has chaired the Developement Project for the Centre agrees. She adds "our vision was to create a Centre that will be a legacy for the next and future generations, to ensure that they will enjoy the same quality of life, opportunities and richness that we, and those before us have enjoyed."

A Project of the Italian Canadian League of Manitoba
The Centre is a project of the Italian Canadian League of Manitoba, an umbrella organization within the Italian community. The league has for years expressed a wish to have a place that would meet the needs of the community. "I think we've met that need with Centro Caboto" says Domenico Romano, League President and the past Chair of the League's Building/Expansion Feasibility Committee. "We've had this dream since we began working on this project almost 10 years ago".

Back in 1989, in conjunction with the League's 25th Anniversary, surveys were conducted within the Italian community to find out what their needs were. Further studies were undertaken in 1992 including surveys and focus groups.

The committee examined three potential options for the community: expand the League's existing facility "Casa D'Italia" on Notre Dame Avenue, purchase an existing building, or build a new Centre. "Our final report, recalls committee member, Mario Audino, Regional Executive Liaison with the Department of Canadian Heritage recommended building a new Centre as the best alternative that would provide a strong message of renewal, ongoing development and community building".

First Critical Step
By 1993, the wheels were in motion. The first critical step occurred on August 26, 1994 with an announcement by Premier Gary Filmon and Lloyd Axworthy, then Minister of Western Economic Diversification of a $900,000 investment, which included equal contributions by the federal and provincial governments, and the League. "The cultural diversity and character of our communities are importnnt building blocks for Manitoba's future," Premier Filmon said. Axworthy added, "The new Italian Centre and piazza will beautify the City and enhance its diverse communities, while creating new jobs and tourism revenue". In fact, the new Centre will create several dozen jobs once its fully operational.

The next step was securing land. Since the early 90's, there had been plans to locate on Wilkes Avenue adjacent to Villa Nova. The location would present the second leg of an Italian village concept that leaders in the community had envisaged. Negotiations spearheaded by the League's legal counsel and project team member Maria Grande of Thompson Dorfman Sweatman began with the City of Winnipeg, which led to finalization of a 70-year lease agreement with

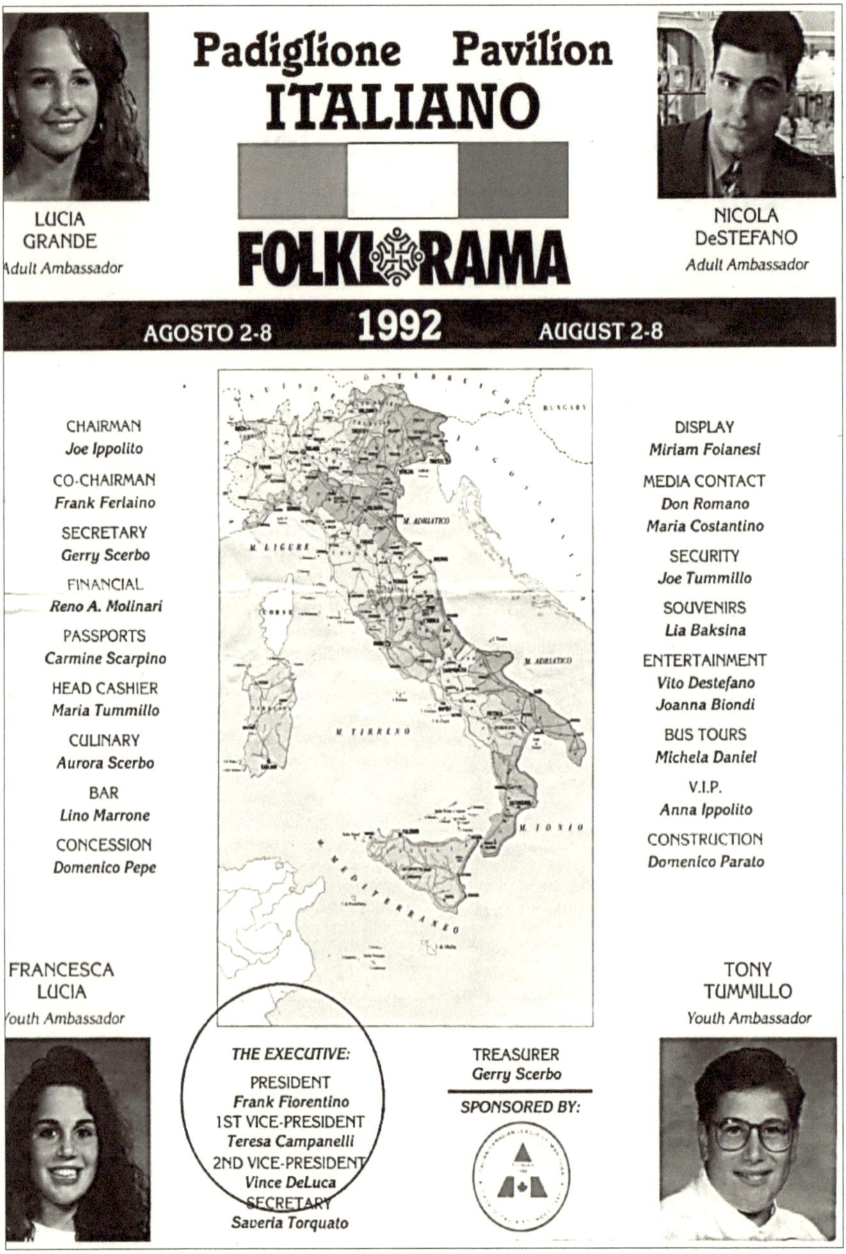

Crescendo to Becoming

Padiglione Pavilion
ITALIANO

LUCIA GRANDE
Adult Ambassador

NICOLA DeSTEFANO
Adult Ambassador

FOLKLORAMA

AGOSTO 2-8   **1992**   AUGUST 2-8

CHAIRMAN
Joe Ippolito

CO-CHAIRMAN
Frank Ferlaino

SECRETARY
Gerry Scerbo

FINANCIAL
Reno A. Molinari

PASSPORTS
Carmine Scarpino

HEAD CASHIER
Maria Tummillo

CULINARY
Aurora Scerbo

BAR
Lino Marrone

CONCESSION
Domenico Pepe

DISPLAY
Miriam Folanesi

MEDIA CONTACT
Don Romano
Maria Costantino

SECURITY
Joe Tummillo

SOUVENIRS
Lia Baksina

ENTERTAINMENT
Vito Destefano
Joanna Biondi

BUS TOURS
Michela Daniel

V.I.P.
Anna Ippolito

CONSTRUCTION
Domenico Parato

FRANCESCA LUCIA
Youth Ambassador

TONY TUMMILLO
Youth Ambassador

THE EXECUTIVE:
PRESIDENT
Frank Fiorentino
1ST VICE-PRESIDENT
Teresa Campanelli
2ND VICE-PRESIDENT
Vince DeLuca
SECRETARY
Saveria Torquato

TREASURER
Gerry Scerbo

SPONSORED BY:

Folklorama and the Eccellenza Awards that we instituted were two major undertakings during the time that I was President of the Italian Canadian League of Manitoba

BECOMING A VOLUNTEER COMMUNITY BUILDER

The Past Presidents of the Italian Canadian League of Manitoba, to 2006
(assembled together by computer)
Front Row, Left to Right: *Franco Grande, Dr. Luigi Villa, Dr. Idris Sabbadini, Luigi Vendramelli;*
Back Row, Left to Right: *Don Pepe, Dr. Sam Loschiavo, Gianfranco Riva,*
Phil DelBigio, Don Romano, Mario Raimondi and me, Francesco Fiorentino

---

April 26, 1993

Carissimo Franco,

I was at a meeting of the Amatese, the ad hoc committee for the Festa di San Francesco, and I was told you were not well. The same thing became evident when you were not able to attend the League" AGM on April 14. I sincerely hope that you feel better now and that you will recover 100% to continue to be the dynamic person that you are.

I read with great interest your report to the League's membership. It's obvious as I had rightly anticipated that you took the job seriously! Determined and resolute, you provided strong leadership. It was through your style, dedication, and savoir faire that in less than a year a profound positive change occurred with in the League. Beyond confines of the Italian community you were able to project a solid and respectable image for both the League and our community. Another year of your active and competent involvement would have performed the miracle. Experience tells me that of all presidents (some of whom occupied the position for several years since 1964) you were the one that left the largest imprint in a short time.

You brought quality, class and distinction to both the League and the community. I thank you for this, and I wish you a speedy recovery.

Ciao!
Mario Audino

My Friend Mario Audino's Caring Letter to me is Self-explanatory

273

Crescendo to Becoming

The above letter by my friend Mario Audino recaptures two important aspects of my status in the Spring of 1993. Firstly, was the impact that I had on the Italian Community only after a little more than one year as President of the Italian League, and secondly, that I reluctantly submitted my resignation as President of the Italian League due to the fact that I had been diagnosed as having a heart condition and would likely have to undergo some form of surgery related to that, although they did not know for sure what that would entail. Although my preference would have been to remain as President for at least another one or two years to see plans for the new cultural center being advanced to the building stage, members of my family and I arrived at the conclusion that a stress-free environment would be best for me personally, given the situation.

A Gift from an Indigenous student in Northern Manitoba

12.
BECOMING "ITALIANISSIMO" AS VICE-CONSUL FOR ITALY

AFTER MY SATISFYING CAREER IN Education, nothing has given me greater personal satisfaction than the nine-year term I served as the Vice Consul of Italy in Manitoba, for I have always been very proud of my Italian roots, much the same way my father was before me. My motivation for the position of Vice Consul of Italy was the fact that it would give me an opportunity to serve Italy and Italians in Manitoba and would also afford me an opportunity to return to my Italian roots that I have always loved so much. For all this, I have Mario Audino to thank more than anybody else, for it was he who started the whole process toward my appointment, with his persistent efforts to convince me to do it, and for initiating and putting forth my nomination for the position.

For the period of three years from 1995 to 1998, Bruno Esposito had been the Vice Consul of Italy for Manitoba, but for some reason he would vacate the position officially as of July 1, 1998. In early Spring of the same year, Mario Audino, who was now the first Executive Director of the Italian Cultural Centre known as *Centro Caboto Centre*, approached me and suggested that I would make a very good Vice Consul, and that I should consider the possibility seriously. He felt that I had all the required attributes for the position and more, and he would personally begin the process by putting forward my nomination. As I gave Mario some indication that I was interested, he began in earnest to do everything possible to make it happen His letter of January 20, 1998 to the Italian Consul-General of the day, Dr. Leonardo Sampoli below, shows clearly his efforts and the process that followed in the selection of the nomination. It also shows the input and

Crescendo to Becoming

support of various components of the Italian community toward my nomination. Finally, it shows that there were eight candidates that were shortlisted and considered, with the recommendation to put forth my name. As well, it shows the rationale and criteria sought in the candidate, which follows Mario's letter to the Consul General of Italy in Toronto.

                                                     Mario Audino
                                                     73 Shorecrest Drive
                                                     Winnipeg, Manitoba, R3P 1P4
                                                     Tel.:   (204) 488-2480 (casa)
                                                                           (204) 983-2592 (ufficio)
                                                     Fax: (204) 984-6996

Dr. Leonardo Sampoli
Console Generale d'Italia
136 Beverley Street
Toronto, Ontario.
M5T 1Y5

20 gennaio, 1998

Oggetto: Nomina Vice Console Onarario a Winnipeg

Egregio Signor Console,

Facendo seguito alle nostre recenti conversazioni telefoniche, ho il piacere d'informarLa che abbiamo completato il processo di consultazione per quanto riguarda la raccomandazione di candidati alla nomina di Vice Console Onorario a Winnipeg.

Dopo una discussione preliminare con il signor Domenico Romano, Presidente della Lega Italo Canadese del Manitoba, ed il signor Marco Cucina, delegato al COMITES ed impiegato presso il Centro Italo Canadese, ho ritenuto opportuno consultarmi anche con la signora Cristina Povoledo che è rientrata dall'Italia il sette gennaio.

A conclusione del mio primo incontro con la signora Povoledo il dodici gennaio, abbiamo deciso di coinvolgere anche la Dottoressa Caterina Cicogna e chiedere il suo parere dato che lei conosce abbastanza bene il nucleo attivo della comunità di Winnipeg, specialmente per quanto concerne l'insegnamento della lingua italiana.
Approfittando della sua venuta a Winnipeg, è stato possibile incontrarci venerdì scorso a casa della signora Povoledo.

Nel condurre l'analisi e la valutazione dei potenziali candidati, si è tenuto conto, sia pure in sommi capi, di un certo numero di fattori (Requisiti/Abilità/Qualità/Caratteristiche) di cui in allegato e non necessariamente nell'ordine in cui appaiono.

BECOMING "ITALIANISSIMO" AS VICE-CONSUL FOR ITALY

Si è discusso delle seguenti persone:
Gianfranco Riva, Adriana Lombardini, Eliana Handford, Santino Viselli, Carmine Coppola, Franco Fiorentino, Caterina Sotiriadis e Cristina Campomanes.

Per vari motivi, e con riferimento alla lista dei requisiti, è stato relativamente facile escludere la maggior parte delle persone dalla raccomandazione alla candidatura. Alla fine della discussione si è concluso che molto probabilmente la persona più raccomandabile sia il signor Franco Fiorentino che però la dottoressa Cicogna non aveva ancora avuto modo di conoscere.
Si decise perciò d'invitarlo all'apertura ufficiale della mostra dei Vetri Veneziani che avrebbe avuto luogo domenica, 18 gennaio, presso la Galleria d'Arte di Winnipeg.
Così facendo, ho presentato il signor Fiorentino ad entrambe; successivamente, loro mi hanno riferito che sono rimaste bene impressionate e che una persona come lui potrebbe essere raccomandabile nel caso fosse interessato.

Ieri pomeriggio ho parlato con il signor Fiorentino il quale sarebbe onorato di essere considerato per la nomina a tale carica. Io personalmente sono convinto che al momento attuale lui sia la persona più idonea per svolgere le mansioni di Vice Console Onorario a Winnipeg e che la sua eventuale nomina sarebbe bene accolta dalla comunità anche perchè, per quanto io sappia, sarebbe ben disposto a stabilire la sede vice consolare al nuovo Centro..

Il signor Fiorentino gode un'ottima reputazione anche al di fuori della comunità italo-canadese; ha l'età di 61 anni; è sposato; ha tre figli ed è ritirato in pensione; è benestante ed autosufficiente; è un tipo affabile, socievole, assertivo e cortese; è un ottimista, sempre pronto e capace a trasformare problemi in opportunità; è stato insegnante, preside ed infine direttore generale (Superintendent) della circoscrizione scolastica di Transcona-Springfield; attualmente lavora per conto proprio dedicandosi saltuariamente all'organizzazione e presentazione di seminari su vari temi che influiscono sulla funzionalità dell'individuo, gruppi, organizzazioni e strutture.

Ecco il suo indirizzo: Franco Fiorentino
1294 Ravelston Avenue West
Winnipeg, Manitoba, R3W 1R3
Tel.: (204) 661-6340
Fax: (204) 661-3834

Naturalmente, il tutto ora dipende da Lei, signor Console. Come Lei ben sa, c'è una certa premura da parte nostra a far sì che si proceda con la nomina al più presto possibile.

Codiali saluti

Mario Audino

Crescendo to Becoming

CONSOLATO GENERALE D'ITALIA

136 BEVERLEY STREET
TORONTO ONTARIO M5T 1Y5
TEL.: (416) 977-1566 • FAX: (416) 977-1119

TO WHOM IT MAY CONCERN

This is to certify that **Mr. Francesco FIORENTINO**, born in Amato (Italy) on February 20th, 1936 was duly appointed and established by this Consulate General of Italy in Toronto to be the **Honorary Vice-Consul of Italy in Winnipeg**, Manitoba as of July 1st, 1998.

Mr. FIORENTINO is therefore rightfully and lawfully entitled, under Italian and Canadian Law, to act in the capacity of Honorary Vice-Consul of Italy in Winnipeg, Manitoba with jurisdiction limited to the territory of the Province of Manitoba.

In such capacity Mr. FIORENTINO is also authorized to open a bank account in the name of "VICE CONSOLATO D'ITALIA - WINNIPEG, MANITOBA" (Vice-Consulate of Italy, Winnipeg, Manitoba).

Toronto, July 9th 1998

Leonardo Sampoli
Consul General of Italy

BECOMING "ITALIANISSIMO" AS VICE-CONSUL FOR ITALY

PREMIER OF MANITOBA
Legislative Building
Winnipeg, Manitoba, CANADA
R3C 0V8

July 23, 1998

Mr. Francesco (Frank) Fiorentino
Honorary Vice-Consul of Italy
1294 Ravelston Avenue West
Winnipeg MB R3W 1R3

Dear Mr. Fiorentino:

    May I take this opportunity to extend warm congratulations on your appointment as Honorary Vice-Consul of Italy.

    I wish you every success in your endeavours and I am sure you will find the position rewarding.

    I look forward to meeting you in the near future and ask that you contact Mr. Dwight MacAulay, Director of Protocol at 945-8845 to arrange a convenient time.

Yours sincerely,

Gary Filmon

Gary Filmon

Crescendo to Becoming

Office of the Lieutenant Governor
Room 235, Legislative Building
Winnipeg, Manitoba, Canada
R3C 0V8

July 20, 1998

Mr. Francesco Fiorentino
Honorary Vice-Consul of Italy
1294 Ravelston Avenue
Winnipeg MB   R3W 1R3

Dear Mr. Fiorentino:

      Congratulations on your recent appointment as Honorary Vice-Consul of Italy in Winnipeg.

      You have demonstrated a caring commitment to our community and I congratulate you for your dedication and enthusiasm to tackle new challenges.

      May I extend my personal best wishes as you prepare to carry out the rewarding duties as a member of the Consular Corps of Winnipeg.

Yours sincerely

W. Yvon Dumont
Lieutenant Governor
Province of Manitoba

BECOMING "ITALIANISSIMO" AS VICE-CONSUL FOR ITALY

March 23, 1999

Frank Fiorentino
1294 Ravelston AV W
Winnipeg MB R3W 1R3

Dear Frank:

Please accept my congratulations on your being named the Vice-Consul of Italy. It must be very gratifying for you to be recognized with this honour and have the opportunity to put your various skills and abilities to good use on behalf of the Italian-Canadian community.

This has been an exciting year for the Italian community both as it strengthens the links in Manitoba through the activities in the CentroCaboto as well as strengthening its links to Italy through the Italian Chamber of Commerce which recently announced its opening. As well there are a number of ongoing activities.

Once again, please accept my congratulations as your MLA for your part in making the Italian-Canadian community of Winnipeg as vibrant as it is and as important to the larger multicultural fabric.

Sincerely,

Marianne Cerilli,
MLA for Radisson.

/ed
opeiu-342

Constituency: 549 Regent Ave. W. Winnipeg, MB R2C 1R9 Tel: 222-0074 Fax: 222-2840 e mail: ers464@freenet.mb.ca
Legislature: 234 - 450 Broadway Winnipeg, MB. R3C 0V8 Tel: 945-1567 Fax: 945-0535 e mail: mcerilli@mts.net

Fratellanza Amatese

November 17, 1998

Mr. Frank Fiorentino
Vice Consulate of Italy
c/o Centro Caboto
1055 Wilkes Avenue
Winnipeg, MB
R3P 2L7

Dear Frank,

On behalf of your Amatese Community and myself, I would like to take this opportunity to congratulate you on your recent appointment as Vice Consulate of Italy. We are confident your expertise and commitment will result in beneficial reward for the entire Italian Community.

If there is any assistance you may require from our membership or myself, please do not hesitate to call.

Once again our sincerest congratulations!

Best Regards.

Stella Mazza
President - Fratelllanza Amatese

BECOMING "ITALIANISSIMO" AS VICE-CONSUL FOR ITALY

BELOW IS THE ITALIAN GOVERNMENT'S DECREE APPOINTING ME VICE CONSUL OF ITALY AS IT APPEARED IN THE ITALIAN GOVERNMENT OFFICIAL GAZZETTA (ROME)

8-10-1998   GAZZETTA UFFICIALE DELLA REPUBBLICA ITALIANA   *Serie generale* - n. 235

2) emanazione di atti conservativi, che non implichino la disposizione dei beni, in materia di successione, naufragio o sinistro aereo;

3) rilascio di certificazioni (esclusi i certificati di residenza all'estero e i certificati di cittadinanza) vidimazioni e legalizzazioni;

4) compiti sussidiari di assistenza agli iscritti di leva ed istruzioni delle pratiche in materia di servizio militare, fermo restando la competenza per qualsiasi tipo di decisione al consolato generale d'Italia in Madrid;

5) effettuazione delle operazioni richieste dalla legislazione vigente in dipendenza dell'arrivo e della partenza di una nave nazionale;

6) tenuta dello schedario dei cittadini e di quello delle firme delle autorità locali.

Il presente decreto verrà pubblicato nella *Gazzetta Ufficiale* della Repubblica italiana.

Roma, 22 settembre 1998

Il Ministro: DINI

98A8734

Limitazione di funzioni del titolare del vice consolato onorario in Winnipeg (Canada)

IL MINISTRO DEGLI AFFARI ESTERI

(Omissis);

Decreta:

Il sig. Francesco Fiorentino, vice console onorario in Winnipeg (Canada), oltre all'adempimento dei generali doveri di difesa degli interessi nazionali e di protezione dei cittadini, esercita le funzioni consolari limitatamente a:

1) ricezione e trasmissione materiale al consolato generale d'Italia in Toronto degli atti di stato civile pervenuti dalle autorità locali, dai cittadini italiani o dai comandanti di aeromobili nazionali o stranieri;

2) ricezione e trasmissione materiale al consolato generale d'Italia in Toronto delle dichiarazioni concernenti lo stato civile da parte dei comandanti di aeromobili;

3) ricezione e trasmissione materiale al consolato generale d'Italia in Toronto dei testamenti formati a bordo di aeromobili;

4) ricezione e trasmissione materiale al consolato generale d'Italia in Toronto degli atti dipendenti dall'apertura di successione in Italia;

5) emanazione di atti conservativi, che non implichino la disposizione di beni, in materia di successione, naufragio o sinistro aereo;

6) rinnovo di passaporti nazionali dei cittadini che siano residenti nella circoscrizione territoriale dell'ufficio consolare onorario, dopo aver interpellato, caso per caso, il consolato generale d'Italia in Toronto;

7) ricezione e trasmissione al consolato generale d'Italia in Toronto della documentazione relativa al rilascio di visti;

8) rilascio di certificazioni (esclusi i certificati di residenza all'estero e i certificati di cittadinanza) vidimazioni e legalizzazioni, autentiche le firme apposte in calce a scritture private;

9) compiti sussidiari di assistenza agli iscritti di leva e di istruzione delle pratiche in materia di servizio militare, fermo restando la competenza per qualsiasi tipo di decisione al consolato generale d'Italia in Toronto;

10) tenuta dello schedario dei cittadini e di quello delle firme delle autorità locali.

Il presente decreto verrà pubblicato nella *Gazzetta Ufficiale* della Repubblica italiana.

Roma, 22 settembre 1998

Il Ministro: DINI

98A8735

Limitazione di funzioni del titolare del vice consolato onorario in Rio Grande (Brasile)

IL MINISTRO DEGLI AFFARI ESTERI

(Omissis);

Decreta:

Il sig. Giovanni Amadori, vice console onorario in Rio Grande (Brasile), oltre all'adempimento dei generali doveri di difesa degli interessi nazionali e di protezione dei cittadini, esercita le funzioni consolari limitatamente a:

1) ricezione e trasmissione materiale al consolato generale d'Italia in Porto Alegre degli atti di stato civile pervenuti dalle autorità locali, dai cittadini italiani o dai comandanti di aeromobili nazionali o stranieri;

2) ricezione e trasmissione materiale al consolato generale d'Italia in Porto Alegre delle dichiarazioni concernenti lo stato civile da parte dei comandanti di aeromobili;

3) ricezione e trasmissione materiale al consolato generale d'Italia in Porto Alegre dei testamenti formati a bordo di aeromobili;

4) ricezione e trasmissione materiale al consolato generale d'Italia in Porto Alegre della documentazione relativa al rilascio di visti;

5) tenuta dello schedario dei cittadini e di quello delle firme delle autorità locali.

Il presente decreto verrà pubblicato nella *Gazzetta Ufficiale* della Repubblica italiana.

Roma, 22 settembre 1998

Il Ministro: DINI

98A8736

Limitazione di funzioni del titolare del consolato onorario in Salisburgo (Austria)

IL MINISTRO DEGLI AFFARI ESTERI

(Omissis);

Decreta:

Il sig. Nicola Nicolelli Fulgenzi, console onorario in Salisburgo (Austria), oltre all'adempimento dei generali doveri di difesa degli interessi nazionali e di protezione dei cittadini, esercita le funzioni consolari limitatamente a:

1) ricezione e trasmissione materiale al consolato generale d'Italia in Innsbruck degli atti di stato civile pervenuti dalle autorità locali, dai cittadini italiani o dai comandanti di aeromobili nazionali o stranieri;

2) rilascio di certificazioni (esclusi i certificati di residenza all'estero e i certificati di cittadinanza) vidimazioni e legalizzazioni emesse gratuitamente ai sensi dell'art. 58 del decreto del Presidente della Repubblica 5 gennaio 1967, n. 200;

3) tenuta dello schedario dei cittadini e di quello delle firme delle autorità locali.

Il presente decreto verrà pubblicato nella *Gazzetta Ufficiale* della Repubblica italiana.

Roma, 22 settembre 1998

Il Ministro: DINI

98A8737

— 29 —

Crescendo to Becoming

I have always considered it a great honor to be the leader of the Italian Community of Winnipeg, to represent the Italian Government in Manitoba and, in addition, to represent the Italian Canadians from Manitoba to Italy. For me, it represents going totally back to my roots, and an opportunity to reconnect and interact more intimately with my *connazionali* in Winnipeg and Manitoba. It was an opportunity to meet many people from many corners of the globe, and from many walks of life. For me personally, it was an opportunity for transformation and self-actualization, to become what I truly longed to be.

So, the moment I took office on July 1, 1998 the first thing I actually did was to move and install the office of the Vice Consulate of Italy into the newly-built *Centro Caboto Centre* at 1055 Wilkes Avenue, for I had already made the commitment that the Vice Consulate of Italy office should and would become henceforth visible and much more easily accessible to all.

The second thing I did was to install **Angela Caputo** in the important position of Vice-Consul Secretary, a person who was well-versed with the needs of the community and knew firsthand most of the people who would be seeking interaction with the office. Her deployment would ensure better delivery of our services to the people, and visible accessibility to the services of the Office.

The third thing I did was to arrange meetings with every group and every organization in the Italian Community, not only to introduce myself, but also to delineate all the functions, services, and responsibilities of the Vice Consul, so that people would be better informed as to what the office was all about. Also, I published a series of information bulletins to give important and timely information on items of interest to those using the services of the Vice Consulate office. (see also below)

BECOMING "ITALIANISSIMO" AS VICE-CONSUL FOR ITALY

Functions of the Vice Consul of Italy (Honorary)

1. PASSPORTS   a. Issuance
                                 b. Renewals
                                 c. Requirements
                                 d. Cost
2. VISA   a. Study
                                 b. Work
                                 c. Tourism
3. ITALIAN CITIZENSHIP   a. First time applicant
                                 b. Re-acquisition
4. VITAL STATISTICS   a. Birth Certificate Registrations in Italy
                                 b. Marriage Certificate "   "   "
                                 c. Death Certificate   "   "   "
5. PENSIONS   a. Old Age
                                 b. Military Service
                                 c. Disability
6. POWER OF ATTORNEY   To Legally Assign Someone:
        (1) A GENERAL POWER OF ATTORNEY OR
        (2) A SPECIAL POWER OF ATTORNEY:
                a. To administer
                b. To Sell
                c. To Buy
                d. To Donate
                e. To Execute a Will and Testament
                f. To Represent someone and carry out whatever is delegated
7. DELEGATIONS   A person delegates someone legally to do something on his behalf
8. DECLARATIONS   To make a legal declarations about something OR AFFIDAVIT (i.e. to declare a loss of a passport)
9. TRANSLATIONS   Translating documents into English or Italian

10. LEGALIZATIONS AND AUTHENTICATIONS OF DOCUMENTS
11. OBLIGATORY REGISTRATIONS FOR MILITARY SERVICE AT AGE 18 (NOTE: Law changed on December 31, 2005 making military service in Italy no longer obligatory but voluntary.)
12. STUDENT EXCHANGES BETWEEN ITALY AND CANADA
13. DEPORTATIONS OF PERSONS "NON GRATA" BACK TO ITALY
14. ARRANGING DOCUMENTATION FOR TRANSFERING OF CORPSES AND URNS FOR BURIAL IN ITALY
15. ARRANGING FOR CITIZENS RETURNING TO ITALY PERMANENTALY
16. ARRAGING FOR RETURN OF MONEY INVESTED OR DEPOSITED IN ITALY
17. SEARCHES TO FIND INDIVIDUALS FROM ITALY IN CANADA
18. LEGAL NOTIFICATION AND DELIVERY OF COURT PAPERS
19. ARRANGEMENTS TO BRING SPECIAL ITEMS TO ITALY (DOGS, GUNS, ETC)
20. BRINGING GREETINGS ON BEHALF OF THE ITALIAN GOVERNMENT TO MANY EVENTS IN THE COMMUNITY

TWO OF MY RESPECTED VICE COUNSULS PREDECESSORS IN WINNIPEG

Domenico Povoledo
Former Italian Vice Consul of Manitoba

Giovanni Mottola
Former Italian Vice Consul of Manitoba

BECOMING "ITALIANISSIMO" AS VICE-CONSUL FOR ITALY

IL BOLLETTINO
Del Vice Console d'Italia

1055 Wilkes Avenue, Winnipeg, Manitoba R3P 2L7 — Telefono: (204) 488-8745 Fax: (204) 487-3460

Anno 1 Numero 1 — Agosto 1998

MESSAGGIO DI FRANCESCO FIORENTINO VICE CONSOLE D'ITALIA IN MANITOBA

CARISSIMI CONNAZIONALI:

Sono lieto porgervi un messaggio e desideroso di informarvi della nomina recentemente assegnatami dal Console Generale d'Italia di Toronto Dr. Leonardo Sampoli, alla carica di Vice Console Onorario per la provincia del Manitoba.
Nell' assumere l'incarico, mi propongo di rendere più accessibile le varie operazioni consolari richieste da tutti voi.
A tale scopo, mi prefiggo di rispondere e risolvere con entusiasmo patriottico le vostre numerose esigenze individuali, recando non solo rinnovamenti essenziali alla carica, ma abbracciando anche il vostro pensiero, e cercando di semplificare tutto a Vostro favore.
Si cercherà anche di promuovere il nostro patrimonio artistico, sociale e culturale italiano, dando la forza e incoraggiando ai giovani a partecipare nella vita comunitaria, gettando le basi alle future generazioni di questa grande provincia canadese.
Gli uffici del Vice Console si trovano presso il nuovo *Centro Caboto Centre*, rappresentando per gli italiani del Manitoba un palazzo da sentire ognuno grande orgoglio.
Ho voluto segnalare un breve commento sul *Centro Caboto Centre*, per rinsaldare sotto unico tetto la vostra presenza distintamente valida al successo degli italiani ed italo-canadesi in Manitoba.
Riportandoci al nostro ufficio consolare tengo a precisare che, s'interessa di pratiche consolari e funziona in maniera **apolitica**, rispetto a qualsiesi altra forma operativa esistente nel *Centro* stesso.
Il Vice Consolato d'Italia a Winnipeg, come è noto,

Frank Fiorentino
VICE CONSOLE d'ITALIA

MESSAGE FROM FRANK FIORENTINO VICE CONSUL OF ITALY IN MANITOBA

I am very pleased to announce my recent appointment as Vice Consul of Italy for the Province of Manitoba effective July 1, 1998. I consider it both an honor and privilege to serve in this capacity. My motivation for accepting the challenging assignment arises out of a real sense of personal satisfaction and fulfillment to provide a much-needed service to Italians and those of Italian descent in Manitoba.
My vision as Vice Consul is quite clear: to create and maintain a knowledgeable and efficient system of delivery of services to all the Italians and Italian-Canadians of this province in an environment that is user-friendly, accessible, open, and visible. Ultimately, the goal is to enhance the quality of our life and lifestyle by developing a strong sense of pride in our rich and glorious Italian roots, culture, and heritage.
Language is the "carrier" of culture and heritage. When a language dies, so does the "glue" and bonding with our traditions, our culture, and our heritage. It is imperative that our language be a living language, used and promoted in every way possible if our very culture is to flourish. It is my declared intent to actively model this belief and promote our precious and most beautiful language. Once again in my life, I am focussing on it as an enthusiastic learner of it, and find it growth-producing and rewarding.
I see my appointment as a new beginning, that coincides with a new era for all Italians and Italian-Canadians in Manitoba. The opening of our new *Centro Caboto Centre* symbolizes this new birth which has consumed our thoughts for many years and is now, a dream come true. It is important, not

Crescendo to Becoming

MESSAGGIO (cont.)

serve circa 20.000 connazionali che sono cittadini italiani o canadesi di origine italiana che risiedono nella circoscrizione di questa vasta provincia.
I compiti del Vice Consolato sono molto numerosi sia nel campo dei servizi al pubblico, sia in quello della tutela degli interessi della collettività e del mantenimento e sviluppo dei suoi legami culturali, linguistici e sociali con l'Italia.

LE FUNZIONI PRINCIPALI VICE-CONSOLARI SONO:

Rappresentanza
Il Vice Console rappresenta l'Italia e le sue leggi a tutti i connazionali del Manitoba, ed è, anche, l'autorità italiana che vi rappresenta in Italia.
Si fara di tutto per assistere e proteggere tutti i nostri connazionali del Manitoba e per creare un rapporto d'armonia in seno alla nostra comunità.

Informazioni:
I connazionali possono considerare il Vice Console come fiduciario del governo italiano, anche per somme elargite ai Club o Società da parte del governo italiano.
Il Ministero degli Affari Esteri di Roma emana sempre nuove leggi che sono a disposizione di Voi tutti in ufficio o tramite Il Bollettino.
Se avete proprietà immobilare in Italia, occorre essere al corrente delle recenti disposizioni legali e i regolamenti concernenti le tasse.

Passaporti:
Il passaporto è un documento personale molto importante. Esso distingue la vostra personale identità agli effetti nazionali, ed internazionali.
Il passaporto serve anche per farvi riconoscere quando desiderate viaggiare in Italia o in altri paesi. Però, il passaporto ha importanza solo se si mantiene aggiornato, cioè se non è scaduto.
Dalla data del rilascio, il passaporto italiano ha una durata di 5 anni e può essere rinnovato per altri 5 anni. Dopo 10 anni, il passaporto deve essere sostituito con rilascio di nuovo libretto.
Il passaporto nuovo costa circa 57 dollari canadesi, mentre il solo rinnovo costa circa 49 dollari canadesi; gli importi possono variare ogni 3 mesi a causa del cambio lira/dollaro canadese o ache per variazioni del costo del servizio deciso per Legge in Italia.

Cittadinanza
Il Vice Consolato segue le vicende di cittadinanza degli italiani che vivono nella circoscrizione del

MESSAGE (cont.)

because it is a new building, but because it represents our collective, renewed commitment to contribute immeasurably to the richness of the Canadian mosaic and to the quality of life in Manitoba and in Canada as we have always done.

We must realize that with the many benefits that we enjoy as a result of being Italian/Canadian we must meet our obligations and/or duties, for there can be no benefits without responsibilities. Our democratic way of life is based on the principle of freedom with responsibility. We cannot have one without the other.

As the direct and official representative of the Italian Government in Manitoba, the activities of the Vice Consul are of particular interest both individually and collectively to all Italian citizens in Manitoba, to those that hold dual citizenship (Italian/Canadian) and to those of Italian descent who have or wish to maintain a bonding with their Italian roots.

The major functions of the Vice Consulate deal with educational, cultural, and social assistance in the following major areas:
Representation
Information Dissemination
Passports Issue and Renewal
Visas (to secondary students and workers)
Academic Information
Social Assistance
Legal Matters
Pensions
Vital Statistics
Education
Citizenship
Military Matters
Other

In order to better facilitate the utilization of the many services outlined above we are pleased to announce the establishment of this periodic publication entitled *"Il Bollettino del Vice Vice Console d'Italia"* which has as its primary purpose, the provision and delivery of information about the operation, services, and programs provided by the Vice Consulate of Italy in Manitoba, knowing fully well that "ignorance of the law" is not a legitimate excuse for what we do, or for what we fail to do. Being a good citizen in a democratic society demands that we keep well-informed. It is our intent to facilitate this process through this bulletin which will be distributed through many city outlets for your convenience. These outlets will include the *Centro Caboto Centre*, the *Holy Rosary Church*, the various Clubs, Associations and Italian-owned businesses.

BECOMING "ITALIANISSIMO" AS VICE-CONSUL FOR ITALY

MESSAGGIO (cont.)

Manitoba. Chi sono i cittadini italiani? Come si acquista la cittadinanza italiana? Cosa bisogna fare per acquistare la doppia cittadinanza? Quali sono i diritti e i doveri dai cittidinani italiani? Queste sono le domande che il Vice Console può chiarire per voi.

Pensioni
Per quelli della "terza età", per quanto riguarda le pensioni, cosa hanno deciso o stabilito a Roma ultimamente? Conoscere gli effetti fa bene a tutti. Il Vice Console fornisce informazioni sul sistema pensionistico italiano, autorizza le visite mediche per coloro che richiedono la pensione di invalidità, notifica gli atti provenienti dall'Italia riguardanti le pensioni, e certifica l'esistenza in vita per quei tipi di pensione per i quali è richiesta.

Assistenza Sociale
Il Vice Consolato tutela quei connazionali che si trovano in difficoltà, e s'interessa di problematiche legate alla situazione dei minori e dei rientri definitivi in Italia. Per il rientro definitivo in Italia, sono previste delle agevolazioni doganali. Per questo tipo di pratica si prega di contattare l'ufficio che vi indicherà i documenti necessari che debbono essere presentati e fissare un appuntamento.

Stato Civile
Lo Stato Civile si occupa delle vicende dei cittadini italiani dalla nascita fino alla morte. Esso si occupa di nascite, matrimoni, divorzi, decessi, che devono essere segnalati ai Comuni italiani di ultima residenza, in maniera tale che le autorità italiane siano informate di ciò che accade ai cittadini italiani all'estero.

Anagrafe degli Italiani all'Estero(A.I.R.E.)
L'anagrafe si occupa di aggiornare i Comuni italiani sui cambi di residenza di coloro che risiedono all'estero. Presso ogni Comune in Italia esiste un ufficio AIRE che tiene traccia di tutti gli italiani residenti all'estero. Questi dati devono esssere sempre aggiornati da parte degli stessi cittadini italiani che sono residenti in Canada.

Funzioni Notarili e Legali
Queste sono le funzioni che in Italia sono normalmente eseguite dai notai, come procure ed autentiche di firma. Si notificano anche gli atti provenienti dai tribunali e dalle amministrazioni italiane indirizzati a coloro che resiedono nella circoscrizione del Vice Consolato.

MESSAGE (cont.)

In addition to my personal involvement, *Il Bollettino* will have other writers on a volunteer basis such as Bernardo Tucci, Mario Audino, Angela Caputo, and others as they come forward.

As to the hours of operation of the Vice Consulate office, we have increased the hours of operation considerably in the hope and expectation that this will provide greater flexibility and access to our services. The new hours of operation are as follows:

MONDAY: 9:30 a.m. - 4:30 p.m.
TUESDAY: 9:30 a.m. - 12:00 p.m.
WEDNESDAY: 1:00 p.m. - 8:30 p.m.
THURSDAY: 9:30 a.m. - 12:00 p.m.
FRIDAY: 9:30 a.m. - 12:00 p.m.

In order to run our office more efficiently and to provide better service to you, we request that you govern yourself in accordance to two basic points:
1) Please make an appointment if you wish to see or to talk to the Vice Consul himself; and
2) The Vice Consul will be present at the office every Monday and Wednesday at the hours outlined above

One of our first priorities will be the creation of a current database of every Italian and Italian-Canadian citizen living in Manitoba. We will be asking you to register with us by providing us with some very basic information about yourself.

To summarize, we have undertaken to make the Vice Consulate of Italy responsive to the needs of the Italians and Italian-Canadians of Manitoba. Keeping in mind that the nature of the functions require meticulous attention to detail and rigid adherence to requirements of Italian law, we are within these constraints, trying to make the often difficult process as "user-friendly" as possible.

It is our intent to make the Office of the Vice Consulate quite accessible, highly visible and interactive with the Italian community of Manitoba. We must demonstrate that we can make a worthwhile contribution to this community by living both individually and collectively, in harmony with each other, and with other ethnic communities.

Finally, I wish to extend my appreciation to those that have made a commitment to sponsor this bulletin.

On behalf of the President of the Italian Republic Oscar Luis Scalfaro, the Ambassador to Canada His Excellency Andrea Negrotto Cambiaso, the Consul General of Italy Dr. Leonardo Sampoli, I add my personal best wishes for your health and happiness.

Respectfully,
Francesco (Frank) Fiorentino
Vice Console d'Italia

Crescendo to Becoming

MY FIRST MAJOR SPEECH DELIVERED AS VICE COUNSUL OF ITALY ON THE OCCASION OF THE SEVENTY-FIFTH ANNIVERSARY OF THE HOLY ROSARY CHURCH HELD AT THE CONVENTION CENTER, WINNIPEG, 1998

Mr. Chairperson, Your Grace Archbishop Wall, religiosi padri, distinguished head table guests, ladies and gentlemen, connazionali ed amici ... buona sera:

E un onore e mio vivo piacere partecipare insieme con voi in questa bellisima e storica serata in occasione del settantacinquesimo anniversario della Chiesa del Santo Rosario. In nome della communità italiana di questa provincia, vorrei rivolgere alcune parole di testimonianza, in augurio e anche per riconoscere l'immenso contributo della nostra parrocchia.

La mia conoscenza personale di questa codesta parrocchia ha incominciato precisamente nel 1949, circa 50 anni fa, arrivato qui a Winnipeg insieme mia intera famiglia che consisteva da mio padre, mia madre e cinque figli. (Il sesto nacque poco dopo, nel 1951).

Ma qual'era veramente lo stato e il pensiero del l'emigrante italiano di quell'epoca? La risposta a questa domanda si contiene, io penso, nei pochi versi di una poesia lirica, scritta da mio padre, felice sua memoria, circa il 1952, che va cosi:

Amato era il mio paese,
Dove suonava l'avvemmaria,
E ogni giorno di ogni mese,
Mamma mia bella pregava in chiesa.

Qui non c'e' questo, non c'e campane,
Non c'e più mamma che mi vuol bene,
Passano i giorni, le settimane,
Ma il conforto, non tanto viene.

Qui non c'e questo, c'e solo pane,
E poi del resto,...so tutte pene.

Ho fatto coraggio a recitare questi pochi righi di questa poesia per farvi sentire più meglio, la forte tristezza, la malinconia e l'angoscia che ardeva nel cuore di mio padre, e penso, certo, nel cuore di molti altri emigranti.

BECOMING "ITALIANISSIMO" AS VICE-CONSUL FOR ITALY

E pensate un pò cosa avrebbe a loro accaduto se non ci fosse stata la chiesa del Santo Rosario, che per tanti di noi era l'unico focolare, il rifugio, e l'appoggio, in questa terra non solo straniera, ma strana a tutti i nostri ambienti.

La nostra chiesa e stata il centro non solo per il mantenimento dei nostri valori, ma un centro ch'era anche il sostenitore che dava coraggio agli emigranti e che facilitava anche la loro propria sopravvivenza.

Si può dire che la nostra parrocchia era il centro che ci riuniva, il centro dove si andava per soddisfare i nostri bisogni non solo spirituali, ma anche i nostri bisogni sociali e culturali. Era solo lì dove eravamo veramente benvenuti, abbracciati, dove ci sentivamo accettati, e graditi. Era li, sul l'incrocio di Sherbrook e Bannatyne, frequentamente sotto al basement, dove si sentiva parlare la nostra bella lingua, dove ci potevamo esprimere con i nostri propri ambienti italiani.

Bisogna ricordare che i nostri parroci religiosi eravamo sempre li, nel centro dell'azione, con noi, a dare vita a tante iniziative a noi interessante. Per esempio, *la Dante Alighieri* fu fondata dal nostro illustro Bernardo Tucci, ma al suo canto era Padre Depalma. Il Club Italo-canadese fu fondato da Tony Bogdanich, Raffaele Cantafio con molti altri di noi, insieme la presenza di Padre Fiore. E mi ricordo anche che nel 1955 al basement della chiesa, che fu lanciata la mia orchestra « Amati 5 » e poi il "Combo Italiano" che cercava di portare un pò d'italianità ed allegria ai nostri connazionali.

E tutto ciò ci fa ricordare che come in Italia la domenica era un giorno veramente speciale. Si andava a messa, e poi s'incontrava e s'incoraggiava i nostri concittadini che arrivavano in gran numero giorno per giorno dall'Italia, e poi si andava a casa ad ascoltare *"La Voce Italiana"* presentata sempre del nostro Bernardo Tucci sulla radio.

In conclusione, la contribuzione della nostra chiesa italiana e stata veramente vasta e incommensurabile sempre a far migliorare la qualità di vita, diciamo, non solo per i membri della communità italiana, ma anche per tutti gli altri parrochiali.

I wish to say a few brief comments in English, not to translate what I have already said, but simply to capture the essence of what I said in Italian.

I can capsulize what I said like this:

Crescendo to Becoming

Never has so much,
Been done for so many,
For such a long time,
By relatively so few.

From Father Furlan in the 1950's to Father Sam Argenziano in the present time, we have been bonded and linked together during the last 50 years in our church by many dedicated, caring people such as the always present Father Fiore, and Peter Maruca the church's choirmaster, who's been a constant since 1947. They all deserve these accolades for their dedication and perseverance. The priests gave us a sense of spiritual harmony with God and provided social and cultural sustenance of our homeland which we all craved.

I wish to testify and recognize that the Holy Rosary Church, from the very beginning, certainly during the past 50 years, has been a veritable pillar of strength and support for the members of the Italian community. If not for the Holy Rosary Church, I am sure that particularly in the early years, many of our people would have found life in the new land, unbearable.

It must be acknowledged that the Holy Rosary Church has significantly contributed to the quality of our very life, and that its role in helping us define who we really are collectively as a people, has been unsurpassed.

In closing I wish to thank all those that have and are still contributing and giving so much for our benefit, both individually and collectively. I thank them with a prayer that I usually reserve for my favorite friends and relatives, which reads:

May the road rise up to meet you,
May the wind be always at your back
May the rain fall softly upon your faces,
And to the end of time,
May the good Lord, hold you all,
in the palm of His hands.

Grazie, e buona sera.

ASS. NAZ. ALPINI
WINNIPEG

BECOMING "ITALIANISSIMO" AS VICE-CONSUL FOR ITALY

Frank Fiorentino "Inducted" as an Honorary Member of the Alpini Group of Winnipeg, 2001. (I am seated front row, second from right.)

Left to Right: Me, City of Winnipeg Councillor Franco Magnifico, and Executive Director of the Italian Chamber of Commerce of Manitoba Anna-Maria Toppazzini, 2004

Crescendo to Becoming

TIPICO DISCORSO DEL QUATTRO DI NOVEMBRE IN ONORE DEI NOSTRI CADUTI IN QUERRA

Padre Sam, Diacono Vince Catalano, Capo Gruppo d'Alpini Gildo di Biaggio e fratelli alpini, signore e signori, connazionali ed amici, buon pomeriggio:

Inanzitutto vorrei esprimere la mia graditudine e riconoscere lo sforzo di coloro che s'incaricano ogni anno ad organizzare questa funzione cosi significativa e solenne per tutti noi. In particolare vorrei riconoscere a lei Signora Presidente Adriana Lombardini incluso i componenti del club Italian Canadian Foundation, a lei capo gruppo degli alpini Signor Gildo di Biaggio e gli alpini qui presenti, a lei Roy Paltronetti, presidente del Centro Caboto incluso gli attuali dirigenti e personale del Centro, e naturalmente ringraziare a lei Padre Sam Argenziano incluso il nostro Diacono Vince Catalano, Pietro Maruca e il nostro coro, e il giovane Andrew Coleman, musicista di tromba --che senza la loro piena cooperazione e disponibilità, questa funzione non avrebbe lostesso significato ed apprezzamento.

In rappresentanza del governo italiano è mio onore partecipare con voi come al solito, è sempre con una certa emozione e con orgoglio che rivolgo ancora una volta un messaggio a tutti i partecipanti in questa importante e sacra occasione del quattro di novembre, un giorno che sempre risuscita in me un sentimento d'impegno morale e di grande affetto, perchè veramente é un giorno questo principalmente di ricordo e di riflessione, e amplificare un pò su i motivi per cui noi siamo qui oggi e sul vero senso di questa memorabile giornata.

Siamo qui oggi per fare il nostro dovere morale, perchè la nostra storia di chi noi siamo ci obbliga e c'impone di ricordare quello che si é stati, e quello che si é fatto per noi.

Siamo qui oggi come dicono gli alpini per "onorare i morti aiutando i vivi" e onorarli con tutto il nostro essere coloro figli della nostra patria che vissero la tragedia di dolorosi, e massimi sacrifici per tutti noi.

Siamo qui oggi per riflettere sulla necessità di non tradire la memoria dei nostri caduti difendendo la pace che i nostri giovani e padri ci hanno consegnato, pagando un prezzo altissimo, e compiendo il loro dovere verso la loro, e la nostra patria.

BECOMING "ITALIANISSIMO" AS VICE-CONSUL FOR ITALY

Siamo qui oggi per riconoscere che abbiamo un immenso debbito che bisogna assolutamente ripagare almeno con un segno di rispetto e di ammirazione una volta all'anno.

Siamo qui oggi per dare testimonianza ed attestare che il grande sacrificio dei nostri caduti non fu in vano.

Siamo qui oggi perchè vogliamo tentare di sanare tutte le ferite, sanarle, senza di nuovo riaprire le piaghe e l'amarezze, che la storia del passato e contemporaneamente ha impietosamente prodotto .

Siamo qui oggi per dimostrare ai nostri figli ed ai figli dei nostri figli il mantenimento della memoria del passato, ma operando nel presente e nel futuro, e sempre con i nostri diversi valori italiani.

Siamo qui oggi per mai dimenticare la memoria, poichè un popolo senza memoria non ha storia, e un popolo senza storia non avrà futuro.

Siamo qui oggi per dare espressione ai nostri valori di dignità umana e fierezza di chi noi siamo.

Siamo qui oggi per parlare un pò dei nostri cari Alpini Italiani perchè come ben sappiamo il quattro di novembre e un giorno molto significativo e caro nei cuori degli alpini italiani. In fatti, per gli alpini il quattro di novembre è, e sarà un giorno veramente indimenticabile. Essi sono i custodi di un' estimabile eredità che discende dall'orgoglio di aver servito nel corpo degli alpini, dalle antiche tradizioni delle genti italiane e di montagna, e da tante gloriose pagine di storia che tramandano il valore in guerra di soldati di ieri, e l'impegno di quelli di oggi in missioni all'estero, per il mantenimento della pace. Questo è il retaggio che ha guidato e guida generazioni di alpini ad offrire incondizionata prova di attaccamento alla patria, e che oggi li spinge, alle popolazioni bisognose, in missioni multinazionali di pace in Ialia, e ai paesi esteri.

Di modo più specifico, colgo l'occasione oggi di onorare la memoria dei nostri fratelli alpini di questo gruppo autonomo di Winnipeg deceduti nei giorni e negl'anni passati di cui mi pregio di far parte con una certa fierezza, e anche di alpino onorario. In questo riguardo vorrei richiedere al capo gruppo un attenti degli alpini presenti per ricordare espressamente gli alpini non più con noi fisicamente ma con noi in spirito.

Capo gruppo, per cortesia, un attenti per ricordare i nostri soci/compagni già defunti:

Crescendo to Becoming

1. *Cenedese Orlando*............ *1972*
2. *Bin Bruno* *1977*
3. *Franz Agostino* *1984*
4. *Altarui Armando* *1988*
5. *Cosentino Agostino* *1992*
6. *Povoledo Domenico* *1995*
7. *Franz Claudio Simone*....... *1996*
8. *Croatto Aldo* *1997*
9. *Rinaldi Giulio* *1999*
10. *Boriero Valentino* *2000*
11. *Busca Giulio* *2003*
12. *D'Angelo Carmine*........... *2004*
13. *Rizzuto Phillip Antonio*..... *2004*

La terza ragione che siamo qui oggi e per ricordare anche tutti i nostri cari familiari ed amici defunti i cui dei nomi sono incisi sulla parete fuori nella nostra piazza accanto a la galleria. Lì, noi assisteremo a Padre Sam che celebrerà una breve funzione religiosa di benedizione in onore di tutti coloro nostri cari familiari ed avi gia defunti, ma che rimangono sempre vicini nei nostri cuori

Ladies and gentlemen,

On the eleventh hour, of the eleventh day, of the eleventh month, we shall remember all who are gone from our lives: soldiers, family members, and personal friends who paid the ultimate sacrifice with their own lives with this beautiful commitment:

In the rising of the sun and in its going down
We remember them.
In the freshness of spring and in the warmth of summer
We remember them.
In the rustling of the leaves and the beauty of autumn
We remember them.
In the chill of winter and the blowing winds
We remember them.
In the beginning of the year and when it ends
We remember them.

BECOMING "ITALIANISSIMO" AS VICE-CONSUL FOR ITALY

In the laughter of a child and in the singing of the bride
We remember them.
When we are weary and in need of strength
We remember them.
When we are lost and sick at heart
We remember them.
When we have joys we wish to share
We remember them.
So long as we live, they too shall live,
For they are part of us .....
They shall grow not old
As we that are left grow old;
Age shall not weary them.
Nor the years condemn.
At the going down of the sun,
And in the morning
We will remember them! *Yes, we will remember them!*
Thank you and grazie

Crescendo to Becoming

ITALIAN CHAMBER MANITOBA NEWS

Carpe Diem

Francesco Fiorentino,
Honorary Vice Consul of Italy in Manitoba

"Carpe Diem", "seize the day", "seize the opportunity". It is a Latin phrase that has always provided great inspiration in my personal life, and a great motivational tool to use as an educator that has empowered and impacted significantly and positively the lives of many of my students.

It is a phrase that has come into clear focus once again in my life with new significance in describing the essence of the exciting movement that is unfolding in Manitoba and Western Canada, largely through the worthwhile initiatives of the Camera di Commercio Italiana del Manitoba, a modern and vibrant organization that thinks globally and acts both locally and globally. As an Honorary Vice Consul of Italy, as an educational and motivational consultant, as community worker, and as a proud Italian Canadian, I have watched with sheer delight, the great efforts of this organization to "seize the opportunity" to make a meaningful contribution to building bilateral partnerships. I am an admirer of the organization's commitment to its stated noble vision and mission to reach out both within and well beyond our borders to promote co-operation, constructive dialogue, and mutual understanding with the people of Italy and people across the globe. As an invited and active "honorary member" of this organization, I am even more appreciative of the efforts of its founding members such as Leonard Copetti, Frank Bueti, Maria de Nardi, Josie D'Andrea, Anna Maria Toppazzini for their vision and for their past and present enlightened and effective leadership they have provided.

In the world of human endeavour human interaction is everything. The Camera di Commercio Italiana del Manitoba has principled leadership both at the Board and Executive levels, leadership based on strategic planning that promotes human and technological interaction with people of countries and regions that have mutual vision and interests, with end-outcomes being not only reciprocal economic benefits, but also invaluable linkages established in the spirit of developing a human and friendly bond between the participating "partners".

In these times of globalization in which we live, those that have an interest in commerce must become well aware that there are today, in fact, two Italys, the Italy we all know with specific boundaries, wonderfully and strategically positioned within the European community, and the other Italy which has no specific boundaries, but with perhaps even more global interconnectedness and influence, an Italy composed of the millions of hyphenated Italians who have legally acquired double citizenship, and all those like me, far from our original roots, who in their hearts still feel a strong attachment to Italy, its people, its places, and its culture.

Yes, Italy today as a fifth leading economic giant, is strategically well-positioned to interact meaningfully with many communities not just in Europe but world-wide. But so is Canada in general, and Manitoba in particular, the "heart of the North American continent", "open for business" and strategically well-positioned for providing new and varied opportunities in an inviting, stable, and positive business climate. Manitoba (and Western Canada) is a relatively new and exciting frontier, offering opportunities for meaningful interactive networks with potential for profitable results, ultimately leading to intrinsic benefits to our collective and individual lives.

In summation, Italy and Canada today are both looking to the future, committed to the promotion of stronger economic and other ties, recognizing the vast potential for new trade and commerce, investment, and more importantly, to fostering greater interactive networking and understanding between the two peoples. Let's not be afraid to seize this glorious opportunity for contributing pro-actively to the enrichment of our lives within the great Canadian mosaic.

"Carpe Diem"

Fall 2002 | Italy Canada Trade

Article Written by me for publication in Italy **Canada Trade** *(now called* **Partners***),*
fall issue, 2002

BECOMING "ITALIANISSIMO" AS VICE-CONSUL FOR ITALY

On the Occasion of the 2000 Diplomatic Forum

The Honourable Gary Doer
Premier of Manitoba
and Ms. Ginny Devine
request the pleasure of your company
at a reception on
Thursday, October 19th, 2000
from 7:00 p.m. to 9:00 p.m.
at the Manitoba Museum of Man and Nature
190 Rupert Avenue

THIS INVITATION IS NON-TRANSFERABLE
PLEASE PRESENT INVITATION AT DOOR   DRESS: BUSINESS SUIT/CULTURAL DRESS

CANADA

On the occasion of
the International Conference on War-Affected Children
The Honourable Lloyd Axworthy
Minister of Foreign Affairs of Canada
and
The Honourable Maria Minna
Minister for International Cooperation of Canada
request the pleasure of your company
at the Opening Ceremony
Saturday, September 16, 2000 at 10 a.m.
Pantages Theatre
180 Market Avenue, Winnipeg, Manitoba

Guests are requested to arrive at exactly 9:15 a.m. with this invitation card
Business Suit   National Dress

MY SPEECH TO THE AMICI ABBRUZZESI CLUB, (2007)

Mr. Chairman, ladies and gentlemen, friends, signore e signori, cannazionali ed amici, buona sera:

In rappresentanza del governo italiano e, in nome della communita italiana che io ho l'onore di rappresentare, mi sia permesso innanzitutto estendere la più sincera gratitudine per l'invito a partecipare insieme con voi in questa piacevole serata, e a dire che mi e particolarmente gradito porgere i miei più distinti e cordiali saluti augurali a lei Signor Presidente Racciatti e a tutti i componenti del esecutivo e a tutti i soci del club **A*mici Abbruzzesi.***

Mi approfitto di questi festaggiamenti da voi organizzati, per unirmi ai vostri e miei amici e concittadini, a farle così giungere non solo i miei voti beneauguranti, ma anche i miei sentiti auguri e le più vive congratulazioni per i notevoli traguardi raggiunti, e per i progetti che grazie al supporto degli abbruzzesi, saranno senz'altro realizzati nel futuro. Si puo oggi attestare che da quasi 10 anni il club si riconosce unito, e che trova la sua identità nei principi di amicizia, di fratellanza e di uguaglianza, e che continua à riscuotere successo tra coloro che vogliono abbinare ai valori lodevoli ed umani in un ambiente ancora di tipo molto italiano. Io non so di preciso lo scopo della fondazione del club A*mici Abbruzzesi*, ma son ben certo che lo scopo fu per non dimenticare mai la nostra cultura, i nostri radici, le nostre tradizioni, per mai perdere la nostra identità di chi noi siamo e da dove veniamo. Per noi lontani della patria che ci ha dato luogo luce e vita, essere insieme in amicizia e una grande ricchezza.

Mi è gradito anche rivolgere un vivo plauso ed apprezzamento a tutti voi presenti uniti in questa atmosfera di amicizia e di allegria.

Infine, vorrei esprimere un sincero ringraziamento verso gli *Amici Abbruzzesi* riconoscendo il loro appoggio visibile e concreto verso le iniziative della comunità italiana intera di questa circoscrizione consolare. Essere uniti per ottenere le visioni della collettività italiana di questa provincia sono e rimangono molto importante per noi tutti. E in un modo di più personale, sarà mio vivo piacere durante queste due o tre ore stasera fare conoscenza con tutti i nostri connazionali ed amici, uno per uno.

Di nuovo, grazie, buona sera, e buon divertimento.

* * *

BECOMING "ITALIANISSIMO" AS VICE-CONSUL FOR ITALY

A SPEECH OF MINE DELIVERED IN 2004 ON THE OCCASION OF THE TWENTY-FIFTH ANNIVERSARY OF FATHER SAM ARGENZIANO, HELD AT THE CENTRO CABOTO CENTRE.

Mr. Chairperson, Your Grace Archbishop Wiseberger, Fathers Sam, Ron, and Olds, Diacono Vince Catalano, ladies and gentlemen, signore e signori, connazionali ed amici, buona sera:

Innanzi tutto vorrei esprimere la mia graditudine al nostro Diacono Vince Catalano ed ai suoi componenti del comitato organizzativo, che si sono prestati Cosi generosamente per garantire il successo dell'occasione, e anche per aver consentito a farmi partecipare insieme con voi, in questa bellisima festa-manifestazione di riconoscimento di Padre Sam. Partecipo dunque con tutto il cuore alla cerimonia, e alla richiesta degli incaricati, e son molto lieto ad assumere il ruolo di portavoce indistintamente di tutti i connazionali italiani di questa comunità. Questo riconoscimento per Padre Sam stasera è senz'altro ampiamente meritato, ed è una testimonianza tangibile del suo immenso contributo sul campo religioso e spirituale, che si esprime con dedicazione e devozione, al servizio non solo della collettività italiana, ma anche della comunità intera di questa città.

Ma in verità, chi è quest' uomo a mezzo a noi così affabile? Questo nostro parroco con un accento così strano? E perchè ci vogliamo tutti tanto bene?

Padre Sam è uno dei primi cittadini della nostra cumunità, e mi accorgo con compiacimento che Padre Sam svolge un ruolo di primo piano sulla scena di questa comunità. Al riguardo del suo impegno si può dire che si svolge non solo nel campo religioso ma anche come grande difensore dei nostri importanti ed apprezzati valori, in un campo che oggi più che mai fortemente accresciutosi sempre di più.

Con grande sforzo, determinazione e passione, Padre Sam si dedica a proseguire le sue azioni con appoggio concreto alle numerose esigenze della comunità, al servizio del benessere dei nostri connazionali, e nei confronti dei quali noi tutti proviamo riconoscenza ed amicizia.

Direi anche che Padre Sam e un uomo di cuore e di animo italiano. La sua distinta italianità si vede sul fatto che lui ama l'italia, e tutto quello che rappresenta l'italia di oggi e del passato. Lui è talmente entusiasto del suo proprio e vero legame con l'italia, e si rende conto che l'italia è la terra dove di più meglio, il corso della storia e delle civiltà è illustrato. Questo lascito culturale è un punto che alimenti il nostro amore verso l'Italia e anche lui si sente nel cuore l'amore e l'orgoglio dei suoi radici italiani che lo attirono visibilmente a noi, e alla terra natia dei suoi genitori. Il suo D.N.A. è italiano al 100 %.

Padre Sam ama la vita e amando la vita Padre Sam ama mangiare all'italiana e lo dimostra con un appetito di tipo vero italiano. Io so che anche stasera lui avrà portato in tasca i peperoncini piccanti come lo facciamo tanti altri di noi. Si, e vero che lui ama la cucina italiana, e la cucina francese, americana, spagnola, cinese, canadese, ecc., ecc. Quando si tratta di mangiare Padre Sam ama la globalizzazione.

Ormai si sa che Padre Sam fa parte della nostra famiglia italiana di questa provincia ed è ormai uno di noi. Lui e sempre con noi e noi con lui. Lui appartiene a noi e noi a lui.

Ma il punto saliente, cioè il fortissimo di Padre Sam è certamente il suo carattere umanitario che si nota nelle sue espressioni d'amicizia infaticabile con tutti e che arricchisce tutti coloro fortunati a fare la sua conoscenza. Infatti, Padre Sam è sempre resoluto con il sorriso in faccia, e ci presenta una prospettiva sempre positiva. Lui dimostra di avere un cuore sensibile, nobile e tranquillo, che rende sempre facile ad avvicinarlo ed a volerci bene. **Il suo viso fiducioso rifletta l'immenso amore profondo che Padre Sam sente nel cuore per Gesù Cristo Nostro Signore, ed in lui, cioè, sul viso di Padre Sam, noi vediamo specchiare lo splendore della luce divina di Dio.**

Padre Sam, chiudo il discorso italiano formulando a lei i miei piu cari auguri sperandomi con tutti qui presenti che la nostra celebrazione di riconoscimento questa sera rappresenta per lei un ricco e prezioso momento di soddisfazione e di gioa, nella tua carriera e nella tua vita.

Ed io, in qualità di Vice Console d'Italia, porgo a lei caro Padre Sam, il mio più rispettoso, e spero di lei gradito elogio, con distinzione ed onore.

Ladies and gentlemen:

On behalf of the Italian Government, its ambassador and consul general, and on my personal behalf, I am delighted to extend heartfelt congratulations to Father Sam on this wonderful occasion of his 25th anniversary as a man of God in the service of mankind. I am also here tonight representing all those clubs and people of Italian descent that wanted to speak and convey their best wishes to Father Sam, but whose role, in the interest of time, was delegated to me to do the honor. Father Sam, please accept these words and thoughts as a sincere expression of our collective and individual feelings of friendship, respect, appreciation and love that we all have for you.

So, Father Sam, how do we love thee? Well, let me count some of the ways:

Father Sam, we love you for your extraordinary sense of humour. Ladies and gentlemen, I don't know if you have ever attended a wedding where Father Sam is officiating? If you have you will have noticed that the bride invariably comes to the alter always with a certain amount of nervousness and anxiety, but somehow after Father Sam is through with the service, the bride is always seen leaving the church with a huge smile on her face. Father Sam is often the best show in town. As you can see tonight, we are sold out, a reflection no doubt of the high esteem we all have for Father Sam.

You may or may not know that Father Sam is an integral part of an infamous trio of their version of men in black. This closely knit trio consists of Father Sam, Father Ron Pasinato, and Father Fred Olds. When together, they remind me as a modern version of a mix between the three musketeers and/or Robin Hood and his merry men in black, of course without the tights. In this fantasy I see Father Olds as the dashing Robin Hood, of course without Miriam, I see Father Sam as Little John the jolly friar, and I see Father Ron as a smart swordsman, something like the brave and intelligent count of Monte Cristo or Zorro. "All for one and one for all" is alive and well with this trio.

Seriously Father Sam, we love the fact that you love everything that is Italian: we know that you have visited Italy, and you can't get enough of it. We know that you are proud of your background and your roots and that too, endears you to us even more, for you make us feel good about who we are and where we come from, and being very proud of you, we relate to you in a credible and intimate way.

Father Sam, we know you love life in many of its manifestations and that your "joie de vivre" is unparalleled in our community. Your enthusiasm is very contagious, and we appreciate the fact that we cannot be sad for long when we are with you, for you lift up our spirits and our hearts.

We also know that Father Sam also demonstrates this "joie de vivre" with food which he enjoys immensely. He just loves Italian food, also French, Amarican, Chinese, Japanese, and German food. He just loves food

Father Sam, we appreciate you for you listen and are very receptive in trying to understand our individual and collective needs, and you respond in a caring way to meet them. The presence of the statues of the various saints in the church's corridor, the Festa of San Francesco di Paola, and the annual celebration and procession in August are three examples of the many ways you have responded to the expressed needs in our community.

Father Sam, I must now confess to you, that we have become accustomed to you, accustomed to your face, and accustomed to your smile, and the whole ball of wax. Father Sam, we love the fact that you are a man of the cloth, a member of the clergy, a man of God. In this role **you are the salt of the earth, and the happy and friendly countenance on your face is likely a reflection of the divine light that constantly seems to shine upon your face, --a reflection no doubt, of your devotion and great love and commitment to God.**

Finally, Father Sam, we love you for all the above, but most of all we love you, period.

May the road rise up to meet you
May the wind be always at your back
And till the end of time immemorial
May God hold you always,
in the palm of His hands.
Father Sam, bocca a lupo, grazie, e buona sera.

MY GREETINGS ON THE OCCASION OF THE OFFICIAL OPENING OF THE NEW "PIAZZA DE NARDI" OF UGO AND MARIA DE NARDI, YEAR 2000

Your Worship Mayor Murray, distinguished guests, ladies and gentlemen, famiglia De Nardi-Romeo, buon giorno:

In nome della communità italiana di questa provincia è mio vivo piacere aggiungere i miei distinti auguri e congratulazioni principalmente ad Ugo, Maria e l'intera famiglia De Nardi-Romeo per questa manifestazione del loro gran successo nel campo del commercio. **Si riconosce che il loro successo è il nostro successo**, un meritevole successo, un bellissimo luogo che da presenza visibile alla nostra communità, la cui ci fà molto contenti e molto fieri. E ne siamo tutti orgogliosi perchè è il risultato non soltanto del loro forte lavoro, e di passione, ma anche della loro generosità verso la communità di questa circoscrizione.

Ladies and gentlemen, on behalf of the Italian community of Manitoba I wish to extend our congratulations to the De Nardi-Romeo family for their great achievement and success in the field of business. We are delighted and proud to see this beautiful modern structure as visible evidence of that success, **for we realize that when one of us succeeds, we all succeed.**

Today we are really celebrating the realization of a dream, the visualization of which occurred many years ago of very meagre beginnings, and the result of a labor of love. I had the pleasure of knowing Maria's father, a dear friend of my own father, who came to Canada many years ago. I also know that those pioneers were very disappointed that when they came here "the streets were not paved with gold" as they had been promised. They chose to stay nevertheless, because they realized that what they had found here, was something perhaps even more precious than gold. They had found a land of freedom and opportunity, where anyone who wants to work hard can find success. This event today is one more testimonial that they were right.

Again, continued success, and thank you.

SPEECH DELIVERED ON THE OCCASION OF THE FESTA RELIGIOSA DEI SANTI ALLA CHIESA DEL SANTISSIMO ROSARIO TUTTI GL'ANNI AD AGOSTO

Archibishop Wiseberger, fathers Sam, Ron, and Michael, ladies and gentlemen, signore e signori, cannazionali e compaesani, buon pomeriggio:

Innanzi tutto vorrei esprimere la mia graditudine per l'invito a partecipare insieme con voi oggi, in questa bellisima festa manifestazione. Mi è particolarmente gradito porgere i miei più affettuosi, distinti e cordiali saluti augurali a lei Arcivescovo, a lei Padre Sam, e a lei Padre Ron e Micheal, e a tutti i partecipanti e credenti qui presenti.

Si, oggi è una bellissiama giornata,...una giornata di felicità, ...ed è mio vivo piacere perchè in effetti, questa è veramente una festa a l'italiana, e quindi ne sono ben certo che a noi italiani questa occasione, si manifesta come una giornata completa e ricchissima di tutto quello che sia di più importante e prezioso, nei nostri cuori.

Bisogna dire in primo, che questa è una giornata importante perchè se non altro, ci fa mettere da parte, almeno per un giorno, la nostalgia, e quell'angoscia che arde nel cuore di tanti di noi emigranti.

Oggi è una bellissima giornata perchè si basa sui giorni più belli che tanti di noi abbiamo vissuto in italia, giorni così gioiosamente ricordati. Di come mi ricordo io personalmente, per dare soddisfazione a tutti i nostri gusti non cerano giornate più belle delle nostre feste nel bel paese: indistintamente tutti partecipavano, e a dirittura tutto si svolgeva in una fantastica atmosfera di festaggiamenti: l'illuminazione del paese, la fiera, le campane che ci attiravano a chiesa per la santa messa cantata, la processione, i suoni della musica d'accompagnamento, poi a casa a gustare la più grande cena di come meglio si poteva a quei tempi, gelati e dolci cosi profumati, lo spettacolo e concerto in piazza, ed in ultimo, nel buio in fine, i bellissimi colori e botte dei fuochi artificiali.

È una bellissima giornata questa, perchè ci permette a passare qualche ora insieme con i nostri familiari, con i nostri connazionali, con i nostri conpaesani, con i nostri amici --tutto in armonia ed in allegria;

È una bellissima giornata questa perchè ci offre a noi qui, la possibilita di dare espressione alla nostra cultura e valori, alle nostre tradizioni ed ambienti, a la nostra fede e religione, pregando e festeggiando i nostri santi patroni, usando la nostra lingua, la nostra musica ed i nostri canti, come è ancora l'usanza ai nostri luoghi in Italia. E per tutte le suddette richezze elencate, in nome di tutti gl'italiani del Manitoba che io ho lonore di rappresentare, voglio sinceramente riconoscere la grande disponibilità del nostro caro parroco che ha messo a disposizione tanto per noi, Padre Sam, la cui comprenzione e cooperazione e ammirata e molto gradita. (si, un grande applauso per Padre Sam e i suoi assistenti.)

Sentiti ringraziamenti anche ai componenti del comitato e a tutti coloro che si sono prestati così generosamente per garantire il successo della giornata che in somma, è una delle occasioni piu belle, e più significativi per noi italiani residenti in questo grande ma lontano paese.

Ladies and Gentlemen,

I am delighted to be here and to share with you all, this most beautiful festa, very much in the Italian tradition, which packs into one celebration, all the emotions, and all the things that we treasure and that we hold most dear in our hearts. When you really think about it, a day such as this gives us an opportunity not only to put aside the nostalgic feelings most of us have for the country where we were born, but a day so special and so well-planned, that affords us an opportunity to give expression to our beliefs, our faith, our religion, our traditions, our customs, our language, our values and our way of life. In short, an event that really helps us define and enhance our self-esteem about who, and what we are.

On behalf of all of you present, and on behalf of all those that I represent, I wish to express infinite thanks to father Sam, Father Ron, and Father Michael for being so understanding and so flexible, and allowing us to relive at least one day doing those things that reconnect us with happy memories of where we come from. As well I wish to thank all of those who accepted the challenge, commitment, and hard work to put this complete package together for our benefit and our enjoyment.

Di nuovo grazie a tutti voi presenti, che cosi bene avete onorato la vostra religione e la vostra italianità.

Grazie, e buona giornata.

MIO MESSAGGIO COME VICE-CONSOLE D'ITALIA NELL'OCCASIONE DEL DECIMO ANNIVERSARIO DI VILLA NOVA

In qualità di Vice-Console d'Italia nella circoscrizione consolare del Manitoba, mi sia gradito innanzi tutto porgere i più sentiti auguri e le più vive felicitazioni a nome dell' Ambasciatore d'Italia in Canada Sua Eccellenza Marco Colombo, del Console Generale d'Italia Dottor Luca Brofferio, e dell'intera comunità italiana del Manitoba che io ho l'onore di rappresentare.

L'anno 1993 sarà ricordato come un anno importante nella storia e sviluppo della collettività italiana del Manitoba perchè fu la data che vede nascere in realtà l'esistenza della *Villa Nova di Winnipeg*. Particolarmente per noi tutti italo-canadesi, anche essa ormai rappresenta un grande sforzo, e direi un trionfo, per la communità italiana, accanto ad altre nostre iniziative, tale quale la Chiesa del Santissimo Rosario, Villa Cabrini, e il Centro Caboto Centre.

Colgo questa occasione dei festaggiamenti di questo decimo anniversario, per riconoscere e ricordare il grande contributo del Signor Gus Cosentino la cui visione e passione per la Villa Nova sono già ben notate. Quello che non tutti sono conoscenti però, è che infatti io assieme con lui, abbiamo iniziato i primissimi passi di ricerche, per scropire la possibilità per la creazione della Villa Nova che lui (mio zio) aveva profondamente nel cuore, e che io come presidente della Lega Italiana del Manitoba, avevo nella mia agenda del giorno già in cammino, discussioni per un nuovo centro culturale italiano che poi devenne infatti, il Centro Caboto. Mi sembra anche doveroso testimoniare amicizia e stima a tutti coloro componenti e membri che dall'inizio si sono prestati a sostenere così generosamente al successo della Villa Nova suscitando sempre di più rispetto, e così facendo onore a tutti gli italiani di questo comune.

Oggi, dunque, è un momento gioioso in cui una comunità intera si stringe intorno a riconoscere ed ad onorare la *Villa Nova di Winnipeg*. Per noi italiani essa rappresenta un maraviglioso successo ed un altro simbolo italiano che alimenti l'orgoglio di tutti noi emigranti, italiani, connazionali ed/o italo-canadesi del Manitoba.

MESSAGE OF THE VICE COUNSUL OF ITALY TO THE SONS OF ITALY, MARCH 19, 2005

I am delighted to bring special greetings and best wishes as the repre-sentative in Manitoba of the Italian Ambassador to Canada his Excellency Dr. Marco Colombo, as well as the Consul-General of Italy Dr. Luca Brofferio. As well, I wish to bring "auguri" and greetings on behalf of the Italian-Canadian community of Manitoba that I am also honored to represent.

I am always delighted being invited to share with my friends, Italian, Canadian and other, in worthwhile activities undertaken by the "*Sons of Italy*" whose noble vision and empowering mission, are both made clear through their bold, humanitarian goals and their manifestations in evidence year after year. Initiatives such as this one this evening, designed for generous contributions to worthwhile community projects, demonstrate how much *"The Sons"* care for the overall wellness of our community and the people within it. They are determined to make a positive and invaluable difference in the quality of life of the people that are affected and directly impacted. As for us Italo-Canadians, it allows us to identify with something wonderfully human and relevant, from which we can only gain a profound personal fulfillment and a heightened self-esteem.

Alfred Martin once said: *"That which constitutes the supreme worth of life is not wealth, not ease, nor fame, not even happiness, but service".* It is always admirable to see Canadians and Italians responding so generously to those in need anywhere in the world, as has been the case recently with the Tsunami disaster. I also note with tremendous satisfaction that the exciting program this evening brings into closer focus the vision and mission of *United Way*, which recognizes that we as a people, though diverse in many ways, are much more alike than different. We as Italians and Canadians see ourselves as world citizens with a caring global vision, characterized by a human and humane responsiveness to those in need regardless of color, creed, race and geography. Together this evening, through the initiative of the *Sons of Italy*, in a truly *"United Way"*, our commitment is on-going community-building at its best for all.

Let me, on behalf of the Italian community, also extend a warm welcome to this evening's guest speaker Mr. Hartley Richardson, a well-recognized friend of all Winnipegers, and himself one of the "giants" who impacts positively in our community in his own distinctive and caring way.

Miei cari connazionali: teniamoci conto che non siamo ancora arrivati a la nostra destinazione, ma senza nussun dubbio, *L'Ordine dei Figli d'Italia / CIBPA* con la loro grande agenda per soggetti umanitari e generosi contributi, ci illumina meglio la strada, e arricchisce non solo la collettività italiana del Manitoba ma la comunità intera di questo (ormai anche nostro) grande paese. Si nota con molto piacere che il programma di stasera si converge e si dedica a farci riconoscere la visione e la missione di *United Way of Winnipeg*, di cui tutti ne siamo riconoscenti e ben fieri, e così ricostruire e sempre milgliorare indistintamente per tutti la grande comunità.

Signed: Francesco Fiorentino

Crescendo to Becoming

*Josie and Me taking part at the Holy Rosary Church
All Saints Procession August 24, 2003*

Ladies and gentlemen,

Although I will not translate what I have just stated, I'll say simply that I have announced that I must retire from the Office of Vice Consul of Italy come February, 2006. I am obliged to do so because (God willing) I will be reaching age 70 when Italian law requires mandatory retirement from the Honorary Consul mandate.

I must tell you that I had set a goal to serve the community in this capacity for 10 years, but that won't be possible. The 8 years that I will have served has been an honor and privilige for me. I remember that I set out to open up the office of the Vice Consul and make it more accessible, more visible, and more open and transparent. Giving service to those in the community has been my goal, and I believe that I have achieved these primary goals.

I have found it a learning and enriching experience one that has brought me back to my Italian roots and for that I shall always be grateful. Your support and the support of the overall community has been overwhelming, and that's something that I shall always cherish the rest of my life. Thank you, and have a beautiful day.

BECOMING "ITALIANISSIMO" AS VICE-CONSUL FOR ITALY

LAST SPEECH TO THE ALPINI GROUP, DECEMBER 3, 2005 AT VILLA CABRINI

Padre Sam, capo gruppo Signor di Biaggio, carissimi Alpini, coniugi e familiari, amici: buona sera. Colgo questa splendida occasione stasera per ringraziarvi profondamente a indistintamente a tutti, uno per uno, per tante varie cose da me molto apprezzate e gradite.

Innanzitutto grazie per il vostro gentile invito, ogni anno a partecipare assieme con voi in questa cena diciamo intima e nostrale, ringraziando anche le mani di coloro che l'hanno preparato.

*Grazie infinite per la vostra rappresentata presenza a la ceremonia del 18 novembre scorso, indimenticabile serata in cui fui conferito l'**Ordine della Stella della Solidarietà Italiana** con il titolo di "**Cavaliere**". Il vostro appoggio incondizionato durante questi otto ultimi anni e stato molto significativo per me che non dimenticherò mai,... mai.*

Come ho detto nel mio breve discorso quella sera, questa onorificenza anche se in mio nome, rappresenta per me non un trionfo, ma un grandioso onore, un onore non solo personalmente per me, ma un onore per tutta la comunità italiana di Winnipeg. Il mio successo personale rifletta semplicemente il successo della comunità intera di cui io sono ma un singolo componente.

Ho detto anche quella sera che questo riconoscimento così prestigioso per me, attesta che il grande sforzo dei nostri avi e genitori per scoprire nuove opportunità di lavoro accompagnati dei loro grandi sacrifici, non furono in vano. Come potrei mai dimenticare il mio caro nonno Arcangelo Sherbo, che nell'anno 1891, a la tenera età di appena 14 anni, lasciò il suo piccolo paesello Amato per andare a traverso un oceano, in cerca di lavoro in Canada. Quindi senza nessun dubbio, il mio riconoscimento attesta, che i grandi sacrifici assaggiati da i mie cari parenti sono cosi riconosciuti.

*E voglio anche ripetere qui stasera un altro punto interessante del mio discorso del 18 novembre. Circa due mesi fa, nell' occasione in cui il Presidente d'Italia Carlo Azeglio Ciampi fu conferito la cittadinza onoraria della citta di Roma, il Signor Veltron, Sindaco di Roma disse: "**Essere nati e vivere in Italia è un dono: a Roma, è un privilegio** ". Anche io, come tutti noi qui, ho avuto la grande fortuna di nascere, vivere e conoscere il dono che è l'Iitalia, e il privilegio di conoscere il mio paese con il più bel nome del mondo: Amato.*

Crescendo to Becoming

Si dice che una persona rappresenta ed è parte di tutto quello che ha incontrato nella sua vita, e in questo caso non c'è dubbio che io sono parte di voi Alpini, come voi siete ormai parte integrale della mia esistenza, e della mia vita.

Carissimi fratelli e sorelle, da quasi otto anni noi abbiamo trascorso assieme delle attività con affiatamento e reciproca stima. Ed io posso aggiungere che sarò sempre fiero di voi, del vostro aiuto, e della vostra ammirata dedicazione, la vostra indispensabile disponibilità, e la vostra elevata italianità su tutte le cose meritevole.

Adesso vorrei chiamare a ciascuno degli Alpini uno per uno a presentarsi a me e così ricevere un abbraccio ed una stretta di mano come simbolo del mio rispetto e grande stima che io ho per tutti voi.

Augellone Primo
Basso Maurizio
Bergagnini, Lorenzo
Bertoncello Walter
Bevilacqua Sergio
Bianchi Renato
Canal Rino
Cendon Mario
Carbone Lorenzo
De Luca Domenico
De Negri G. Battista
Dei Cont Umberto
Di Biaggio Ermenegildo
Di Curzio Sebastiano

Di Lazzaro Vittorio
Grande Pasquale
Magnifico Giuseppe
Menei Paolo
Peluso Valentino
Piana Franco
Porco Gabriele
Scaletta Franco
Silvestrin Dante
Tomasi Eugenio (Ugo)
Toppazzini Luciano
Tozzi Franco
Trentin Pietro

Infine, con l'avvicinarsi delle Feste Natalizie, porgo a tutti voi ed ai vostri famiglairi i miei più sentiti e cordiali auguri di Buon Natale e felicità, e che nei prossimi anni goderete ottima salute con l'augurio di.

sempre un migliore futuro .

Grazie e buona sera

BECOMING "ITALIANISSIMO" AS VICE-CONSUL FOR ITALY

Holy Rosary Church Procession

CONSOLATO GENERALE D'ITALIA
TORONTO
IL CONSOLE GENERALE

Prot. n. 5519

Toronto, 4 maggio 2005

Caro Sig. Fiorentino,

pochi giorni or sono ho rilevato che il 20 febbraio 2006, ossia tra meno di un anno, Lei compira' 70 anni, che, secondo le regole stabilite dal Ministero degli Affari Esteri italiano, rappresentano l'eta' massima per lo svolgimento dell'incarico di Vice Console onorario, decorsa la quale non sono possibili ulteriori proroghe.

In considerazione di tale situazione, e tenuto conto che beneficiamo di un certo anticipo, La prego di voler sin da ora avviare una ricerca a Winnipeg, che permetta una rapida individuazione di un Suo successore nell'incarico che Lei attualmente ricopre, cosi' da evitare vuoti e discontinuita' nel funzionamento del Vice Consolato onorario, cosa che inciderebbe negativamente sulla Comunita' italiana del Manitoba.

Restando a Sua disposizione per eventuali chiarimenti ed in attesa delle indicazioni che Le ho richiesto, Le invio i miei migliori saluti unitamente ai miei complimenti riguardo al modo in cui sta gestendo l'Ufficio consolare di Winnipeg. *(pero' non ci credo che l'anno prossimo compia l'eta' fatidica: sembra ancora un ragazzino!)*

Min. Plen. Luca Brofferio

Gent.mo Signor
Francesco Fiorentino
Vice Console onorario d'Italia
WINNIPEG

Crescendo to Becoming

CONSOLATO GENERALE D'ITALIA
TORONTO
IL CONSOLE GENERALE

Prot. n. 5848

Toronto, 12 maggio 2005

Caro Sig. Fiorentino,

tra poco meno di un anno la Sua lunga esperienza di Vice Console onorario d'Italia a Winnipeg avra' termine, per sopraggiunti limiti d'eta, limiti imposti dal Ministero degli Affari Esteri e che vanno percio' rispettati, senza, purtroppo, possibilita' alcuna di deroga.

Le confesso che l'idea di perdere un valido collaboratore come Lei mi dispiace molto e mi da' qualche apprensione per il futuro. Lei aveva accumulato, in anni ed anni di onorato ed efficiente servizio, una competenza vastissima nelle numerose e complesse pratiche consolari, divenendo un punto fermo e fidato di tutta la Comunita' italiana che vive in Manitoba. Lei ha contribuito, con il Suo rigore e la Sua innata disponibilita', ad alleggerire – e non di poco – i gravosi compiti che fanno capo a questo Consolato Generale. Di cio', mi creda Le sono profondamente grato.

Come sempre accade, la fine di un'epoca della vita puo' rappresentare l'entusiasmante inizio di qualcos'altro. Tempo fa ebbe occasione di dirmi che e' Sua intenzione scrivere un libro di memorie. Non rappresenta forse questo un nuovo inizio, che la condurra' lontano nei tanti ricordi accumulati e che arricchira' ulteriormente i Suoi interessi?

Sono quindi molto lieto di formularLe i miei migliori auguri per questa nuova sfida, nella quale la Sua esperienza di Vice Console onorario occupera' senza dubbio un posto estremamente importante. E poi, comunque, prevedo che la Comunita' italiana di Winnipeg continuera' a vedere in Lei un interlocutore di riferimento imprescindibile nella soluzione dei suoi problemi.

Tutto cio' premesso, desidero ancora una volta ringraziarLa di cuore per tutto cio' che ha fatto, per noi e, soprattutto, per gli Italiani del Manitoba: sia certo che non dimenticheremo ne' Lei ne' il Suo egregio lavoro, che lascia un'eredita' apprezzata, significativa e pesante su chi prendera' in mano le redini del Vice Consolato.

Con i miei migliori e più' cordiali saluti,

Min. Plen. Luca Brofferio

Gent.mo Signore
Francesco Fiorentino
Vice Console onorario d'Italia
<u>WINNIPEG</u>

BECOMING "ITALIANISSIMO" AS VICE-CONSUL FOR ITALY

Although I had done some bits and pieces of volunteer work over the years, my volunteer work focus began again in earnest after 1991, shortly after I retired as the Superintendent of the Transcona-Springfield School Division No.12, for that was when I began to devote a significant amount of time to this worthwhile undertaking. Because most of these events have been noted previously elsewhere, I will focus here on only five of the most current.

ADULT AMBASSADOR FOR THE 2009 WINNIPEG FOLKLORAMA FESTIVAL

In the spring of 2009, I was asked by the Board and staff of the *Centro Caboto Centre* to be the Adult Ambassador for the upcoming *Folklorama Festival* that takes place annually in Winnipeg in the month of August. Because they had no other potential candidate in mind and thinking that the role only meant a commitment of the week the Italian Pavilion would be open, I accepted.

What is *Folklorama*? Perhaps a bit of history on the outstanding event that is now an annual celebration, and the Italian community relationship with it, would be in order here.

The Official Opening of Folklorama, 2009
Left To Right: Mariella Di Santo, Father Sam Argenziano, Angie Boehm, Maria Marrone, Me, and Cristina Ardita

Crescendo to Becoming

Remarkably, *Folklorama* was celebrating its fortieth anniversary in 2010, and the *Italian Canadian League of Manitoba*, the voice of the Italian community of Winnipeg, was already well-entrenched and very supportive of the multicultural concept that was *Folklorama*. Today, as in the past, the Italian community is still very proud to have been actively associated with *Folklorama* since its inception in 1970.

It is believed that it was Stephen Juba, the City of Winnipeg Mayor in 1970, who originally had the vision for what was to become *Folklorama*. Dr. Sam Loschiavo, a most outstanding member of the Italian Community and an Amatese to boot, was one of Folklorama's founding members, a man who had vivid recollections of its interesting beginnings. Before he died, Dr. Loschiavo when asked about the beginning of Folklorama, he wrote: "*Folklorama was supposed to be a one-time multicultural festival to celebrate Manitoba's centennial in 1970. It was so popular that the sponsoring group, the Manitoba Folk Arts Council decided to repeat it in 1971. It was loosely structured in 1970 with venues on the street and in the old civic auditorium. In 1971 there were 19 venues or pavilions. In 1972 there were 26. It continued to grow in popularity and in 2010 marked its 40th anniversary and is an internationally recognized event*". Dr. Loschiavo goes on to say that "*The name was borrowed from the Lakehead Folk Arts Council, which had an event called Folklorama '67 to commemorate Canada's Centennial. They had local talent but invited two groups from Winnipeg, the Philippine Dancers and the Italian Canadian League Dancers under Angela Lake. The Lakehead group gave us permission to use the name Folklorama and later it was incorporated by the Manitoba Folk Arts Council. The concept came from the annual festival called Caravan in Toronto held under one roof. In Winnipeg, Folklorama was held initially in church halls, clubrooms or community clubs. Visitors were issued passports that were stamped with visas at each pavilion, thus allowing people to "travel the world" and sample the history, music, dance, and cuisine of many cultures.*" . . During the forty years of *Folklorama*, the Italian Pavilion has been there all the forty years except one, but its venue has been in various locations in Winnipeg: (1) the Basement of the Holy Rosary Church, (2) the Southern Arena on Osborne Street, (3) the Grant Park Collegiate, and now (4) the Centro Caboto Centre in the beautiful airconditioned Italian Canadian Cultural Centre on Wilkes

Avenue... Winnipeg's *Folklorama* has evolved magnificently to become the greatest folk festival in North America due in part, to its noble and great mission, i.e. *"Celebrating diversity: promoting cultural understanding"* It is now an enriching multi-cultural phenomenon where various diverse ethnic communities live and celebrate their distinct cultures and traditions in unity, harmony and with respect one for the another. The ultimate result of all this positive interaction is an enriched quality of life for all of us in Canada, our home.

Left to right: Youth Ambassadors: Cristina Artdita, Cella Lao Rousseau and Adult Ambassadors: Maria Marrone and me

MEMBER BOARD OF DIRECTORS HEART AND STROKE FOUNDATION OF MANITOBA

One of the most meaningful endeavors that I have undertaken was to compete for and be selected as a member of the Board of Directors of the *Heart and Stroke Foundation of Manitoba*. The motivation for joining such a group is obvious, in that we must do everything possible in eradicating the devastating disease. The information below speaks volumes about why I got involved.

"Every seven minutes in Canada, someone dies from heart disease or stroke. Heart disease and stroke are two of the three leading causes of death in Canada. These statistics are based on 2008 data (the latest year available from Statistics Canada).[1]

In 2008 cardiovascular disease accounted for:29% of all deaths in Canada (69,648 deaths – or more than 69,500)

- *28% of all male deaths*
- *29.7% of all female deaths*
- *In 2008, of all cardiovascular deaths:*
- *54% were due to ischemic heart disease.*
- *20% to stroke*
- *23% to heart attack*

The Mission of the Heart and Stroke Foundation, *a volunteer-based health charity, leads in eliminating heart disease and stroke and reducing their impact through:*

- *the advancement of research and its application.*
- *the promotion of healthy living; and advocacy.*
- **The Values of the Heart and Stroke Foundation are:**
- **Collaboration** *– committed to working together collaboratively for a common cause across the federation and with our partners*
- **Excellence** *– committed to excellence in all we do*
- **Innovation** *– a passion for and the courage to explore, stimulate and engage in new ideas, behaviors and approaches*
- **Integrity** *– acting ethically to ensure transparency, accountability and public trust*
- **Respect** *– respecting, appreciating and recognizing our donors, volunteers, staff and partners who help us achieve our mission*

The photo below shows me receiving a large donation of $80,000. from the *Sons of Italy* organization on behalf of the *Heart and Stroke Foundation of Manitoba.*

Pictured above: (L to R) Tom De Nardi, Dinner Chair; Franco Petrelli Dinner Chair; Monique Gravel, CIBC Wood Gundy; Frank Sottana, District Vice-President; CIBC Retail Banking; me Frank Fiorentino; Debbie Brown; Wendy Bullock; John Giavedoni, SOI Gala Treasurer; Justin Bova, SOI president (011)

My motivation for joining the Heart and Stroke Foundation of Manitoba was (and is) to help finding a cure for the eradication of this dreaded disease that takes away so much precious life from so many of us.

MEMBER OF THE TRANSCONA CENTENNIAL CELEBRATION STEERING COMMITTEE (2012)

The Town of Transcona was incorporated on April 6, 1912, its new charter and received Royal assent on April 12, 1912. Thus, on April 12, 2012, Transcona (which has been part of Winnipeg since 1971), celebrated its 100 years anniversary as a community which still seems distinct from Winnipeg probably because of its geographic separation from the big city.

The official program took place on April 12, 2012 at the Canadian Legion site on Regent Avenue East, a truly memorial function with all the dignitaries from the three levels of government, and complete with the historic CNR nostalgic whistle (which was blown for some 70 years precisely a 12:00 to announce the noon break, and which was resurrected specifically for this commemorative occasion).

As I have been a Transconian since 1960 the year that I got married, i.e. the same year that I began my teaching career in Transcona Collegiate, and the same year I moved into the community. During these past 64 years I got to know many Transcona pioneers and many young people, and because I was in fact the co-author of From Slate to Computer, a book about the history of the Transcona-Springfield School Division, I enjoyed my association with the 2012–2013 project.

I now consider myself one of its citizens, and on that basis, I volunteered as a committee member to help them, among other things, to find a way for the inclusion of all the students who are attending Transcona schools during this centennial year. One of my specific roles in the committee was to design a Commemorative Certificate which would be presented to every pupil and student who wass actually attending a Transcona School on April 12, 2012

MEMBER OF THE WRHA RIVER EAST- TRANSCONA COMMUNITY HEALTH ADVISORY COUNCIL (2012 -2016)

Originally an "Advisory Council", the name was changed to *Local Health Involvement Group* shortly after I began my term. This is an initiative of the Winnipeg Regional Health Authority (WRHA) and my role was to "represent" the River East-Transcona community and provide feedback to the large health authority which is trying hard to be more responsive to community needs in an area that is very emotional, costly and difficult to change.

13.
BECOMING HONORED AND ESTEEMED

I HAVE BEEN VERY FORTUNATE in my life for I have been blessed with many things, things and events that have given me a great deal of personal satisfaction and fulfillment. Intrinsically without question, the greatest of these is my own immediate family which includes Josephine, my wife of almost 64 years (August 20, 2024), my son Tony, my daughter Franca and her husband Rob, my daughter Elisa and her husband Mark, and my treasured and wonderful 12 grandchildren: Amanda, Dylan, Frankie, Adriana, Evan, Austin, Ethan, and Adam, and 4 great-grandchildren: Finlay and Halldor, Winnfield and Ellis Rae. There is no way of stating the great significance, personal satisfaction and unconditional love that I have received from all the members of my wonderful family.

As well, I have received extrinsic recognition and awards that have also contributed in defining who I am and how I feel. These include the following:

Outstanding Young Man Award Nomination Issued by Transcona Jaycees, 1970

Long Service Recognition (25 Years) Issued by Transcona-Spring-field School Division No. 12, 1985

The Queen's Golden Jubilee Medal Issued by Her Majesty Queen Elizabeth II, 50th Anniversary, 2002.

The Order of Italy (Ordine Della Stella Della Solidarietà Italiana) Issued by the President of the Italian Republic, Carlo Azeglio Ciampi, June 2, 2005 for my work as a Vice Consul of Italy in Manitoba, my outstanding career in education, and my volunteering efforts.

Reco***gnition of Outstandcing Career*** Issued by the Province of Catanzaro, Italy ***and Community Achievement Award***, June 10, 2007.

Eccellenza Award Issued by the Italian League of Manitoba and presented to me October 5, 2007

Eccellenza Award Issued by the Italian League of Manitoba November, 2011 as an honorary member of the Alpini Group of Winnipeg.

Naming of Street in my honour "*Fiorentino Street*" put forth by Councillor Russ Wyatt of the City of Winnipeg in 2011 but actual naming took place in September, 2015

Leaving my "footprint" in Transcona, a street named after me!

Nomination for the Transcona Jaycees Outstanding Young Man Award, 1970

The Transcona Jaycees, a vibrant organization in the Transcona community had established an *"Outstanding Young Man Award"*, to recognize *"young men in their community for their outstanding achievement in their chosen pursuit, and ... in their endeavor to illustrate the important role young men are playing in building a better life, and ... to encourage greater leadership amongst young Canadians"* I was then nominated for the award *"for the excellence he has displayed in his field and for the exemplary leadership in his contributions to his community, his country and to mankind."*

> The TRANSCONA Jaycees having selected young men in their community for their outstanding achievement in their chosen pursuit, and ... in their endeavor to illustrate the important role young men are playing in building a better life, and ... to encourage greater leadership amongst young Canadians
>
> acknowledge that MR. FRANK FIORENTINO has been nominated for
>
> **Outstanding Young Man Award**
>
> for the excellence he has displayed in his field and for the exemplary leadership in his contributions to his community, his country and to mankind.
>
> Dated this Seventh day of APRIL - 1970 at the City of Transcona.
> Ed Nickerson, Unit President
> Jim Parks, O.Y.M. Chairman

1. Long Service Recognition (25 Years)

PRESENTED BY
TRANSCONA-SPRINGFIELD
SCHOOL DIVISION NO. 12

TO

> > > > > * < < < < <

Frank Fiorentino

ASSISTANT SUPERINTENDENT

> > > > > * < < < < <

IN APPRECIATION OF TWENTY-FIVE
YEARS OF DEDICATED SERVICE
1960 – 1985

"THANK YOU FOR CARING"

JUNE, 1985

This is the Plaque in the form of a wooden scroll presented to me to commemorate the occasion of Long Service Recognition with the Transcona-Springfield School Division No. 12, June 1985

BECOMING HONORED AND ESTEEMED

The above photo shows Mary Andree, chairperson of the school board, presenting the Long Service Recognition Award to me at the Harold Hatcher School, June, 1985

To Recognize and Honour

Frank Fiorentino
Superintendent
Transcona-Springfield School Division #12
1990–1991

For your years of service to the children, parents, staff and community of one of the historical divisions in River East Transcona School Division.
Dated this 1st day of June, 2018

River East Transcona

Colleen Carswell
Chair of the Board of Trustees

Vince Mariani
Secretary-Treasurer/CFO

The Queen's Golden Jubilee Medal Issued by Her Majesty Queen Elizabeth II

The commemorative medal Majesty Queen Elizabeth Golden Jubilee Medal was issued by Canada Heritage to mark and highlight her 50 years as Queen of England and of Canada. It was *"awarded to those people who have made a significant contribution to Canada, to their community, or to their fellow Canadians."*

On the occasion of the fiftieth Anniversary of the accession of

HER MAJESTY THE QUEEN

to the Throne the Golden Jubilee Medal is presented to

À l'occasion du cinquantième anniversaire de l'accession de

SA MAJESTÉ LA REINE

au Trône la Médaille du jubilé est remise à

Mr. Francesco Fiorentino

CANADIAN   LES GOUVERNEURS

BECOMING HONORED AND ESTEEMED

The Queen's Golden Jubilee Medal

The Commemorative Medal for Her Majesty Queen Elizabeth II's Golden Jubilee was created to mark the 50th anniversary of the accession of Her Majesty to the Throne on February 6, 1952.

It is awarded to those persons who, like you, have made a significant contribution to Canada, to their community or to their fellow Canadians.

The obverse side of the medal bears the current Canadian effigy of Her Majesty; the reverse side, the Royal Crown above a single maple leaf on which is superimposed the Royal Cypher. The medal is suspended from a ribbon on which the outer stripes appear in red, followed by broad royal blue stripes, white stripes and a red stripe in the center.

This Commemorative Medal is part of the Jubilee year celebrations organized by the Department of Canadian Heritage.

La Médaille du jubilé de Sa Majesté la Reine

La Médaille commémorative du jubilé de Sa Majesté la Reine Elizabeth II marque le 50ᵉ anniversaire de l'accession de Sa Majesté au trône le 6 février 1952.

Elle est conférée aux personnes qui, comme vous, ont apporté une contribution exceptionnelle au Canada, à leur collectivité ou à leurs concitoyens.

L'avers de la médaille porte l'effigie canadienne actuelle de Sa Majesté; le revers, la couronne royale surmontant une feuille d'érable unique sur laquelle est superposé le chiffre royal. La médaille est suspendue à un ruban dont les rayures extérieures rouges sont suivies de rayures larges bleu royal, de rayures blanches et d'une rayure rouge au milieu.

La Médaille commémorative s'inscrit dans le cadre des fêtes du jubilé organisées par le ministère du Patrimoine canadien.

2. Knight of the Order of the Star of Italian Solidarity (Cavaliere Dell'Ordine Della Stella Della Solidarietà Italiana)

On June 2, 2005 the President of the Italian Republic, Carlo Azeglio Ciampi, announced the names of those Italians living outside of Italy upon whom he had conferred the title of Cavaliere, i.e. *Knight of the Order of the Star of Italian Solidarity* who have distinguished themselves highly in a career or in their line of work. Included in that list was the name of Francesco Fiorentino, whose name had been submitted by the Consul General of Italy in Canada, Luca Brofferio and his Excellency, the Ambassador of Italy in Canada, Marco Colombo. In a letter dated October 21, 2005, Luca Brofferio, Consul-General of Italy in Toronto wrote the following letter (translated from the Italian) on the next page.

Toronto October 21, 2005

Dear Knight Fiorentino

It is a great pleasure for me to inform you that the President of the Italian Republic has conferred the award of merit entitled *"Knight of the Order of the Star of Italian Solidarity"* awarded to Italians abroad who have distinguished themselves very highly in their work or careers, and made an outstanding contribution in their respective areas of excellence, and who have made a high contribution toward the Italian community in Canada.

I am delighted to congratulate you for having received this distinguished high recognition and honor of the Italian state and kindly invite you to attend and participate in the Gala Dinner Event organized by the Italian Chamber of Commerce of Manitoba that will take place on the next November 18, 2005, during which His Highness, Marco Colombo, Ambassador of Italy, will be bestowing upon you with the Certificate and the Insignia of the tribute itself.

I extend to you, dear Knight, my warm and loving greetings,
Luca Brofferio

BECOMING HONORED AND ESTEEMED

CONSOLATO GENERALE D'ITALIA
TORONTO
IL CONSOLE GENERALE

Toronto, 21 ottobre 2005 - 13542

Caro Cav. Fiorentino,

è un grande piacere per me infomarLa che il Presidente della Repubblica Italiana Le ha concesso l'onoreficenza di Cavaliere dell'Ordine della Stella della Solidarietà Italiana per gli elevati meriti che Ella ha maturato nei confronti dello Stato italiano grazie al Suo lavoro ed alla Sua attività verso la comunità italiana in Canada.

Mi congratulo vivamente con Lei per aver ricevuto questo alto riconoscimento dello Stato Italiano e La invito a voler cortesemente partecipare alla cena di gala della Camera di Commercio Italiana del Manitoba, il prossimo 18 novembre, nel corso della quale S.E. Marco Colombo, Ambasciatore d'Italia in Canada, Le consegnerà il diploma e le insegne dell'onoreficenza stessa.

Le invio, caro Cavaliere, i miei affettuosi saluti

(Luca Brofferio)

Cavaliere dell'Ordine della Stella della Solidarietà Italiana
Frank Fiorentino
Vice Console Onorario d'Italia
1055 Wilkes Ave.
Winnipeg, Manitoba
R3P 2L7

Crescendo to Becoming

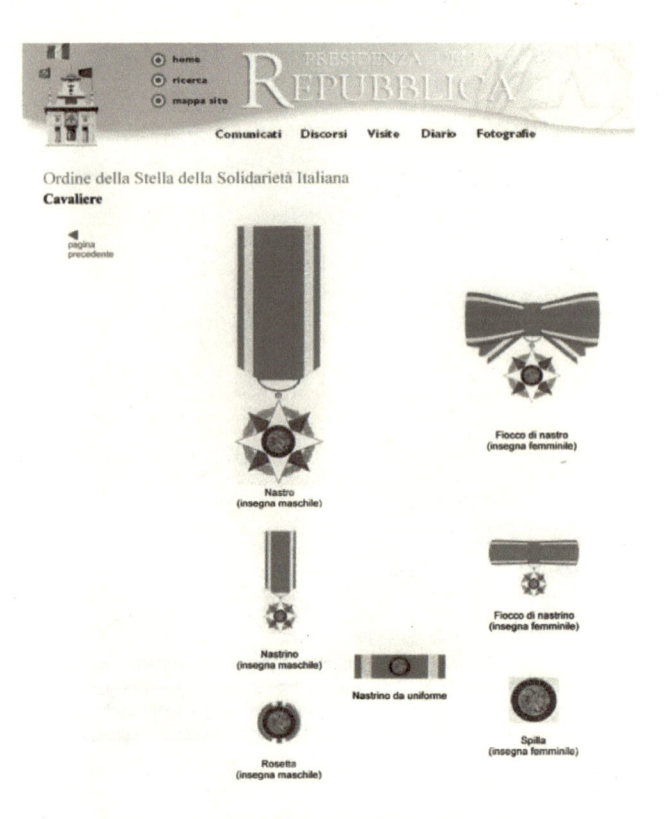

The Order of Italy Award as Cavaliere (Knight), 2005

BECOMING HONORED AND ESTEEMED

The Italian Chamber of Commerce of Manitoba Newsletter "ICCM Network News", June, 2005

Crescendo to Becoming

My Wife Josie Fiorentino and Me, Upon Receiving the "Knight of the Order of the Star of Italian Solidarity" Presented by the Ambassador of Italy Marco Colombo And Consul General of Italy Luca Brofferio, at the Fort Garry Hotel Gala Dinner, Held by the Italian Chamber of Commerce of Manitoba, November 18, 2005

Note: Of all the awards I have received in my life, none has had the significance and meaning as the ***"Order of Italy"*** above, not so much for the personal recognition that I received, but primarily for what it would have meant to my father who was a very staunch and proud Italian. There is no doubt in my mind that this recognition and award issued by the Italian Government would have made my father immensely happy and proud. This award would have justified my father's own decision to leave his beloved Italy some 56 years earlier, in 1949, with everything he gave up in his own life, and all the hard life and sacrifices he had to endure, in order to have the opportunity and ensure a better-quality life for me and all his children in Canada.

BECOMING HONORED AND ESTEEMED

My Speech at the Fort Garry Hotel Gala Dinner, November 18, 2005 upon Receiving of the "Knight of the Order of the Star of Italian Solidarity"

Mr. Chairman, Eccellenza Marco Colombo, Ambasciatore d'Italia, Dottor Luca Brofferio, Console Generale d'Italia, Premier Doer, special guests, ladies and gentlemen, signore e signori, connazionali, amici, buona sera.

Colgo l'occasione innanzitutto di esprimere auguroni al nostro Cavaliere Bueti ed al Commandatore Tolaini, riconoscendo la loro ben meritata onorificenza.

Aggiungo anch'io un vivo, e caloroso saluto di benvenuto a lei Ambasciatore d'Italia Sua Eccellenza Marco Colombo, a lei Console Generale d'Italia Dottor Luca Brofferio, la cui gradita presenza amezzo a noi, anche se brevissima di appena un giorno, ci allegra e profondamente ci onora

In breve maniera, mi sia gradito descrivere qual'è la vera significanza di questa onorificenza per me, puntandomi su due o tre punti più salienti:

Questo riconoscimento anche se in mio nome, rappresenta non un trionfo, ma un grandioso onore non solo per me, ma per tutta la comunità italiana di Winnipeg. Il mio successo personale rifletta semplicemente il successo della comunità intera di cui io sono ma un singolo componente. Senza l'esistenza della Camera di Commercio Italiana, la collettività italiana di Winnipeg, la vostra italianità, e senza il vostro appoggio, nulla sarebbe stato possibile di quello che io personalmente godo in questo momento magico della mia vita. Per tutto questo vi offro i miei voti benaguranti e le mie grazie riconoscente.

Questo riconoscimento così prestigioso per me, attesta che il grande sforzo dei nostri avi e genitori per scoprire nuove opportunità di lavoro, cominciando di mio nonno Arcangelo Sherbo nel 1891, e l'arrivo in Canada della mia famiglia nel 1949, attestano che i dolorosi sacrifici da loro assagiati, non furono in vano.

In occasione in cui il Presidente della Repubblica Carlo Ezeglio Ciampi li fu conferita la cittadinanza onoraria di Roma, il Sindaco di Roma il Sig. Veltroni disse :*"Essere nati e vivere in Italia è un dono: a Roma, è un privilegio ".* Anche io ho avuto la grande fortuna di nascere e conoscere il dono che è l'Italia, e il privilegio che fu ed è tuttora il mio paese con il più bel nome del mondo: Amato.

Cari connazional, credo che già sapete che il mio D.N.A. e le mie radici sono al 100% italianissime ed è vero che l'innesto può permettere all' albero una diversa qualità di rami, di fiori e di frutti, ma in fondo ciò che sostiene la vita

Crescendo to Becoming

dell'albero come anche dell'uomo, sono le proprie radici, e i mie radici sono al 100 percento italiane.

Ladies and gentlemen,

In closing I wish to recognize the following who have contributed enormously and made a significant difference in my life:

My grandfather Arcangelo Sherbo who, at the age of only 14 demonstrated remarkable courage by venturing out of Amato Italy and ended in Winnipeg working for the Grand Trunk Railway as a waterboy;

My father whose passion and intense love of Italy as expressed through his music and his poetry. He helped me appreciate the gift of what it means to be Italian.

The founders of the Italian Chamber of Commerce of Manitoba, whose creative vision to build human and interactive bridges between Manitoba and Italy, and the incredible commitment of the staff: Annamaria, Marco, Chiara, Arsen, Antonietta e Fabrizio, whose efforts and dedication made this beautiful evening possible.

"I am a part of all that I have met" and like Ulysses I am a part of all of you, as I am part of the Alpini group of whom I am particularly proud for they represent the best of Italian virtues and values. Finally, I thank my lucky stars that I have such a wonderful and understanding wife and family members. A good chunk of this honor tonight really belongs to my wonderful wife of 45 years Josie, my children, grandchildren, my brother and sisters and all the extended family members most of whom are here tonight. You all have been my unfailing support base, my source of strength and inspiration, and for that, I shall cherish and love you always.

Thank you and good evening

BECOMING HONORED AND ESTEEMED

Consolato Generale d'Italia
Toronto

Toronto, 13 dicembre 2005 — 175 79

Caro Cavaliere,

    prima di partire desidero ringraziarLa di tutto cuore per la costante, generosa, efficace, responsabile collaborazione che ha assicurato sia al Consolato Generale che a me personalmente durante il periodo della mia permanenza in questa sede.

    Le sempre aggravantesi ristrettezze finanziarie che si sono verificate in questi ultimi anni hanno reso ancora piu' arduo e, contemporaneamente, sempre piu' necessario il Suo lavoro per venire incontro alle richieste dei nostri connazionali e di questo Ufficio; mi auguro proprio che questo periodo finisca al piu' presto in modo che Lei, e tutti noi, possiamo tornare a lavorare, liberi da questo assillo, in maniera piu' serena.

    Desidero assicurarLe che la Sua attivita' e' giustamente apprezzata da questo Ufficio, dalla nostra Ambasciata, dal Ministero degli Affari Esteri perche', lungi dall'esaurirsi nelle mere pratiche burocratiche, essa si estrinseca in una importantissima funzione di indirizzo e di guida della Sua comunita', di esempio e di stimolo ai nostri connazionali a comportarsi ed a vivere in modo da fare onore alla nostra Patria ed al buon nome degli Italiani in questo grande paese che ci ospita.

    Confido che Ella vorra' assicurare al mio successore in misura inalterata la Sua preziosa collaborazione e, nel ringraziarla nuovamente, invio a Lei ed ai Suoi familiari *mille cordiali saluti ed auguri di buone Feste.*

IL CONSOLE GENERALE
LUCA BROFFERIO

CAV. FRANCESCO FIORENTINO
VICE CONSOLE ONORARIO D'ITALIA
VICE CONSOLATO D'ITALIA
WINNIPEG

A letter from the Consul General on the occasion of the completion of his assignment in Canada. (see translation below)

Toronto, December 13, 2005

Dear Knight,

Before leaving Canada, I wish to thank you wholeheartedly for your constant, generous, effective, and responsible collaboration to the Consul General and to me personally during the period of my assignment in Canada.

The always very restrictive and worsening financial situation that we have witnessed during the past few years made things even more difficult and arduous and at the same time made your work even more necessary in order to meet the needs of our Italian countrymen of this jurisdiction. I sincerely hope that this period is coming to an end as soon as possible in order that you and all of us, can assume our duties free of this worrisome situation.

I wish to reassure you that your work is truly appreciated by this office, by our Embassy in Ottawa, by the Ministry of Foreign Affairs, because far from being exhausted involved in simple level of bureaucratic work, he is involved in extremely important work of giving assistance and direction to your own community, providing a model and stimulus, to our countrymen, to lead exemplary lives that bring honor to our fatherland and that gives a good reputation to our countrymen that live in this great country (Canada) that hosts us.

I trust that you will give my successor your loyalty and the same precious cooperation that I enjoyed. Again, may I convey my appreciation and send to you and members of your family my very best wishes and happy Christmas Holidays.

Luca Brofferio
Consul General of Canada

BECOMING HONORED AND ESTEEMED

"Live a good life now as it happens and when later you think back, you will enjoy it even more."
—Unknown

His Honour the Honourable John Harvard, P. C., O.M.
Lieutenant Governor of Manitoba
and
Her Honour Lenore Berscheid
request the pleasure of the company of

Mr. Francesco Fiorentino and Mrs. Josephine Fiorentino

at a **Dinner** in honour of the **Consular Corps of Winnipeg**
on
Tuesday, the 24th day of January, 2006
at 6:30 p.m.

Government House		Please respond by January 16th
10 Kennedy Street	Business Attire	945-4334

Crescendo to Becoming

> **RIDEAU HALL**
> **OTTAWA**
>
> THE GOVERNOR GENERAL
> LA GOUVERNEURE GÉNÉRALE
>
> July 19, 2000
>
> Dera Mr. Fiorentino:
>
> As part of our first official visit to Manitoba, John Ralston Saul and I would like to invite you and your family to attend the Governor General's Summer Levee which we will be hosting in Brandon at the Brandon Armoury on Wednesday, August 2 from 5:00 p.m. to 7:00 p.m. The event is open to the public; light refreshments will be served. Performances by *Pride of Manitoba*, *Brandon Troyanda School of Ukrainian Dance* and *Miss Tara Abbott*, soprano, will also be part of the programme.
>
> For additional information on the event, please contact Government House in Ottawa at 1-800-263-0816 or visit our website at www.gg.ca.
>
> We look forward to seeing you on this occasion.
>
> Yours sincerely,
>
> Adrienne Clarkson
>
> Mr. Francesco Fiorentino
> Honorary Vice-Consul of Italy
> 1294 Ravelston Avenue
> Winnipeg MB   R3W 1R3

Invitation by the Governor General of Canada, July 19, 2000

BECOMING HONORED AND ESTEEMED

Consular Corps of Winnipeg

c/o 101 - 1200 Pembina Highway Winnipeg MB R3T 2A7

February 1ˢᵗ, 2006

Dear Colleague,

We have the pleasure of inviting you to the next function of the **CONSULAR CORPS of WINNIPEG**, taking place at:

CABOTO CENTRE
1055 Wilkes Ave. (you can only approach from Waverley St. – off Kenaston closed)

Friday, February 24ᵗʰ, 2006
6:30 p.m. Reception, 7:30 Dinner

Your host, **Mr. Francesco (Frank) Fiorentino, Honorary Vice-Consul of Italy** is issuing a cordial invitation to all members and spouses or escorts and special invitees to attend this function.

The **cost of the dinner is $ 35.00 per person.**

KINDLY NOTIFY BY TELEPHONE at 269-0525 **if attending**, or you could send your cheque, made payable to the Consular Corps of Winnipeg, c/o above mentioned address or bring along to the function once you have booked. In any case advise **AS SOON AS POSSIBLE**, so that your host may complete the necessary arrangements.

Your attendance to be booked with the Secretary-Treasurer by LATEST, Tuesday, February 21ˢᵗ. Reservations after this date must be made directly with the host.

Your hosts Frank & Josie Fiorentino are looking forward to see you on February 24ᵗʰ, 2006.

Yours respectfully

G. (Gerry) Spindler
Secretary-Treasurer

The Above Announcement Refers to Last Dinner Hosted by me for the Consular Corps of Winnipeg as Vice Consul of Italy

Crescendo to Becoming

Recognition of outstanding career and Community Achievement Award from Province of Catanzaro, Italy, June 10, 2007

Camera di Commercio Italiana del Manitoba | Italian Chamber of Commerce of Manitoba

Winnipeg, May 29, 2007

Mr. Frank Fiorentino
1294 Ravelston Ave. W.
Winnipeg, MB
R3W 1R3

Dear Mr. Fiorentino,

On behalf of the Chamber of Commerce of Catanzaro and the Italian Chamber of Commerce of Manitoba, we are pleased to inform you that you have been selected for the **Recognition of Outstanding Career or Community Achievement Award**.

Your Award will be presented to you at the **"Flavours of Calabria Award Dinner"** that will be held at the Centro Caboto, 1055 Wilkes Avenue, Winnipeg, on June 10th, 2007. Cocktails will start at 6:00 pm, followed by a dinner created by our guest chef from Calabria.

You will be a guest for dinner, but any additional guests you wish to bring will be charged $60.00 for dinner.

Please RSVP to the Italian Chamber of Commerce of Manitoba by noon on Monday, *June 4, 2007* by phone **(204.487.6323)** or e-mail (contact@iccm.ca) whether you will be attending and the number of guests you will bring.

Please accept this award as a small token of our gratitude for your exemplary commitment to our community.

Again, our heartiest congratulations. If you have any questions, please feel free to contact me at *204.487.6323*.

Sincerely,

Sebastiano Baglione
Executive Director
Italian Chamber of Commerce of Manitoba

1055 Wilkes Avenue, Unit #113
Winnipeg, Manitoba, Canada R3P 2L7
TEL: 001.204.487.6323
FAX: 001.204.487.0164
EMAIL: info@iccm.ca
WEB: www.iccm.ca

BECOMING HONORED AND ESTEEMED

Programme for the Catanzaro Outstanding Achievement Recognition Dinner, June 10, 2007.

Crescendo to Becoming

Italian Canadian League of Manitoba Inc.
Lega Italo Canadese del Manitoba

1055 Wilkes Avenue
Winnipeg, Manitoba R3P 2L7
(204) 487-4597

President
Greg Fiorentino

1st Vice-President
Dr. Brett Carter

2nd Vice-President
Antonio Di Geronimo

Secretary
Vivian Albo

Treasurer
Katia von Stackelberg

Public Relations Officer
Teresa Campanelli

Past President
Carmine Coppola

Honourary Counsel
Mario Grande

Presidents
– Member Organizations

Marietta Pellettieri
– Associazione Basilucana Di Winnipeg Inc.

Giovanni Racciatti
– Amici Abruzzesi

Frank Caligiuri
– Fratellanza Amatese

Vivian Albo
– Giovanni Caboto Society Inc.

E. (Gildo) Di Biaggio
– Gruppo Alpini

Mario Audino
– Italian Canadian Foundation Inc.

John Yunyk
– Italian Youth Association

Caterina Sofriadis
– La Lupa Di Roma Lodge

Cosmo Rocano
– Order of the Sons of Italy – Garibaldi Lodge

Anna Maria Puleri
– San Mango D'Aquino Society Inc.

Linda Romeo
– Società Culturale Dante Alighieri

Gerarino Conte
– Società Roma

September 6, 2007

Mr. Frank Fiorentino
1055 Wilkes Avenue
Winnipeg, MB R3P 2L7

Dear Frank:

Re: Eccellenza Awards

We are delighted to inform you to confirm that the Eccellenza Awards is being planned for Friday, October 5th at the Centro Caboto. As you know, we will be honouring you as the recipient of the Eccellenza Awards for the category of **Business, Trades & Professions**. This category recognizes outstanding achievement in business, trades and or the professions in private, public or not for profit companies and/or organizations. The event will begin with a reception followed by dinner and the awards presentations.

We have enclosed two complimentary tickets for the event, and in addition, 4 more tickets that you indicated to Vivian Albo that you wish to purchase. You may give Vivian a cheque for the tickets when you next see her.

In the event that you will need additional tickets to the Awards Gala Dinner, you can contact John Yunyk at the Centro at 487-4597.

Again, congratulations on your selection for an Eccellenza Awards. We look forward to seeing you on October 5th.

Yours truly,

Teresa Campanelli
Eccellenza Awards Chair

National Congress of Italian Canadians (Manitoba Region) - Congresso Nazionale degli Italo Canadesi (la regione del Manitoba)

BECOMING HONORED AND ESTEEMED

The Italian Canadian League of Manitoba
presents

2007

Eccellenza

Awards

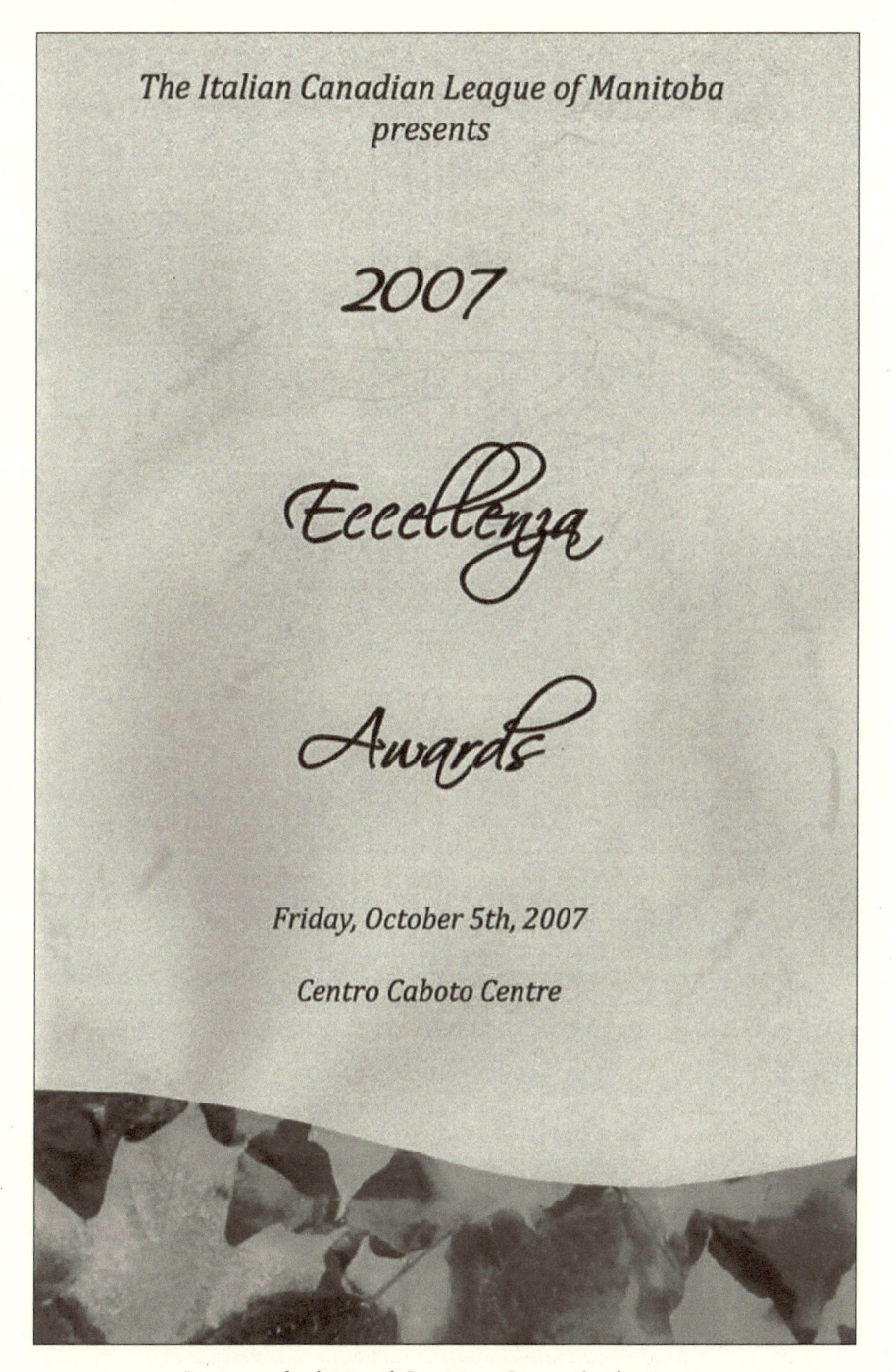

Friday, October 5th, 2007

Centro Caboto Centre

Programme for the Awards Recognition Dinner, October 5, 2007

Business, Trades & Professions
Frank Fiorentino

Francesco Fiorentino was born in Amato (Catanzaro) in 1936 and came to Canada i 1949. He graduated from university with impressive scholastic and academic achievements including a B.A., a B.Ed., a Master of Education degrees, a Permanent Professional Teaching Certificate, and a Certificate in Education Administration.

    He has had a remarkable and illustrious career in the field of Education tha started out as a High School Teacher in 1959. He went on to become a High School Principal, Assistant Superintendent, Superintendent and C.E.O. of the Transcona-Springfield School Division. He was the first Italian-Canadian to reach that level in Manitoba. He is presently a part-time Consultant of Education with People Develop ers, a company that he founded in 1992. In the Italian community, Frank Fiorentino was a founding member of the Italian Canadian Club in the early 1950's. In 1992, he served as President of the ICLM. In his role as President of the League he convince his Board to sell the Casa d'Italia on Notre Dame Avenue, and, together with his unc Gus Cosentino, they initiated discussions with representatives of the three levels of government seeking financial support for both the Cultural Centre and Villa Nova, both which are now standing in this site. In 1998, he was appointed by the Italian Government as the Honorary Vice Consul of Italy for Manitoba and remained there until the age of 70. Frank presently sits on the Boards of *Villa Cabrini* the *Centro Caboto Centre*.

    Frank's proudest moment as an Italian was his induction into the Order of Italy, the *"Ordine Della Stella Della Solidarietà Italiana"* as "Cavaliere", i.e. "Knight", conferred to him by Carlo Azeglio Ciampi, President of the Italian Republic, in 2005

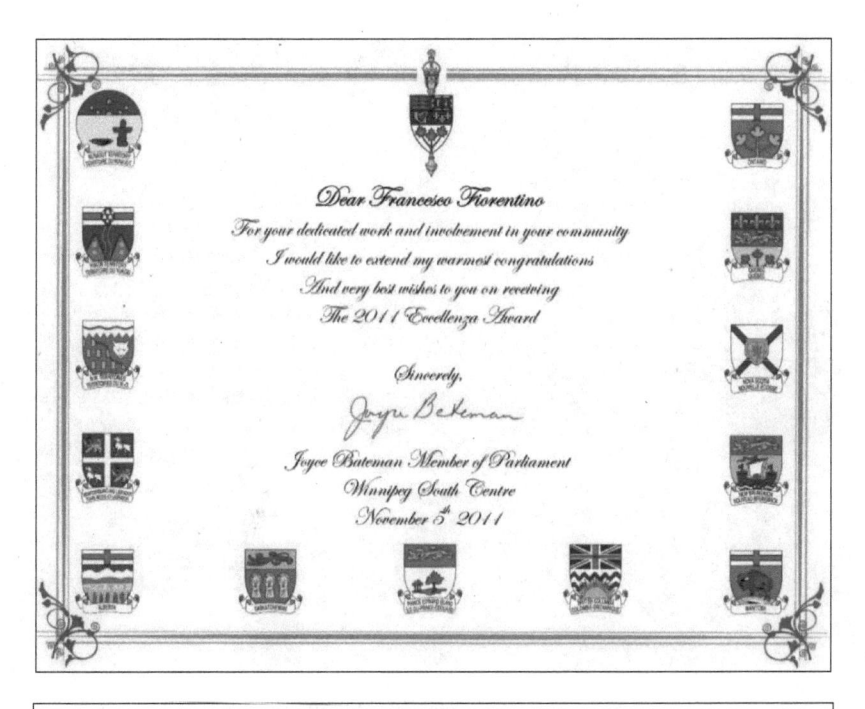

BECOMING HONORED AND ESTEEMED

> Dear Francesco Fiorentino
>
> For your dedicated work and involvement in your community I would like to extend my warmest congratulations And very best wishes to you on receiving The 2011 Eccellenza Award
>
> Sincerely,
>
> Joyce Bateman Member of Parliament
> Winnipeg South Centre
> November 5th 2011

Ottawa Office
Room 311 Justice Bldg.
Ottawa, Ontario
K1A 0A6
Tel: (613) 992-9475
Fax: (613) 995-9586
Joyce.Bateman@parl.gc.ca

Joyce Bateman, M.P.
Winnipeg South Centre

Constituency Office
102-611 Corydon Avenue
Winnipeg, Manitoba
R3L 0P3
Tel: (204) 983-1355
Fax: (204) 984-3979
Joyce.Bateman@parl.gc.ca

Friday, November 3, 2011

Dear Francesco Fiorentino,

I am writing to send you my personal congratulations on receiving the 2011 Eccellenza Award for you participation in the Gruppo Alpini di Winnipeg.

It is so important to be able to acknowledge and celebrate those who are striving to make a difference in their own community.

I wish you all the best in your future life endeavors, whatever they may be.

Sincerely,

Joyce Batman, M.P.
Winnipeg South Centre

A Second Eccellenza Award Awarded to Me as a Member of the Group Alpini of Winnipeg and the Accompanying Congratulatory Letter from Joyce Batemen, Member of Parliament, October, 2011

Frank and Josie Fiorentino, Eccellenza Awards, 2005

My Eccellenza Award Speech

Madam chairperson, distinguished honored guests, ladies and gentlemen, signore e signori, connazionali e compaesani, amici, a tutti buona sera:

Mi sia gradito innanzitutto formulare e porgere ogni voto augurale a lei Signor Greg Fiorentino includendo naturalmente i componenti della vostra oganizzazione. Mi rendo conto certamente, che questi eventi non occorono da soli, se nonchè qualcuno li crea e li porti in conclusione. E per questo porgo grazie infinite alla Signorina Vivian Albo, Teresa Campanelli, Rosanna Caruso, Jonathan Yunyk, e il personale in cucina Louis and Tammy i quali si son prestati cosi generosamente ad organizzare questa bellissima e significativa serata manifestazione.

Colgo l'occasione a me consentita per aggiungere i miei più sinceri voti augurali alle distinte e meritevole persone riceventi del premio *Eccellenza Award* che mi affiancono qui stasera, cioè ai fratelli Amadeo ed Alberto Capone, a Giuseppe De Natale, e a tutti i miei compaesani e soci della

BECOMING HONORED AND ESTEEMED

organizzazione Fratellanza Amatese, ch'è composta dei miei amici compaesani, la cui presenza qui stasera mi fa grande piacere.

Credetemi, e veramente una grande soddisfazione condividere questa bellissima occasione assieme con tutti voi presenti qui stasera. Nulla sarebbe stato possibile di quello che io personalmente godo in questo momento così signicativo, se avrebbe mancato la vostra attiva partecipazione. Per tutto questo, vi offro i miei voti benauguranti e i miei profondi ringraziamenti.

Come nominativo, vi assicuro che è vero che non c'è più bella cosa che di essere apprezzati a propria casa dai nostri cari familiari ed dai nostri amici. Di più, questo autentico premio a me conferito stasera dalla collettivita italiana, è un premio creato del talento del dotato Signor Pino Regina, e dunque rappresenta qualcosa d'accezzionale che riconosce la nostra grande italianità che ci unisce e ci lega insieme per sempre. Il mio piu grande dono rimarrà la vostra cara ed inestimabile amicizia.

Ladies and gentlemen,

First of all, I am delighted to extend heartfelt congratulations to the honored members of our community for the great achievement, recognition, and accolades which they are receiving this evening. I know for a fact that these honored guests, are held in very high esteem and they should know this evening that I share in their moment of joy and happiness, for tonight after all, we are part of one other.

To Amadeo and Alberto Capone, Giuseppe DeNatale, and the 60 years old Fratellanza which consists of wonderful friends from my home town of Amato and their children, to all of you I extend my sincere congratulations and say also that you are truly an intrinsic part of our Italian community and our collective family. But even more so to me, you are an intrinsic part of all that I have been, *and of who I am today*.

You can be justly proud, for you have been community builders in the very sense of the word. You should also know that you, like many Italians like you, from the time of your arrival to this community, you and the organizations that you belong to, have actually helped shape and change the character of this community, and in so doing, you have contributed significantly to the quality of life in this community and in this great country.

Finally, I wish to acknowledge the contribution and support of a few very special people in my life. First and foremost, Josephine, my wonderful and

Crescendo to Becoming

understanding wife of 52 years. Without her support and love, little of whatever success I have would have been possible. Secondly, my more vocal but solid support base consists of my son Tony, and my two princesses Franca and Elisa, including their respective husbands Rob Kiz and Mark Charbonneau. And thirdly, our beautiful and oldest granddaughter Amanda, first of my seven (now eight) delightful grandchildren, . . the only real thing that makes our senior age a golden one. And last, but not least, I wish to thank two very special, and supportive friends here tonight at our table, Steve Kiz and Dolores Gibbons.

Just one more thought. It is said that it is in giving service from the heart that we receive the greatest meaning in our lives. As for me, yes, I may have given some, but I have received much, much, much more in return.

I have rediscovered the innate love of my country of origin, I have received the privilege of living in this great country, and ladies and gentlemen, I have received your unfailing support over the years. Above all else, I believe I have received your greatest gift of all: --your friendship and your respect, -- and these two I shall always cherish and hold them close to my heart. Di nuovo grazie, and God bless.

Me, with Friend Tony Tascona, Famous Italian-Canadian Sculptor, 2004

14.
BECOMING A VICTIM OF HEART AND CANCER DISEASES!

I THANK GOD THAT OVERALL, during my whole life I and all members of my immediate family have enjoyed relatively good health for the most part. In the latter years, however, as a family we have fallen prey to the two most threatening medical diseases in the western world: heart disease and cancer. I know now why they say that *"your best wealth is your good health"*.

My very first indication of illness occurred in 1950 shortly after we arrived in Winnipeg. We all found the extreme cold weather quite intolerable, and it wasn't long before I developed a case of bad tonsillitis, and as was customary in those days, I was hospitalized for a couple of days to have my tonsils removed.

Then later, when I was about 21 years of age, I succumbed to smoking, a filthy habit that was almost universally accepted and sought after in the 1950's. The prevalent opinion of the years before this was that you weren't a man unless you smoked, and so almost everybody smoked, especially men and young women.

Ironically the Fiorentino family had historically always been non-smokers. According to my father, no one in our family had ever cultivated the habit of smoking, until he himself started smoking at the mature age of 50. Soon after, I started as well but it had nothing to do with my father smoking. Actually, the influence to smoke came from the members of my dance band who all smoked, and they all seemed to enjoy a cigarette so much whenever we had a break, and smoking cigarettes seemed to be such a 'cool', relaxing thing.

I remember that when I started to smoke, I got sick and found it anything but pleasant. But I persevered (as I did with everything else), and I became a smoker, eventually a heavy smoker of close to two packs a day, especially on days when we had a booking with the dance band, which was almost every Saturday. I became so addicted that at one time the first thing I did upon rising every morning, was to smoke a cigarette. It got so bad that I often had a troublesome and persistent cough, especially in the morning. When I went to see a specialist for some other matter, the doctor told me that the fellow that he had just seen before me had terminal cancer due to smoking. Turning to me he said: "That fellow doesn't have a chance to claim his health back anymore, but you still do. You should think very seriously about quitting, before it might be too late for you too."

So, on July 29, 1981 we had gone to one of my niece's wedding in Montreal, and on the way home from the wedding party precisely at 3:30 a.m., I recall very vividly that we were over the Jacques Cartier Bridge over the St. Lawrence River, and I noted that I had smoked two packs of cigarettes on that long day, and was about to start out a third pack. As I was about to place the cigarette in my mouth, I realized in my dismay that I already had a cigarette burning in my mouth. It was the moment when "the rubber hits the road" as they say, and in grand fashion, I announced out loud to those in the car with me (Josie, Elisa, brother-in-law Pasquale and sister-in-law Carolina) that I was quitting smoking right there and then. So, in such dramatic fashion, I threw the new pack of cigarettes into the river, along with the new cigarette I was about to light up, and the partially smoked cigarette I already had in my mouth. Upon my announcement everybody began to laugh, for they had heard the pronouncement before. But I was very serious. In fact, I am happy to say that to this day, I have not touched a cigarette since, i.e. 43 years ago. Quitting smoking was such a momentous decision that I have never forgotten the date, the place, and even the time when it actually occurred.

Healthwise the next significant health event occurred in the Spring of 1988. One day in early May I got up not feeling well at all. One moment I would feel hot and sweaty, and the next I would feel cold and trembling. Because I was allocating the number of staff to each of the school principals for the following year, I felt I had to go to work. While I was at the superintendent's planning meeting in mid-morning, I felt hot and faint and so I got up to go to the washroom to freshen up. When I got to the washroom,

BECOMING A VICTIM OF HEART AND CANCER DISEASES!

I looked at the mirror and I hardly recognized myself. I looked extremely pasty and sickly. I came out of the washroom because I thought that if I were going to pass out, I did not want it to happen in the washroom where nobody would see or find me perhaps for hours. I took a few steps, and as I was going past the office of the Secretary-Treasurer Todd Baraniuk, I stopped and told him I felt like I was going to have a heart attack. As if on cue, I collapsed right there and then on the floor, and Todd and the whole office staff quickly gathered around to see what was wrong. As I lay on the floor, Gail Bagnall, who was our secondary program consultant at that time, held my very cold hands and I can still remember how warm her hands were by contrast. Somebody quickly called for an ambulance and within a few minutes, paramedics were attending to me. All my vital signs were very weak (as I heard them talk) but I knew that it could not be a heart attack because I had no pain in my chest nor in my left arm. As they began to stabilize me, they placed me in the ambulance and immediately took me to Concordia Hospital, the closest hospital to my house. I faintly told them that I wanted them to take me to St. Boniface Hospital, but they said that because my vital signs were quite poor, they had to take me to the closest hospital as per their policy, and that was the Concordia Hospital.

On the way to the hospital the ambulance went down Kildare Avenue and then carried on west through Ravelston Avenue West. I could see my house "flying" by as we passed it, and I remember that moment so vividly still today, for that's the instant that I made myself a promise, namely that if I were to come out of this alive, I would make some lifestyle changes in my life, and consider my health a much bigger priority, and stop neglect it.

Once in the emergency ward, they administered some EKG tests, and the results were conclusive that I had not had a heart attack. Then quickly, they were pumping out my stomach which contained a considerable amount of "blackened" blood. The attending doctor at my side asked me what I did at work, and as he heard my answer, he quickly realized what the problem was. "Mr. Fiorentino" he said, "I think you have some pretty bad habits. You probably work long hours and often get home quite late. You get home around midnight, you try to unwind and you go into the fridge and have something to eat and drink, and then you go right to bed. Correct?" "Yes, doctor, you are right on!" I said.

Crescendo to Becoming

He explained to me that once you do that for several years (over 20 in my case) the food that you eat sits in your upper stomach and builds up acidity there. The result is an ulcer, not a classical type of ulcer, which he explained are located usually at the bottom of the stomach, but one that sits closer to where the esophagus pipe enters into the stomach. In time the acid actually causes a perforation there and releases a lot of blood in the stomach, which becomes visible through a black-colored stool.

I was given a blood transfusion and prescribed some new and rather effective medication, and in two days I was sent home. On the third day after the "collapse" I invited all those principals who had appointments with me to come to my house and we would complete their staffing allocation there. In the summer of the same year, (1988), I sought the advice of a financial planner to look at the possibility of reducing stress in my life, and with the view of considering an earlier retirement or both, if possible.

Just over a year after this episode, I officially retired from the Transcona-Springfield School Division No. 12 in November of 1991. At the same time, I began to experience serious threats to my health. On several occasions I had to be rushed to the hospital because of heart problems such as irregular heartbeat, speeding heartbeat, shortness of breath, and some angina. What eventually followed was a battery of tests such as stress tests and angiograms. It soon became evident that I had some considerable blockages in two of the main arteries to my heart.

In May, 1993 I underwent a medical intervention known as an *Angioplasty*, an invasive procedure that consists of placing a thin, cable-like instrument in the main artery through the groin that is carefully pushed up through the artery in the direction of the heart, guided by the ultra sound instant images on a television monitor, to locate the end of the medical instrument exactly at the place where there is a blockage. The mechanism at the tip of the instrument was referred to "a balloon" which can be expanded to enlarge the artery by pushing outward the cholesterol build up that restricts and impedes normal blood flow to the heart.

BECOMING A VICTIM OF HEART AND CANCER DISEASES!

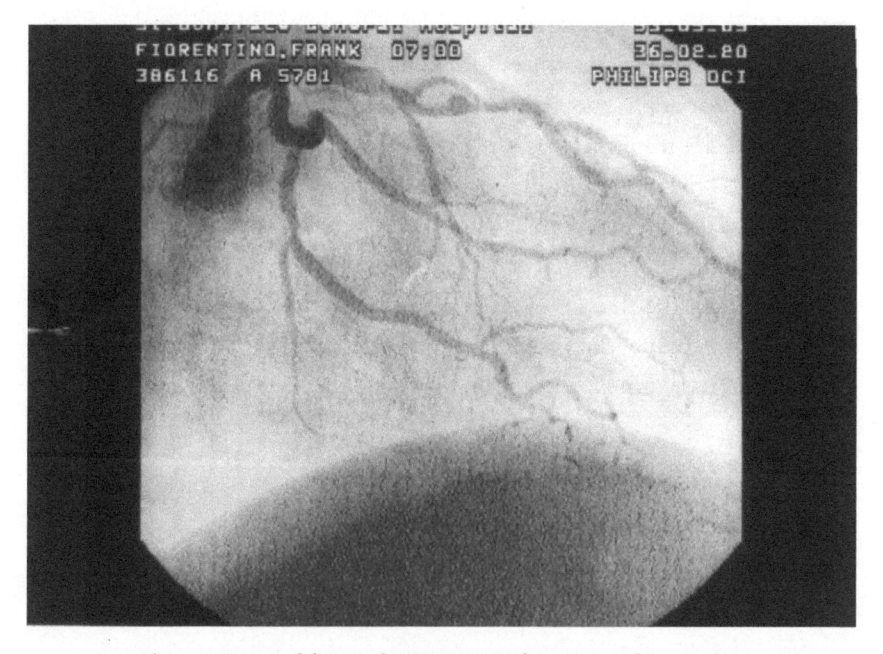

This is a negative of the actual angiogram test done prior to the angioplasty on May, 1993. Through this, the trained eye is able to see where the blockage is. The angioplasty (balloon) is used to widen the passage by pushing outward, the plaque buildup in the artery.

In 2024, it has been almost thirty–one years since the administration of angioplasty and things still appear to be good and under control, thanks to the technical advances in medicine.

But the biggest scare in my life occurred in the year 2001. Two years prior to that, in 1999, I had gone to my family doctor for a routine physical at which time I asked the doctor to check my prostate gland, based on the fact that I had read several times, that every male person over fifty years of age should do this test routinely. As I had not done this for quite a while, and even though I had no indications of any symptoms, I wanted the procedure done just to be on the safe side.

In addition to the doctor's physical check of the prostrate, he ordered a PSA, a blood test which revealed that the results were borderline, not high but not low either. So, every three months I was asked to go back for more PSA tests and invariably the test results would fluctuate and sometimes erratically, but always marginal, that is to say, borderline. After about two

Crescendo to Becoming

years of this, the specialist told me that he didn't know what to make of these inconclusive test results and would like to do a biopsy to see if there is any evidence of cancer in the prostrate. The biopsy consists of extracting eight samples directly from the prostrate through a syringe, and I can tell you that part of it was the most painful procedure I have ever experienced. The result showed that in two of the eight samples there was some cancer alright. The good news was that the cancer was diagnosed and caught quite early, and because of that, the chances of arresting the cancer were quite good. Even so, however, I still went into some kind of shock, but after a couple of hours I rationalized everything and went on living as if little had changed.

• •

"WHAT CANCER CANNOT DO"

"What cancer cannot do:
Cancer is so limited.
It cannot cripple love.
It cannot shatter hope.
It cannot corrode faith, and
It cannot destroy peace.
It cannot kill friendship.
It cannot suppress memories.
It cannot silence courage.
It cannot invade the soul.
It cannot steal eternal life, and
It cannot conquer the spirit"

—Author Unknown

• •

Interestingly enough, it was during this early period that I came in contact with the poem (quoted above) that helped me with the rationalization of the whole affair, and made me realize that I would not let this setback impact negatively upon my life.

In any case there were several options that had to be considered, ranging from radiation treatments to removal of the prostrate altogether. Because of

BECOMING A VICTIM OF HEART AND CANCER DISEASES!

the early detection, it was believed that I was an ideal candidate to receive a procedure that was still quite new, which consisted of "implanting radiation seeds" in and around the prostrate, and slowly but surely these "seeds" would "burn" and destroy the malignant cancerous cells over a period of a year or more.

As the procedure was still not available in Winnipeg, we had to decide to go to either to Toronto or Quebec City to have it done. We finally chose Quebec City because the doctor there who performed the procedure was the first in Canada to do so, and his success rate with the procedure was quite high. And so, Josie and I took a week off and went to Quebec City. As we were reassured by the attending doctor that everything had gone well, we decided to spend two or three days there as a holiday. Then on the way home we stopped by Montreal to visit Carolina, Pasquale Loschiavo, and family.

As of now, after 23 years, everything seems to be still under control, with the last PSA results being at .02, which is very low and almost negligible, and therefore very good.

In two different and separate occasions, both occurring while vacationing in Hawaii during the month of January, the first time I came down with a good case of "shingles" and two years later I contracted a severe case of pneumonia on the third day after our arrival there. The interesting thing about the latter is that it was necessary to be hospitalized for two and half days, and after being discharged from Honolulu Hospital, I was presented with an invoice totaling $27,000. Thank God I was covered by medical travel insurance, and the only loss that we incurred, was in fact the price of the flight for both of us.

Another scare occurred to me in early October 2011 when I and members of my family noticed a black spot on my face that seemed to get bigger and bigger. It was odd shaped, thin, and was both black and brown in color. When I asked my doctor about it, he suggested that we should have it removed, for he did not like the shape and color of it and wanted to ascertain whether it was cancerous or not. He arranged a referral to a skin specialist, and consequently an appointment was made for me four months from that date. I called a couple of times to check if there were any cancellations to advance my date as soon as possible. On the second call, I lucked out with a cancellation and my appointment was rescheduled soon in a few days. But

Crescendo to Becoming

when I went to my appointment with the specialist, he re-scheduled me two weeks further down and informed me that I had to be off the blood thinners such as *warfarin* and baby aspirin that I was taking as part of the regimen for my heart condition.

I underwent the minor surgery to remove the spot on my face on October 26, 2011 and was told that I would have to go back to see the specialist in two-months' time, unless the doctor wished to see me because the finding of the analysis were positive, in which case he would call me.

On November 9, 2011, exactly two weeks after the intervention on my face, I called the specialist office, thinking that by now I was 'out of the woods" since I had not received a call from his office. But I was wrong. I was told by the nurse/secretary that the results had just arrived that morning, and the doctor had not had a chance to see them as yet. The very same day at 1:30 p.m. I received a call from the specialist's secretary telling me that the specialist doctor wanted to see me "right away", and asked me if I could be there at 4:00 p.m. Because he wanted to see me so urgently, I thought the worst of everything. I went on the internet and discovered that *melanoma* skin cancer is often "deadly" and must be attacked early if one is to survive. I also learned that in Canada there are about 6000 cases of melanoma diagnosed every year, and that about 950 of these cases, (or 16%) result in death.

So, at 4:00 p.m. Josie and I were at Dr. Ali's office, and he quickly told us that indeed the spot that he had removed was *melanoma* cancer, but the good news was that the results showed that the cancerous cells had been totally removed, and that I should be o.k. from it. He did, however, referred me to the *melanoma* department at the Winnipeg Health Sciences Hospital for further assessment and monitoring.

But on my first appointment in the *Cancer Care Manitoba Unit*, the melanoma cancer specialist suggested that margins were too close where the first incision was made, and therefore the procedure should be redone, this time removing a bigger junk of flesh to reduce the possibility of the *melanoma* expanding as it likes to do. So, as a precautionary move, I was slated for the bigger procedure on January 4, 2012, but thank God, as of 12 years later, January 2024, the corrective measures taken have all been successful.

BECOMING A VICTIM OF HEART AND CANCER DISEASES!

MY DEAR FRANCA'S TRAGEDY

My daughter Franca, husband Rob, and Austin, Adriana, and Evan in much happier times (2005)

The worst day of my then seventy-three-year life and of those I love most, occurred on August 12, 2009, around noon. This was the unforgettable day when the "roof fell in" and "all hell broke loose" as our lives were filled with the worst devastating and excruciating pain and anguish imaginable. **That was the day when our dear first daughter "princess" Franca was diagnosed with advanced phase four breast cancer.**

When Franca's husband Rob phoned Josie that late morning and told her that he wanted to meet with all the family that evening together so that he could tell us about "a health issue" regarding Franca, Josie knew instinctively that it was serious and began to cry. (She already knew that Franca was awaiting the results of some tests). Shortly after, she phoned me at work and in disbelief, I came home immediately. When we impressed Rob that we could not wait for that evening to find out the facts, we urged him to tell us the situation. When Josie found out, she went into despair and shortly after went into so strong a denial that she literally blanked everything from her mind and in the process, everything that had happened that morning disappeared

Crescendo to Becoming

from her conscious mind. Because we thought that she might have suffered a stroke of some sort, my daughter Elisa called 911 and two rescue vehicles appeared on our driveway and gave Josie all kinds of tests but felt that her problem now was emotional, psychosomatic or whatever. Shortly after, Rob, who is also a Doctor of Medicine, gave Josie a couple of valium-like pills and she pretty well dozed off the rest of the day and overnight till noon the next day. A few days later her memory seemed to have returned, but she still had real difficulty remembering the specifics of the morning before she was totally devastated by the news that Franca had advanced cancer..

The nine-hour surgery to remove the tumor and to reconstruct the two breasts occurred on September 29, 2009, followed by almost a month of recuperation from the ordeal, and this was followed by medical tests and CAT Scans to ascertain the status of the cancer. The results of all these frightening tests would be revealed in a month's time, precisely on Thursday October 22, 2009, along with the plan of attack to destroy the cancers in her cancer-ravaged body.

On March 16, 2010, I wrote the following update: "One of Franca's very first thoughts when she was diagnosed was this: "Well, I will look after all of you guys from up there when I am gone." Amazingly, Franca is fighting valiantly against her cancer, although as expected, she has her miserable moments especially since her last chemo treatment was so much stronger and therefore so difficult to cope with. I remember that on one such occasion, she asked: *"Why me, dad?"* and then she answered her own questions with: *"Then, on the other hand, why not me?"* While it was great in a way to see her being able to rationalize the cruel fate she had been dealt, I must admit that I have spent many hours buried in my own thoughts, contemplating the same question.

I am very proud that she takes part in many activities that involve her children in their varied activities such as hockey, soccer, ringette, music, dance, and others. She has also gone with all her family members on a cruise and other holiday activities much like before she was afflicted by the devastating cancer. And just a few days ago, March 12 to 14, 2010, all the family, except Rob, Dylan, and Frankie, went across the U.S. border to Grand Forks for the weekend and it was a fantastic feeling of having all my children and grandchildren together. But for all intents and purposes, we are now, all of

BECOMING A VICTIM OF HEART AND CANCER DISEASES!

us in our family, living one day at a time, focusing, and squarely facing the realities as they come up. What we do have still is our faith and our prayers, to help us face the unknown future. I now pray for a miracle, ...often.

As of September 2011, Franca is courageously fighting a constant battle and the emotional roller-coaster continues as insidious as ever. Several months ago, she had undergone some CT scans and MRI, and she was told that there was *"no evidence of any cancer lesions in the brain"*. This was great news and therefore reason to celebrate, and this we did. However, the last MRI that she had three months ago again revealed that the cancers had returned much the same as before, in her lungs and in her brain, but in the liver, there was no change (a good thing). The reality though is that Franca has undergone all kinds of difficulties, and I can see that overall things are getting visibly worse by the day.

Cancer, because of its threat to life itself, brings out the worst elements that one can imagine. One day, in early summer 2011, Franca, with the direct help of her best friend Debbie Loschiavo, began planning for such things as her own funeral. As a father and mother, both I and Josie felt crushed by this development, for that is one subject that no parent wants to hear, let alone deal with. She decided on the kind of legacy she wanted to leave her children, reviewed her will and testament with her husband, met and spoke with our priest Father Sam Argenziano of the Holy Rosary Church, and purchased and paid for all other items that would be needed to the very last detail, even what dress she would be wearing. But in the end, Josie and I had to try and get over that as well, for, we wanted to meet her expressed needs, regardless of how we felt, and regardless of how difficult it was to accept.

It is now December 9, 2011, and Franca has been in the palliative care unit at the *Riverview Health Centre* in Winnipeg for just over two weeks. We are incredibly grateful that it is a health-care place where professional healthcare providers really seem to care about the patients under their care. I believe that a person is very lucky if he or she has 3 or 4 really good friends in her lifetime. Well, Franca has at least ten super friends, some of whom are more like sisters to her. It's an unbelievable support base, the result I think, of her having always been a caring, people person. These great friends include Debbie Loschiavo, Heather Werner, Felicia Kriegl, Fran Mulhall, Helga

Lessak, one of them, Patti Lesey, felt compelled to express her feelings and gave her a beautiful card containing the following heart-felt thoughts:

"Franca,

I don't know how to start this. I have been trying to come up with the right words but I'm not sure what those are.

What I do know is that to know you is to love you. Your kind, gentle and generous nature has been a blessing and touched many lives including mine.

Sometimes people come into our lives for a reason, and some for only a season, but you know from that point on, you are changed because of it.

You and I have taken a journey of "self" and "spirituality" together, a journey by which I am forever changed. Knowing you has changed my life. Anytime I listen to my sita Dookuan mediation CD, hear Deepak Chopra's name or pick up my copy of "The Shack," I think of you. I am forever changed and grateful to know you. Thank you for sharing a part of your life with me.

You are a gift
God bless you Franca, and may peace and love be with you.
Patti"

Amazingly, a quote was given to Franca by a teenage friend of her daughter Adriana on November 28, 2011, and posted on the wall in Franca's hospital room. The significance of this quote is the foundation of our Christian belief that death is not the end, for there is no end, but a new o.k. beginning:
"Everything is o.k. at the end . . .
If it's NOT o.k.,
Then it's NOT the end."

Josie and I are now frightened by our own thoughts. We have trouble sleeping at night and fear the worst for our dear Franca. God help us!

More definitely, the beginning of the end started on November 23, 2011, when Franca decided and insisted that she was ready to go to the palliative care ward of the *Riverview Health Centre* in Winnipeg. From that date until her last breath on Thursday December 15, at 5:19 a.m., Franca was never left

BECOMING A VICTIM OF HEART AND CANCER DISEASES!

alone, as we made sure that there was always some family member with her, day and night, often with too many friends and relatives in her room.

One of the many things I shall never forget, was what happened the night before her passing, when her three children came in with their father to say the last goodbye to their mother. It had to be the most painful event that I have had the misfortune to witness.

I thank God that she went away to heaven so gradually, so peacefully, ultimately lowering her head to the side, and fell to eternal sleep on my shoulder. I gently embraced her, cheek to cheek, told her several times that I loved her forever which previously had always answered back in similar fashion, and whispered softly into her ear: *"Jesus, into thy hands I commend her soul."* And then I could no longer hold back and cried the greatest loss I have ever experienced in my 75-year-old life.

Our dear Franca Maria Carmela Kiz
January 17, 1966 – December 15, 2011

• •

"What we have once enjoyed we can never lose.
All what we love deeply becomes a part of us."
—Helen Keller

• •

The funeral was held at the Holy Rosary Church on Monday December 19, 2011, with Father Sam Argenziano and Father Ron Pasinato officiating. The number of people in attendance of all ages was estimated at well over 800 people. It seemed that all those there were very much touched by the service, but particularly by the eulogy delivered by one of Franca's best friends, Felicia Kriegl (nee Torchia) and especially moved by the letter written by Franca herself for the occasion, both which follow below:

MY TRIBUTE TO MY DEAREST FRIEND, FRANCA WRITTEN WITH LOVE, BY FELICIA KRIEGL

Franca Maria Carmela Fiorentino Kiz was born on January 17, 1966. She grew up in Transcona and graduated from Transcona Collegiate in 1983. She obtained a degree at the University of Manitoba in 1987 and RN certification in 1989 through the St Boniface Nursing program. She enjoyed a rich and varied nursing career. Franca married in 1995 and went on to have 3 beautiful children. Left to cherish her memory are her parents Francesco and Josephine Fiorentino, her husband Robert, her children, Adriana, Evan and Austin, her siblings Anthony, Elisa and Mark, as well as numerous aunts, uncles, cousins, nephews and a niece.

I am lucky to be able to say that Franca has been my friend for almost my entire life. We were childhood friends, our grandparents were cousins, neighbors back in Amato, Italy. Our friendship really began to grow though, once we were in high school and university. You see, we had something in common, we were the daughters of Italian parents – which wasn't always easy at that age. But thankfully we had each other. It was over 25 years ago when we had our first jobs at Kildonan Place mall that we started our birthday dinner tradition. A tradition that Franca also shared with her other longtime friends, Debbie, and Heather. We knew that the greatest gift that we could give each other was the gift of time, great conversation and laughter. Franca was the type of friend that you could share everything with, the friend that knew all your secrets. The friend that you could laugh so hard with, until it hurt...or cry so hard with, until it hurt. Supportive and caring, generous and loving.

I remember when Franca told me about Rob during one of those dinners. The day she married him was the happiest day of her life. She was so in love

BECOMING A VICTIM OF HEART AND CANCER DISEASES!

with him, that only he could convince her to move away from all her family and friends to Minneapolis and then later to St. Catharines. And thankfully, he loved her enough to bring her back after their three children were born. Franca loved being a mother – she often told me that her children were the best thing that ever happened to her. They were such a tremendous source of pride for her. Each having their own special qualities…**Adriana**, the beautiful young lady with beauty both inside and out – always showing empathy and kindness to others. **Evan**, her sensitive, thoughtful, son who has become such a handsome gentleman. And **Austin** who brought her so much joy and laughter with his spirit and energy. He always brightened up her day, even on those days when she was not feeling particularly well.

There are many stories that I could share with you about Franca. But there is one in particular that stands out in my mind which so beautifully illustrates the type of person she was. It was July, 1998 and Franca, Rob and one year old Adriana were living in St. Catharines. My husband, Fred and I decided to celebrate our 10-year wedding anniversary with them and visit Niagara Falls. You see, Franca had been one of my bridesmaids. She was beyond thrilled that we were coming out to see them – and we were bringing along our 15-month old son, Adam! Of course, she insisted we stay with them. She had every day planned with meals and activities. She made us feel so welcome – it was easy.

For our anniversary, she planned a day at the spa for her and I, helped arrange for my husband to send me flowers, made dinner reservations for us at a beautiful restaurant in Niagara-on-the-Lake, baby sat Adam while we went out, had a bottle of champagne sent to our table, and if all that wasn't enough, we came back home to a beautiful table set with desserts and Inniskilling ice wine. We were overwhelmed at her thoughtfulness and generosity. You could see that it brought **her** so much joy to make **our** day special.

I'm sure many of you are now thinking of your own special stories about Franca…and I know that is exactly what she would want you to do. Remember her and the good times that you shared. That is how we will keep her alive in our hearts. Remember her smile and her laughter, her zest for life and living each and every day to the fullest. She was a loving wife, mother, daughter, sister, aunt, and friend.

In the past year, Franca had come to terms with her diagnosis. She had a lot of time to reflect on her life. She knew that she had a great life with a loving husband who was an amazing, dedicated father, wonderful children, incredibly supportive parents, siblings, family and friends. She had the opportunity to fulfill so many of her dreams of travel. Our family was lucky enough to share a few of those vacations with Franca and her family. And we will hold those memories forever dear.

In closing, Franca asked me to share with you, a letter that she wrote in her final days…

LAST LETTER FROM FRANCA

I thank you all for being here today to share in the remembrance and celebration of my life.

To my beloved children Adriana, Evan, and Austin, please know and remember that you were my life and I will **always** be with you in your hearts.

Please be inspired to become good, kind, happy, and strong people. Always love and respect yourselves so that you will grow to be loving and respectful adults. Promise me that you will always be responsible and make smart choices. This will mean that my life stood for something.

Be there for each other and take good care of your dad…let us also not forget Meowi, Bella and Rocky.

Please do not be sad for long. I am in a happy place, free from the cancer that took me away from you. Always remember how very proud I am of all of you and how very much you were loved.

To my family…Mom, Dad, Tony, Ellie and Mark, Amanda and Leith, Dylan, Frankie, Ethan, Adam, Steve, and Dolores…Please know and remember how much I loved you all and how much I appreciated your strength and support especially during these last few years.

Mom, I do not even know where to start to thank you for everything you have been and done to Rob and I and the kids. I will always cherish our long talks over cups of coffee, especially first thing in the morning on the deck at the lake. You are truly my best friend.

Dad, thank you for the strength and wisdom you so willingly shared over the years. Thank you for your sense of humor and the many laughs. You always knew how to put a smile on my face. P.S.…and yes, it is true; I did forget to look at my watch all those times I got home late! I will forever be

BECOMING A VICTIM OF HEART AND CANCER DISEASES!

your princess. Tony, Ellie, and Mark always know and remember how proud I am to call you my sister and brothers. There is no way to thank you for your love, support, and occasional, when needed, "kick in the pants".

Tony, you always were and will be the "wind beneath my wings". I am so proud of you for raising your children on your own to be such wonderful, good people.

Amanda and Leith, Dylan, and Frankie, I am reassured knowing you will continue to be there for my children to comfort, protect and guide them.

Ellie and Mark always know and remember how much I loved and cherished you both and your two boys. I thoroughly enjoyed spending time with your beautiful, loving family. Watching Ethan and Adam grow up brought me great joy.

Steve and Dolores, you are the very best in-laws a girl could ever ask for. And yes Dolores, I always considered you to be my mother-in-law. You both have always been there for us. The loving relationship you have with my children means the world to Rob and me. I am assured that you will continue to be there for them. And yes Steve, you were always my favorite father-in-law.

To my dearest, long-time friends, Debbie, Heather, and Felicia, I thank you for your never-ending love, encouragement, and support, especially during this difficult time in my life. To Fran, Helga, Barb, Linda, Noreen, and the many other friends who I have been blessed with in this life, you know who you are; you will never know how much I cherished you all.

I want you all to know that I am at peace knowing I can count on every one of you to continue loving and supporting my family. I encourage you to live life to its fullest. Celebrate all occasions, remember old traditions, have fun making new traditions. Speak of old times, tell funny stories, and fill each and every day with laughter. By doing this you will keep my memory alive in the hearts, minds, and souls of all those I held dear.

To all my caregivers and new friends at Cancer Care Manitoba, in particular the gals in my Tuesday support group, I was blessed to have you all to walk with me through this difficult journey. We were each other's confidants, support, and strength. Never give up hope. Continue to fight the good fight. I pray that a cure will be found.

Last but not least, To Rob. Thank you for being my rock. You gave me the courage to endure the last few years. I could not have made it through

Crescendo to Becoming

without you. You were always my strength, my voice of reason, and my best friend. You gave me a life that a girl could only dream of. Please don't be sad for long. Promise me that you will move forward and find happiness in your life. Together we made our dreams come true. Our children are living proof of that. Live well, laugh often, and love always…I will love you forever,

Franca

It is now June 15, 2024, 13 years to the day in December 15, that my dear Franca passed, and the cruel reality that befell on us is still difficult to accept. On many occasions, I fall back into a deep disappointment and conclude that the whole scenario is totally unjust, for no parent should be expected and required to outlive his children. No parent should be expected to bury their own children. Why is it so, remains one of the greatest mysteries for man and certainly I cannot decipher the rationale for this unbearable pain. Each of us has a cross to bear, but mine/ours seems to be one of the most difficult to accept.

15.
BECOMING LOVING AND LOVABLE: THE ULTIMATE HUMAN

"I don't want to get to the end of my life and find that I have just lived the length of it. I want to have lived the width of it as well."
—Diane Ackerman

THIS CHAPTER REPRESENTS THE CONCLUSION, the culmination of my story and of my thoughts. After all said and done, the "bottom line" and the essence of my existence, is hopefully captured and summarized in this chapter. I hope that this will be the true legacy of yours truly, Francesco Fiorentino.

It is said that it's never too late in life to be or to become who you intended to be in the first place. Another way of putting it, is as Erich Fromm once said: *"Man's main task in life is to give birth to himself, to become what he potentially is."* The sure thing is that as the quote above states, I don't want to get to the end of my days on earth and know that I have lived just the God-given length of it, without reaching the main reason for having lived my life.

At this point of my "life's journey", at 88 years of age, it is my strong conviction that the greatest miracle on earth is man (and woman) himself, and that the greatest innate intention and drive of man, is to become all he or she can be, that is, a loving and lovable human being. It's part of a belief that says that **being kind is more important than being right.** Accordingly, I want to "give birth to myself", to re-invent myself, and become what I think that I am, and what potentially I can still become.

It's important to note that everyone you meet is probably "fighting" some kind of battle or "demon", for no one has an exclusive to this reality. Winston Churchill said that *"if you're going through hell, keep going"*. That is probably the best advice for me, for *"going through hell"* is in fact the case for me, as I have gone through hell since the loss of my dear daughter Franca. In this reality, my highest priority becomes to treat all people with kindness, and thus be and become more loving and lovable in all my relationships with people.

Nothing in this world is more important than unconditional love and love shared, and nobody has stated the case better than St. Francis of Assisi, in my most favorite guiding prayer of all:

PRAYER OF SAINT FRANCIS OF ASSISI

*Lord, make me an instrument of Your **peace**.*
*Where there is hatred, let me sow **love**.*
*Where there is injury, **pardon**.*
*Where there is doubt, **faith**.*
*Where there is despair, **hope**.*
*Where there is darkness, **light**,*
*And where there is sadness, **joy**.*

Divine Master, grant that I may not so
*Much seek to be consoled, as **to console**;*
*To be understood, as **to understand**;*
*To be loved, as **to love**.*
*For it is in **giving** that we receive—*
*It is in **pardoning** that we are pardoned;*
AND IT IS IN DYING THAT WE ARE BORN TO ETERNAL LIFE.

Becoming loving and lovable has been and remains a life-long mission of mine, and I am fully aware that some people can never get it right. I tried to be loving and lovable to some measure all my life, often with success and sometimes without success. I have now, once again actually, recreated a vision for myself: to become as loving and lovable as possible. What a super achievement it would be for me personally, and what a legacy it would be, if I could

BECOMING LOVING AND LOVABLE: THE ULTIMATE HUMAN

become a satisfied loving and lovable person before I leave this earth and this life. I am so sure now, that the ultimate state that man could achieve is to be governed in all things by love, to love life, to love himself and all other beings, and to love with all his heart, our loving and lovable God.

I recognize that "love shared is actually love gained," and sharing love unconditionally results in an abundant life of love. And yes, no doubt about it, a loving and lovable foundation is everything in everybody's life. I am now sure that love, like life itself, must be always nurtured if it is to grow. I am sure that such endearment is a way of life that probably gives the greatest personal fulfillment and satisfaction.

Having said that, I believe that having been empowered with the power of choice and the ability to love, man has the potential to be the greatest being in all of creation, for we also know that conversely and unfortunately, man is his own or mankind's worst enemy. Historically, man has demonstrated that he is capable of both love and hate. I believe that in my lifetime, I have tried to eradicate hatred from my heart, and have developed to a great extent, a true appreciation for life, for people, and for all living things.

For me trying to be lovable and loving also means being closest to those that I love most, and those that I feel love me. These are the people that can really attest to whether I am lovable or not. What they think in this regard is of paramount importance to me.

Henry James once said: *"Three things in human life are important. The first is to be kind. The second is to be kind. The third is to be kind."* Amazingly, this can be obtained without a lot of money and without a lot of power. I have no doubt that we become most human, when we reach the ultimate state of being most loving and lovable.

Crescendo to Becoming

* * *

The highest reward for a person's toil is not what they get for it, but they become by it."
—**John Ruskin**

* * *

When once you tasted flight, you will forever walk the earth with your eyes turned skyward. For there you have been, And there you will always long to return."
—**Leonardo da Vinci**

* * *

16.
AT THE END: A NEW BECOMING?

I HAVE CONCLUDED THAT LIFE is much more than it appears to be, and with that in mind, I believe that I am today pretty well what I have always wanted to be. While I haven't totally reached the destination (which may be elusively impossible to do in this lifetime), I can honestly say that I feel substantially satisfied that I have reached most of my important goals that I planned along the way in my life's journey: a great and wonderful family, a good and rewarding career, economically self-sufficiency, positive self-esteem, and lots of respect and integrity. In short, a meaningful, and even happy existence that only became unraveled upon the untimely death of my wonderful daughter, Franca, now thirteen years ago in December 15.

I think I knew when I came to Canada that I had to grow and make myself a great deal more than what I was. I believe that I have been able to design my life much as I planned, and I am now satisfied that to this point I have experienced a great existence consisting of two distinct lives, two loves, two languages, and two cultures. I was born Italian, but I am now both Italian and Canadian, and I feel accepted and embraced by both countries. I have travelled upon "two roads" and many paths and I have been impacted and enriched by a true mosaic of meaningful experiences which all, except one, have given me a great deal of satisfaction and contentment. In short, I can honestly say that I have experienced life in all or most of its manifestations, both joyous and painful, and in the process, I have been transformed into the new me that I am now.

I may have not gone everywhere I intended to go at the beginning of my "journey", nor have I likely become everything I may have wanted to be, but I think I have come very close for I ended up pretty well where, what, and who I wanted to be and therefore I am very much satisfied with my end-outcomes to date. Throughout the living of my life, I have learned who and what I am, and that which I think, feel, and have experienced, has a great deal of value to me. In fact, its true value is a priceless gift that often one calls success or happiness.

There are real rewards that result from writing your autobiography. Some would say that it is risky to commit to paper factual information of your own story, but I believe that writing from the heart for me, has been a revealing, therapeutic process, which has given me richly rewarding understanding about myself and the world around me. And the benefits of knowing oneself are empowering, invaluable, and self-actualizing.

I am enormously proud of my accomplishments in the world of academia, music, sports, community volunteering, education, and career. But I am particularly proud of my family, especially members of my immediate family, the ones I had the most and closest interaction with including all my "grand" kids. They too have become who and what I was always hoping for: super loving and lovable human beings.

All I want now is to let me be what I am, hopefully a loving and lovable, ethical, and moral being, until the end of my life upon the earth. I expect that the end of life will be the greatest new beginning that goes well to eternity. **In our end is our new beginning, and no doubt, a new becoming.** At this end, the resurrection awaits, and I will be ready to *become* part of God's energy and eternal plan. That's when the best of everything will really begin to be. **At long last, hopefully, our (my and man's) greatest victory.**

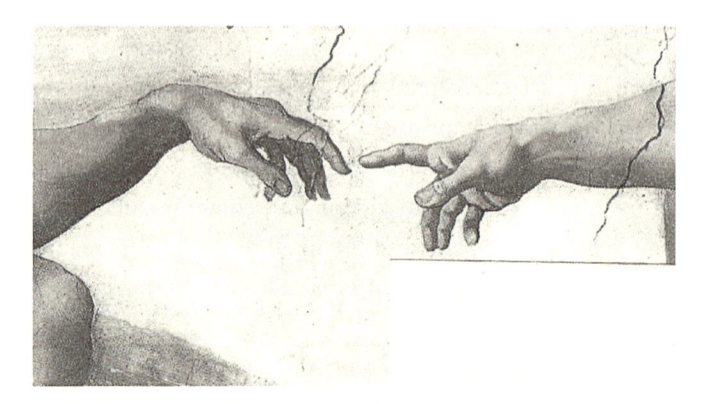

Michelangelo Buonarroti's. . . RECREATION!

POSTSCRIPT: SOME OF MY SPECIAL PEOPLE

MY DEAR MOTHER AND FATHER
ANTONIO AND CARMELINA FIORENTINO

THE FIORENTINO-GRAZIANO FAMILY, CIRCA 1984

MY BROTHER ONOFRIO FIORENTINO AND SISTER DELFINA

MY BEST MAN AND BEST FRIEND, FRANCO MASI

POSTSCRIPT: SOME OF MY SPECIAL PEOPLE

GIOVAN-BATTISTA (TITTA) MASI AND HIS WIFE ASSUNTA,
UNFORGETABLE, GREAT FRIENDS

MARIO AND JOSIE AUDINO
In Great Company!
Front Row, Left to Right Josie Audino, Mario Audino
Back Row, Left to Right: __ ____ Josie and Artibano Lucidi, me, and my wife Josie

Crescendo to Becoming

The letter from my friend Mario Audino to me is another example of being loving and lovable

A TESTIMONIAL FROM MY FRIEND MR. BERNARDO TUCCI

Bernardo Tucci

Parlare del Dr. Francesco Fiorentino, non bastano pagine intere che, racchiudono il modo eloquente né tratteggiare le individuali capacità intellettuali in un contesto di distinte sensibilità verso l'essere umano.

Sul piano operative unendo cultura e musica, in un binomio d'altissime dimensioni, proiettano e livellano le caratteristiche del Fiorentino, nelle moderne e tradizionali visioni di nobiltà di spirito, mente e di cuore.

Figlio di emigrante, di un padre valente cultore con un curriculum di ben 17 pubblicazioni di poesie in versi regionali di stampo calabresi.

Inizia in carriera da insegnante, affiorandone capacità prodigiose da raggiungere incarichi di direttore scolastico.

POSTSCRIPT: SOME OF MY SPECIAL PEOPLE

Tali preparazioni specifiche, lo confrontano professionalmente contri-buendo nell'ambito degli studi acquisiti l'alta carica di Superintendente alle scuole nella divisione di Transcona-Springfield. Nel campo musicale, una passione sbocciata in giovane età, si tratta di personale abilità nel suonare il clarinetto, strumento musicale a fiato che lo vedono coinvolto in vari gruppi orchestrali, partecipando a numerosi spettacoli, sia popolari che classici, con esibizione di alto riconoscimento da solista.

Noi lo ricordiamo con il complesso Combo Italiano con Angelo Ferla, il famoso batterista piemontese. Franco Fiorentino allora studente faceva parte del gruppo come leader, rendando le serate sociali di grande richiamo nella comunità, e di Invito alla partecipazione. Merita attenzione anche nel campo agonistico sportivo in qualità di giocatore di Pallone, portiere della prima squadra Italia di Winnipeg.

Ho cercato di rispondere in breve il lungo e brillante cammico conseguiti nei momenit di identificazione culturale sociale e nel trattenimento, da aggiungere le numerose partecipazioni in qualità di conferenziere, sia in argomenti scolastici, improntati da guida in maniera capillare nei giovani, attingerne evidenti concetti che rispondono a dei quesiti, sempio "Non esistono aspetti sociali, separate da sviluppi di sostegno ai ceti deboli nelle comunità umane". Merita anche eloquente attenzione, prefissa ll'esperienza e responsabilità acquisita esercitare nei giovani in basi indispensabili all'approfondmento delle proprie competenze utili a stimolare qualitative carriere prescelte. Nell' insieme aggregazioni apprezzabili legittimando un rinnovato sentimento che coltivava da sempre, l'occasione lo ha valorizzato nel dimostrare tenace volontà da orgoglioso cittadino di origine italiana, riallocciando legame affettivo nel rendersi doveroso al servizio della comunità italiana in qualità di Vice Console Onorario per il Manitoba.
Bernardo Tucci

Crescendo to Becoming

<u>(I DID IT) MY WAY</u>

And now, the end is near;
And so I face the final curtain.
My friend, I'll say it clear,
I'll state my case, of which I'm certain.
I've lived a life that's full.
I've traveled each and every highway;
But more, much more than this,
I did it my way.

Regrets, I've had a few;
But then again, too few to mention.
I did what I had to do
And saw it through without exemption.
I planned each charted course;
Each careful step along the byway,
But more, much more than this,
I did it my way.

Yes, there were times, I'm sure you knew
When I bit off more than I could chew.
But through it all, when there was doubt,
I ate it up and spit it out.
I faced it all and I stood tall;
I did it my way.

I've loved, I've laughed and cried.
I've had my fill; my share of losing.
And now, as tears subside,
I find it all so amusing.
To think I did all that;
And may I say - not in a shy way,
"No, oh no not me,
I did it my way.
For what is a man what has he got
If not himself then he has not

POSTSCRIPT: SOME OF MY SPECIAL PEOPLE

To say the things he truly feels
And not the words of one who kneels
The record shows I took the blows
And did it my way, Yes, it was my way

Source: Khajadourian, Joe/Golan, Ross/Schwartz, Alex Breezy

Printed in Canada